LEA & FEBIGER: Portion of chart "Frame Size by Elbow Breadth for Females Ages 35–74" from *Modern Nutrition in Health & Disease*, Seventh Edition, by Maurice E. Shils and Vernon R. Young, 1988, Lea & Febiger, Malvern, Pa. Reprinted by permission.

WARNER/CHAPPELL MUSIC, INC.: Excerpt from the lyrics of "My Back Pages" by Bob Dylan. Copyright © 1964 by Warner Bros. Inc. (ASCAP). All rights reserved. Used by permission.

DR. WULF H. UTIAN: Excerpts from *Managing Your Menopause* by Dr. Wulf H. Utian and Ruth Jacobowitz, Prentice Hall Press, 1990. Reprinted by permission of Dr. Wulf H. Utian.

Library of Congress Catalog Card Number: 91-50065

ISBN 0-449-22190-3

This edition published by arrangement with Villard Books, a division of Random House, Inc.

Manufactured in the United States of America

First Ballantine Books Edition: February 1993

Contents

Acknowledgments

We wish to thank the following people without whom this book could not have been written: Dan Wakefield, for his guidance and his unwavering belief in us; Alison Acker and Emily Bestler, our editors, for their critical eyes and available ears; Carol Mann, our agent; Ruth Marcus and Julie and Alissa Paige for their encouragement; Stephen Ditmore, for his ideas and for his commitment; Tom Fiffer, for his support; Shideh Sedgh, for being relentless with us; J. Kenneth Young, for introducing us; Eileen Behan, Beverly Jablons, Margaret Klacik, and Rena Lobosco for reading the manuscript in its various stages, and especially Dian Barrett for her ongoing support and incisive critiques; the numerous doctors, researchers, and experts who gave us their time and knowledge, in particular, Dr. Lois Goodman of Newton-Wellesley Hospital in Massachusetts; and most of all, we thank the women we interviewed, who so generously told us their stories and who, in many ways, were the ones who wrote this book.

Introduction:
So This Is Menopause

This book grew out of a contradiction.

At the age of forty-six I was finally looking forward to having a good time. Having gone back to college in my thirties, I was now the chief dietitian at a major urban hospital. My daughters were moving out of the house. I was single. I'd had a bad divorce and my love life hadn't been very good, but now I was starting over. Anything was possible. Except what my gynecologist suggested during my annual checkup.

"Had any hot flashes?"

"What?" I was indignant as I looked behind me to see if she was talking to someone else. "No," I told her and thought, What nerve. She thinks she's talking to an old lady. I've finally gotten everything together in my life. Is my body going to act up and give me trouble?

Within a year of my doctor's question, it happened. I was counseling a husband and wife on a cholesterol-reducing diet when suddenly my office grew hot. Heat climbed up from my chest and neck to my face and I started to sweat. I looked around the room for a clue. All I saw were my clients, cool and calm, waiting intently for their diet plan. My first thought was, I do not want these people to know what I'm going through.

I could not believe this was happening to me. I was too young. After my initial indignation in the doctor's office I had brushed the notion of menopause aside. My periods had become irregular and then stopped, but I attributed that to the excitement of new responsibilities at work and to my daughters' moving out. Besides, my periods had started up again. Perhaps these overheated sensations were caused by something I had eaten. An allergy. Or maybe nerves. But the intense heat and then a full breakout of sweat was not like anything else I'd ever felt. When the hot flashes began coming often, and without my knowing when, I could not deny them any longer.

One thing was certain: whatever was coming was going to overtake me and I had nothing to say about it.

Ultimately, menopause was nothing like what I had expected. I was concerned that my skin would age rapidly, that changes in my body over which I had no control would occur, and that I would no longer be considered beautiful. And I was particularly afraid that menopause meant going into a depression. I had been depressed during my twenties. Although I now felt further away from depression than I had ever felt in my life, I did fear a return to that misery.

It never happened. I had some mood swings, menstrual irregularities, and hot flashes, which were the most annoying sensations, mainly because I was certain they were obvious and I found that embarrassing. But for the most part, the momentum of other events in my life overshadowed the difficulties of menopause.

BREAKING INTO MODELING

The year I had my first hot flash was the year my daughters began encouraging me to become a model. On vacation that summer they pointed out pictures of Tish Hooker, forty-seven years old and gray-haired, in *Vogue*. "You look as good as she does," they insisted. I laughed them off. "Sure I do." I had worked hard to get where I was at my age among young women in the nutrition profession. The competition in modeling was certainly much tougher. But my daughters wouldn't forget the idea. Throughout the winter they asked me when I'd give it a try, and I finally began to take them seriously.

When I heard about a weekend modeling course offered by Ford Models in Boston, I decided to take it. Afterward, Ford called and asked if I'd like to do a photo session and be in their annual book. I jumped at the chance. The photographer was very supportive. He told me I looked gorgeous and that I was great in front of the camera, all of which was encouraging—until I got my pictures back. I was shocked. The photos had to be of someone else, or else that supportive photographer had wrinkles on his lens. The bottom line was that while I looked good, I was not as smooth-skinned and fresh-faced as I had assumed. But Ford wanted to sign me and they told me to look through magazines for input on how to build my portfolio.

I spent a day combing through all the magazines in the library. By the end of it, I was well aware that I didn't fit in anywhere. The ads I had seen featured young girls modeling bikinis with legs cut to the waist, young mothers loading kids into station wagons, and grandmothers baking cookies. Where was the woman around my age who was lively, good-looking, wearing sexy but not necessarily provocative clothes, hard at work, and having fun? According to the media, the image I had of myself did not exist. That would not make much of a portfolio.

Yet realizing that there were few images out there of the woman who was not young but also not old was inspiring. It occurred to me that this was someone I was able to represent—the woman who knew who she was but who didn't see herself reflected anywhere.

It was a risk, but I decided to leave the job I had held for several years and work as a nutrition consultant while I pursued modeling. My plan was to make a big point about how I looked—great and almost fifty. I wasn't about to shout from the rooftops that I was in menopause, but

I assumed that women in their forties and fifties who might identify with my image would know that menopause was a factor in there somewhere.

While I knew all about the woman I was hoping to represent, I also knew that not everyone was aware of her. No one would be banging down the doors just because I had announced, "Hello, world, here I am." Getting started in modeling would require hard work, particularly at my age.

I had already experienced skepticism about "older" women and work. While applying for nutrition internships after graduating from college at the age of forty, I was told that program directors were concerned about taking me because of my age. And when I applied for my first job as a nutritionist, I was told that my age was a disadvantage. Indeed, I was the oldest employee in the department on my first job.

I considered my age an advantage, however, when it came to working hard. Any woman who has raised a family, managed a home, and worked at a long-term marriage has an enormous range of skills, and after returning to school in my late thirties, I had observed that such skills transferred to any endeavor. I was able to concentrate on several things at the same time, to manage a number of projects at once, and to see a difficult situation through to the end. Under pressure I found myself able to handle stress in ways the younger women around me could not.

I took the summer off to prepare for my new career as a model and had a wonderful time taking the first vacation I'd ever had just for myself. I read, I took walks. And in the fall I began my campaign. I joined the Ford Agency in Boston, had pictures taken, got together a portfolio, and made the rounds to see photographers. I pursued everything that seemed like a lead.

Then I heard about a new magazine called *Lear's*, for "the woman who wasn't born yesterday," and I got very excited. Frances Lear, the magazine's publisher, was putting together an entire publication geared to women in their forties and fifties. I wasn't the only one who considered this part of the population untapped. I called *Lear's* and spoke with China Machado, who said, "I'd love to meet you but I can't use you. You're too short to model." She did add that if I was ever in New York I should drop by. A week later I just happened to be in New York.

When China met me she asked, "How tall are you?" and I said, "Five-six."

"No, you're not," she answered. "You're five-five," and I thought, Does this woman have a tape measure in her head?

"So what?" I said. "So I'll wear high heels. So I'm almost five-six." Actually, I'm almost five-five.

At least I had made contact with an organization that seemed to be doing what I was trying to do. I continued pounding the pavement with my portfolio, through that fall, winter, and spring. At times I felt that I had made a colossal mistake. Organization and persistence, my two formulas for success, didn't seem to be paying off in this situation. In the past I had known what I was striving for—a degree, a job, a relationship, and a family. What I was trying to accomplish now didn't even exist.

On certain days I figured I should forget the whole thing. After all, I already had a successful career. I had good friends and a great family. I was better off settling down and enjoying the fruits of a hard-won middle age than leaping into a new world that didn't seem to want me. Being satisfied with my situation seemed a more appropriate choice for a woman nearing fifty.

Finally, after months and months and months, I landed my first job, in May, in Boston, for the Saddlebrook Bank. One of the photographers I had seen on my rounds needed someone to portray a bank president. I was certain the photographer and art director knew this was my first job, and I felt like a kid wearing squeaky new shoes on the first day of school. But after that job, other things started to come through.

Ironically, in those early months I was trying to "make the case" for being middle-aged and beautiful, but I was also trying to get work in a limited market. I seemed for a while never to have the right look. I was too young for the traditional squinty-eyed, gray-permed grandmother but not right for younger roles. Shortly after my first shoot for the bank my agency called and said, "The *Herald* is doing a story on senior-citizen styles." The photographer had seen my picture and liked my look but thought I was too young.

"I am not," I assured my booker, not wanting to miss the opportunity. "Look—my hair is gray, my chin is beginning to drop, my neck looks like an escalator."

"Okay, okay," the booker said. "I'll tell the photographer." I got the job.

In June, China Machado called and asked me to be interviewed for a promotional video *Lear's* was making in New York. About twenty women, all over forty, from various parts of the country, were to be interviewed individually about their lives. We gathered in Frances Lear's Manhattan apartment. Her living room was set up with lights and cameras, and the air crackled with excitement. The camera crew was astonished. "Where did you get all these great women?" they asked.

"What do you mean?" China responded. "They're everywhere. You just don't know about them."

By midsummer *Lear's* had called again and asked me to come down and do a shoot with a famous photographer. Hiro was his name, and the shoot was for *Lear's* original ad campaign, which consisted of four ads, one woman in each ad, nude from the hips up. Two of the ads pictured a model looking over her shoulder. The other two, of which I was one, featured a woman looking directly at the camera, her arms crossed over her breasts.

I had a few more modeling jobs that season. One was for hospital pajamas, and I was photographed in a rocking chair. My friends thought that was hysterical. They said I looked like I was sitting on a bed pan. That ad was quite a change from the stylish photographs Hiro had taken for *Lear's*. Once again I was made aware that not everyone knew fifty-year-old women could be sexy.

In November I went to the library to find *Advertising Age*, because I knew the Hiro picture was scheduled to run. I opened the magazine to a double-page poster of myself, screamed, and then closed it fast, looking around, not wanting anyone to know. I bought a copy and brought it home, and when my younger daughter saw it she said, "Ma, you have no clothes on," and I said, "Grow up, kid." That picture was building my reputation as a model without my even knowing it. Initially out in the advertising trade magazines, it led to a lot of publicity. *Ad Week* wrote a story on me. I was on *Evening Magazine*. And everyone wanted to know about *Lear's*.

The power of that series of the four women, beautifully photographed, who were definitely not young, made a real impact. And caused some controversy. *The New York Times* wouldn't print the two front-view photos, one of which was mine. *Advertising Age* did an issue on women working in advertising, and *Lear's* ran the full series, which looked fabulous. The next week letters poured in to *Ad Age* saying, "How could you have these nude women next to articles about the smartest women in advertising?" I immediately wrote a letter, which they published the next week, letting them know I was not exactly a nincompoop and that considering brains and beauty to be mutually exclusive was not the trend of the times.

That ad campaign was tremendous and it made its point. Boldly and tastefully, it said that older women are beautiful, sensual, and sexual. And it picked a way to make that point forcefully because, given American culture, the point *has* to be made with force.

Without knowing me, Hiro captured my personality so completely that my own mother said, "You could step out of that picture.'' She and all her friends said, ''We never knew you had all that strength.''

From the start, I had thought of modeling on a national and international scale, because I knew that with the attitude the advertising business had toward older women, if I worked only locally my modeling career would be what the IRS calls a ''hobby.'' I also knew that 90 percent of modeling work goes to people between the ages of six months and twenty-nine years. Today's Woman is Ford Models' division for models over thirty-five. Ford in New York was my goal from the start.

Federico Fellini's famous movie $8\frac{1}{2}$ was made in the 1960s. In one dream sequence, Marcello Mastroianni is in a house filled with his former wives and girlfriends. With a whip he is forcing one of them upstairs because she has passed the age of thirty-five. She cries and begs but he doesn't care. ''*Upstairs*,'' he insists as he whips the steps and she trudges on up. Ford's Today's Woman division is on the top floor of a four-story building, and as I climbed and climbed I half worried, half wondered about what I would find there.

I expected to see some New York vamp with a long cigarette holder waiting to take my name. Instead, I met some very regular people. The director of Today's Woman is nicknamed T. She told me, ''We believe in the market but we already have a large group of strong models in your category. We'll have to think it over. Call me next week.''

I was on pins and needles. I drove my friends nuts with questions like ''Should I call Monday, wait until Wednesday, or what?'' I came home on Tuesday to a huge scribbled note: ''T called. Ford Models. Call her back.'' I screamed and ran down the stairs, out the front door, down the walk, back up the walk, and up the stairs. I banged some walls and ran back down again. I finally made it to the phone, dialed the number, and said, ''Hello. T?''

I signed with Ford in New York and began working

regularly. After a year of persistence and effort, at the age of forty-eight, I had broken into the field of high-fashion modeling.

I was a model, I was in menopause, and I was having the time of my life. The irony of earning a living because of my looks, when my looks were supposedly fading at the same rate as my estrogen levels, was not lost on me. I was so caught up in the excitement of a new career, however, that it seemed as if menopause was no big deal. It wasn't until I wrote this book that I began to understand the numerous ways I was reacting to the process.

THE INSPIRATION FOR THIS BOOK

My first reaction to menopause was to be insulted that my doctor considered me close to the age of such a thing. As it turns out, I did start the process early. Women I interviewed who hadn't gone through the event until their mid-fifties were less surprised, and often had an attitude of "All right, already, let's get on with this."

After my initial indignation, I quickly dismissed the whole idea. Now that I look back I see that I had some free-floating notions about what to expect, but as far as concrete facts went, I knew nothing. I had never read anything about it. What I vaguely remember hearing from my mother and aunts while growing up might not have been about "the change" at all, since the entire subject seemed so hush-hush. Somehow, though, while I was denying the whole process and ignorant of it to boot, I was also scared. I was frightened of depression. And I harbored a slight suspicion that menopause might signal a decline into the second, downward half of my life.

Then, right in the middle of that confusing time, I found myself imbued with a level of ambition and creativity that I had never experienced before.

I have come to see that some of my ambition and creativity was in reaction to the silent fears I wasn't fully aware I had of the loss and the aging menopause might bring. Again, through writing this book as well as speaking with dozens of women on the subject, I have come to identify the unspoken concerns I had about going through "the change." My stubborn response to such concerns was a determination to remain vital and active. Perhaps that is why I pursued modeling, a career that by its very nature defies the loss of beauty I assumed menopause brought with it. I could laugh in the face of that loss by distinguishing myself in a field where great looks, energy, and enthusiasm were the name of the game.

Whatever my hidden motivations were, as my new career gathered steam I had never felt so good. Adolescence, I had read years before, was supposed to be the most creative time of a person's life. I had long since passed that benchmark. In fact, in my twenties and thirties I assumed I was just not creative at all since the only thing I remembered creating in my teens was boyfriends. Yet here I was in menopause, in the middle of what I would call the first creative spurt in my life. Suddenly I was creating a public image as a model, and I had started writing nutrition stories for *Shape* magazine. It was no surprise, then, that when I went looking for information on menopause and found very little available, and when I tried to talk about it and barely got past the word, the idea for this book came to me.

I began to notice that friends and colleagues who were my age, undoubtedly at the same threshold, were not saying anything about "the change." When I did bring up the subject, it was agreed that it shouldn't be discussed, and under no circumstances should a single woman in menopause talk about it with any man she was dating.

While most of us were not exactly sure what menopause was and rarely spoke about it, many of us were certain about how it would affect us physically and how it would affect our relationships. These "facts" we thought we knew included permanent weight gain, unbearable mood swings, wrinkles, overnight aging, loss of both desirability *and* sexual desire, crankiness, and depression. Menopausal women, it was known, couldn't be relied on to make sane decisions; we got hysterical, our opinions vacillated, we were unstable, erratic, and dissatisfied.

Where did these "facts" come from? My personal experiences supported what I already thought I knew:

- When I mentioned the words "hot flash" to a friend who had had a hysterectomy, she said, "I'm telling you, your hormones go crazy and your whole body changes."
- I asked a colleague how his wife was and Ed answered, with a look of resignation, "Well, you know, she's having The Change," and I said automatically, "Well, yes, I know, I know."
- I remember my aunt having a hysterectomy at age forty-two and retiring to her bedroom with a kind of chronic flu from which she recovered at around age seventy. She is more active now as an elderly woman, but her middle years were lost.
- A cousin who had always been troubled began calling people in the middle of the night after her husband left her, and people explained it as The Change. She was hospitalized for a short period of time and given pills that, if taken regularly, would supposedly make her well.
- As a nutritionist I often heard this account: "I got married, had children, gained some weight, had The Change, and became a blimp."
- In my own mind, I was certain that if the man I was dating found out about me, he would leave. If my modeling colleagues knew I was going through menopause, I would be seen as On-the-Way-Out. And I was so convinced my face would fall that every time I glanced in the mirror it looked as if it already had.

* * *

Once it was undeniable that I was in menopause, I discussed the situation with my doctor and decided to begin hormone-replacement therapy, a solution that has worked very well for me. Soon I was free of the overt signs of menopause, such as hot flashes. But as a model I was concerned about what changes might occur in my looks in the next few years. And I became curious about what to expect in general of this stage of my life. So far middle age felt like a time to discover new freedoms and gather strength. At the same time, I had never given this time of life any thought and I felt unprepared for it.

I was lucky enough to trust my gynecologist for all my basic medical needs, but for some reason, I didn't consider speaking to her about my range of feelings about menopause. I didn't think she would be able to give me the real scoop. What I wanted to know was what other women were going through—what other women were thinking and feeling about the subject and what was happening to them. So I stopped trying to hide and I brought "it" up wherever I went, with friends, with other models, with colleagues in nutrition, and I saw that many of them were hungry to talk.

Notes and ideas for a possible book began to accumulate. Women in their forties and fifties were obviously experiencing the inevitable physical changes that I was experiencing, and they wanted to talk about them. These same women seemed also to be going through an exciting time in their lives. Everywhere around me I saw great women in my age group, looking wonderful, being active and productive. Some were seeing adult children move away from home while some were having children for the first time. Others were starting to take care of elderly parents. Some started new careers, others started new relationships, still others were meeting the challenges and pleasures of marriages that had lasted through the ups and downs of several decades. Few fit the image I was discovering many of us still had of the depressed, overweight, resigned, and washed-up menopausal woman. We were somebody else entirely.

Something had happened to my generation in the past thirty years. We had been raised to be pretty daughters, loving wives, and devoted mothers. Many of us fulfilled those expectations quite nicely. Now we found ourselves in the middle of our lives with opportunities no other generation of women had ever had before. Instead of arriving at a midlife crisis, the women around me were starting life anew. Where, then, did this unspeakable stage known as ''the change'' fit in?

I set out to find the answer to that question. I teamed up with writer Pamela Gordon, who became my collaborator, although we chose to write the book from my point of view. Our first step was to look for material that substantiated what everyone already ''knew.'' What we found was a good deal of scientific and medical information in journals in the library, once we hunted for it, much of it contradictory and some of it controversial. We also found a number of recent books on the shelves of bookstores and a smattering of out-of-print books in the library for women who were not inclined to comb through scientific journals. These books offered a lot of medical information, often excellent. Some were slanted toward doing the best for oneself given the terrible circumstances. No popular book was available that chronicled what we women felt, in our own words.

For that information, Pamela and I would have to go directly to the source. Thus began a series of interviews with sixty women from around the country. Most of our interviews were with women in their forties and fifties, although we also spoke with women in their thirties, sixties, and seventies and a woman of ninety-nine. We crossed class, race, and state lines. We interviewed women on either coast, in the South, Midwest, and Southeast. We interviewed black women and white, teachers, waitresses, doctors, assembly-line workers, secretaries, artists, nurses, corporate executives, psychologists, homemakers, writers, housecleaners, and entrepreneurs.

Along with these women, we conducted interviews with and read the research of leading experts and practitioners in gynecology, psychology, psychiatry, women's studies, history, exercise physiology, nutrition, skin care, and beauty. We spoke with officials in the Food and Drug Administration as well as marketers of health and beauty aids. The more research we did, the more outdated older information appeared. At the same time, new research that supported our observations about the quality of life during menopause was becoming available with greater frequency. Major studies such as *The Massachusetts Women's Health Study*, which you will read about in Chapter Five, involved 2,500 Massachusetts residents. Among the study's conclusions about menopause was that "somewhere between the ages of 45 and 55 women typically experience a year or two of irregular periods, fluctuations in body temperature, and some sleepless nights—and often, that is that."

Through it all, the richest source of information and ideas for this book has been the words of the women who opened their homes and their hearts and spoke in detail about areas of their lives many of them had never revealed before. Their stories, shared over tea or coffee, around kitchen tables, in living rooms, on porches, in offices on lunch hours, by tape, by phone, by questionnaire have given this book its life and its shape. Not only did those interviewed reveal what they were going through in menopause and in midlife, they revealed what they wanted to know about menopause as well as what information they needed in order to take the best possible care of themselves.

This book has been designed to address these needs. It clarifies much of the information that is already out in print but that can sometimes be confusing. It attempts to provide what I found missing in the current popular literature. And it offers lists of relevant books, studies, and resources. The entire book is meant to be used as a source to which you can turn again and again.

To best facilitate that, the book is divided into four sections. The first two sections explore the history, the mythology, and the medical facts regarding menopause. The third section provides step-by-step programs in beauty, nutrition, and exercise for women in the menopausal years.

Sections One and Two comprise Chapters One through Seven. Chapter One identifies and introduces the woman in her menopausal years and asks the question, How did we get here? Chapters Two through Six take several steps back in time to examine the myths surrounding menopause and the history that encouraged such myths. These chapters explore prevalent attitudes toward menopause and how such attitudes have shaped our expectations of the event. Interwoven throughout are the experiences of the women interviewed, experiences that sometimes support and sometimes contest the myths.

Chapters Six and Seven lay out the medical facts. These chapters let you know what to expect and to what extent, as well as explaining what you are currently going through or have already experienced. Specifically, Chapter Six provides an in-depth discussion and analysis of physical and emotional signs, while Chapter Seven examines the continuing controversy surrounding hormone-replacement therapy. Throughout these chapters are the voices of women sharing what happened to them during their menopause and the variety of ways in which they have responded.

Section Three of the book, The One-Hour-a-Day Guide to Self-Care, is a beauty, nutrition, and exercise guide, providing step-by-step programs. Menopause is but one of many changes in our lives during middle age. This section offers a comprehensive, integrated approach to staying healthy and being beautiful that also fits into an active, ever-changing lifestyle.

In Chapters Nine through Thirteen you will find easy-to-use, effective, and time-saving systems that I designed based on my years as a nutritionist and my experience as a yoga teacher and a model. These specific systems fill two health and beauty needs that women have said are important to them in midlife. The first is an approach to maintaining health and looks that fits easily into the daily routine. The second is a system specific to women whose bodies are changing. Well-known methods of caring for skin or hair, for wearing makeup and clothes, or for exercising, depended on reliably for years, may no longer apply to the new you. Thus, a daily food, exercise, makeup, and skin care program designed specifically for women at menopause is offered. The entire program, including food preparation and cooking, can be completed in under one hour a day.

In this section are tips from experts in the fields of exercise, nutrition, and beauty, interspersed with the words of the women introduced in the first half of the book—on their attitudes to health and beauty in midlife and what programs, plans, systems, and ideas have worked for them.

In Section Four, Taking Risks, Making Noise, Being Courageous wraps up the findings of the interviews and research and propels us into the future.

Putting together this book involved two years of research and writing. In that time, remarkable strides have been made in public attention to the medical and psychological needs of women in midlife. Menopause clinics are growing in number, from Gainesville to Cleveland to San Francisco. The National Institute of Mental Health is studying the psychological transition from the pre- to the postmenopausal years. And the first major government-funded study on the effects of hormone treatment for menopausal women got under way in 1990: the three-year, 10-million-dollar Postmenopausal Estrogen-Progestin Intervention Trial is being conducted by the National Institutes of Health.

For my part, when I began this book two years ago, I thought I knew what I wanted to say, based on my own experience of menopause. The all-encompassing event that I feared would overtake me never occurred, so I set out on this project with the assumption that menopause was no big deal.

As with most large projects, however, this one soon took on a life of its own. The interviews and the research seemed to move the book in its own direction. I had not anticipated the range of experiences reported to me by women of different ages and backgrounds. Their stories, chronicled in the pages ahead, added infinite layers of depth and complexity to my original assumption.

Throughout the book these women affirm that a vital, rewarding, and productive life is possible during and after "the change." During menopause there *are* physical changes and there *are* hormonal changes. But the physical event itself does not deeply affect the rest of our life. What often contributes to the emotional and physical indications of menopause is our approach to them. For some, when the circumstances of life are particularly difficult, physical changes may signal a breaking point. Yet, by and large, women in their menopausal years are doing just fine. In fact, as most of the women in the book attest, as we get older life gets better.

Sometime after the *Lear's* ad in which I was featured became popular, *Ad Week* published a picture of Brooke Shields in a pose similar to mine, with my picture next to it. The caption read: "Brooke, here's what you're going to look like in thirty years." I have a picture of myself at my senior prom over thirty years ago. All dressed up for the big night, I look tentative and expectant on the arm of my date. I certainly had no idea what awaited me in life. In the *Lear's* photo I am very much awake, present, and conscious. Alive and, yes, beautiful.

The girl in the prom picture never gave growing older a thought, and she never would have imagined the changes the thirty years ahead of her were destined to bring. If prompted to think about menopause, she might have seen it as an end to something. At some point in our history maybe it was. Now, however, it is a signal that we are in the middle of our lives, with years of productivity to come. Maybe we used to be old when we reached menopause, but we aren't anymore.

CHAPTER 1

Who We Are and How We Found Ourselves Here

Life is very rich for me right now and it's not money we're talking about. I'm rich in my ability to enjoy the experiences I have. I don't feel guilty about enjoying myself like I did as a younger woman. I can live my life much more fully without the old worries. I have a lot more fun than I ever did before.

These are not the words of a teenage girl or even of a woman in her early twenties, away from home and on her own for the first time. These words were spoken by Mickie Kramer, a forty-eight-year-old entrepreneur whose sentiments match those of almost every woman who had a chance to speak her mind to me. Life is better as we get older, more interesting, more available. We are less self-conscious, less confused, and infinitely more adept at taking control of our destinies. And that, we insist, has happened over time.

''Better'' does not mean that life has necessarily gotten easier or less complicated. In fact, a claim I heard repeatedly was that as young women few of us had been adequately prepared for the twists and turns our lives were to take. How could we have been prepared, considering the expectations with which we were raised?

We came of age in the 1950s and 1960s. We fell in love to *South Pacific*, *West Side Story*, Frank Sinatra, and early rock and roll. We married, raised families, and never gave a thought to the future, which would take care of itself as long as we followed the rules. What we didn't know was that sometimes rules change.

DIFFERENT ROADS TAKEN

The time of life considered middle age spans roughly two decades, between the ages of forty and sixty. If you are between fifty and sixty, you probably grew up expecting to marry and have children. Yet women who are close to sixty and women currently in their forties have different approaches to this expectation, approaches influenced by the change in culture between the 1950s and the 1960s.

Fifty-nine-year-old Carolyn Sutton married her high school sweetheart when they were both twenty. Their marriage has lasted almost four decades. When she first married, Carolyn put her dream of being a lawyer aside in order to support her husband through law school. Being a wife and mother was her first, unquestioned priority. Although she was committed to her marriage and children, having them as her only focus left her unfulfilled. In her forties Carolyn found personal and professional satisfaction when she began writing one-act plays and performing them in schools and libraries.

Linda Avery, on the other hand, is forty-five, and grew up on the boundary line between the housewives of the 1950s and the rebels of the 1960s. A striking combination of the two, she got married the year she completed law school, when she was twenty-eight. Her husband already had two children from a previous marriage, and she simultaneously became a stepmother and an attorney. She felt confident at the time that she could take on many different roles without difficulty. Yet, in her thirties, once she had her own children, she realized how demanding a full-time career and a full-time family could be. Over time, she and her husband worked out a schedule that balances their careers with child rearing.

Both Carolyn and Linda eagerly embraced the possibilities offered them in their twenties. And neither of them thought about their future. "Thought? Who thought?" said Carolyn. "I don't think I ever looked ahead." Linda agreed. "I never thought that my role as an attorney and my role as a mother might conflict or compromise each other."

Despite some confusion and struggle, each woman has achieved a level of satisfaction in both work and family— satisfaction due perhaps to having the courage they might not have had as younger women to play by their own rewritten rules.

Diana Ramsay's situation exemplifies this point. These days her husband, once a fast-track executive, is starting a consulting business, while Diana is the one carrying the family's financial responsibility. At fifty-one, she is a vice president at Citicorp Bank. Yet, remembering back, she noted, "I didn't think about my forties and fifties at all. And if I had thought about them, it would have just been a carryover of how much further my husband would have gotten and therefore carried me materially. He would be doing better and I would be 'Mrs. Doing Better.' "

AN UNPRECEDENTED FUTURE

Why did we have such a limited view of our own future? One of the reasons is that there was no future to look toward. No generation before us has had the opportunities we have. No generation has had the time or the health to forge midlife ground.

As women experiencing middle age in America, we are at an unprecedented threshold in the history of the human life cycle. In 1900, the average female life expectancy was 49.2 years. Life expectancy did improve once a woman lived into adulthood, since this average age reflects early death rates due to disease and high infant mortality. But life spans have increased considerably and now more than half of all American women are over forty. Women today can expect to live an average of 28.6 years past the age of fifty.

We have been given a gift of thirty extra years. The second half of our lives, our third stage, can be lived as choice years, a time to develop interests and fulfill dreams we might have put aside until now. And yet, as all pioneers on the edge of an unexplored frontier, we do not arrive unencumbered. The history and myths about being a woman may silently influence the explorations ahead. In examining where that history and those myths come from, we can uncover how and why we view middle age the way we do. And no discussion of middle age can be separated from a discussion of menopause.

While woman after woman let me know that she was coping with midlife very well, she still felt unprepared for menopause. What was this dark unexplored event that meant she could no longer have children? What effect would it have on one of her most dependable resources— her body? And what would thirty more years of life beyond the ability to have children be like? Even for those of us who know that we have given birth as many times as we plan to, no longer being able to get pregnant changes our definition of ourselves. And therefore where we are headed. Thus, an examination of the history and myths surrounding the event sets us free to create a new future.

MENOPAUSE VERSUS "'THE CHANGE"

What, exactly, is menopause? I asked that question of Pauline Worlen, a systems analyst who is divorced, in her fifties, with two children who are living on their own. She seemed to know a lot about it. She used medical terms to describe the signs and said that the minor discomfort she experienced as her menstrual cycle changed had not affected her life in a negative way.

She sat across from me as we talked, in the living room of her small comfortable house on a peninsula in

Maine. Growing up in Chicago was a lifetime away from this community, and if she had thought about it then, Pauline would not have imagined herself living as she does now—unmarried, living alone, near the ocean instead of in the city or a suburb. At fifty-seven, she says her life has been a series of surprises, born out of the tensions of expecting one thing (the perfect marriage and family) and living another (self-sufficiency and a successful career that has let her freelance in recent years). A well-developed sense of irony allows her to take pleasure in the way things have worked out. "Whether it's the age I am or not, whatever's got me to where I am, this is the best part of my whole life."

Occasional sun from the blustery October sky wavered across books, records, and knitting work casually lying about the living room. Everything in the room fit together, although nothing conventionally matched, and I had the sense that here, you could do anything you wanted, day or night, without concern for getting in someone's way. Pauline was telling me a story about her mother and she used the phrase "change of life." Something struck her when she said that, something that hadn't occurred to her when she used the word "menopause." "When I say 'change of life,' " she mused, "now there's a whole other story. I knew nothing about 'the change,' except it was when women got weird.

"I remember when I was in high school and I came home one day. In the basement we had a bunch of closets built into the wall. There was one that my father kept his stuff in. He'd been to Europe and come back and put away his attaché case. So I came home and went downstairs and my mother had taken this case out of the closet. She had, in a frenzy, ripped it open to see what was inside because it was locked. And I remember that my brother and I talked about it and we decided it must have been the 'change of life.' "

Pauline also remembered sitting quietly among the racks of dresses hanging in the front room of her childhood home. Her mother was a seamstress, and Pauline would listen to the women who came to have their dresses altered talking back and forth. "Women came in, and they would try things on while talking to each other and I heard a whole lot of stuff. The change of life was a very unpleasant time, they would say, and women got very upset and they got hysterical and crazy. And then that was the end for them, the end of their life. After that their lives were over because they couldn't have children anymore."

I pictured wizened ladies with arthritic limbs coming into her mother's front room, but when Pauline looked back she recalled that these women weren't elderly. In fact, they had not even reached menopause yet. They were just thinking about what menopause would be like, talking about what they expected. Yet they seemed old at the time. "They were heavy, tired. So maybe it was true for them, in a sense, that it did mark the end of their lives."

THE FIRST WORD THAT COMES TO MIND

How did other women answer the question I had posed to Pauline? To get us started I asked, "What is the first word that comes to mind when I say 'menopause'?" The reaction I got was as varied as the experience itself. For a good number of women the first response was, literally, a pause. Nothing came to mind. Others associated the word with "something new" or "change." Another said, "Kotex," another, "The next thing," and for one woman, "Yippee!" But a lot of the associations were negative.

"The first thing that comes into my head is sickness," someone said, and then laughed, a little embarrassed. "Horrible," said another, and others added, "Terrible," "Crotchety," "Slowing down," "When you get depressed," "Going crazy," "Getting all nervous," "Dry, wrinkled skin," "You can't do what you did ten years ago because you are weaker,'' ''Dark,'' ''I don't want to talk about it,'' ''You shouldn't bring it up,'' ''I don't understand,'' ''The beginning of old age.''

Ironically, the women who offered these responses were active, energetic, lively, some at a crossroads in their relationships or making decisions about earning a living, but not depressed and not crazy. Where did these bleak descriptions come from? Certainly not from the lives of the women who spoke them. Diana, the Citicorp vice president, who supplied the descriptions ''crotchety'' and ''slowed down,'' revealed her gut reaction to the term menopause: ''You get depressed. You get emotional. You certainly don't have the vitality you once had. You're a changed woman and less than a whole person.'' Yet Diana also said, ''Menopause has not affected me at all. And I have no emotional highs or lows because of it. I'm functioning just the same with the same energy level as before.''

THE MYTHS

The idea of a debilitating menopause seems justified by the lives of the tired women who came for dresses and conversation to Pauline's mother's front room. Living in a working-class section of Chicago, just a generation away from us, those women must have cooked, cleaned, and taken care of families until they were worn out before their time. But Pauline recalled that those women were actually younger than Pauline is now. They had not yet reached menopause. Their talk about what they were certain was going to happen to them came from images passed down through generations. Those images, strong enough to exert influence on us today, come from five powerful myths, which I will explore in the next chapters. These myths emerged from my conversations with women as well as from historical and medical research:

Myth 1. Postmenopausal women have lost their femininity.

Myth 2. Postmenopausal women are no longer sexy.

Myth 3. Menopause is a medical disease.

Myth 4. Menopause is a psychological crisis.

Myth 5. Menopause signals the onset of old age.

Myths act as the transmitters of a culture's values. While they may originate as tales that explain what cannot easily be understood or controlled, all myths have the potential to be mistaken for the truth eventually. Scientist Evelyn Fox Keller writes in her book *Reflections on Gender and Science:* "Unexamined myths, wherever they survive, have a subterranean potency; they affect our thinking in ways we are not aware of, and to the extent that we lack awareness, our capacity to resist their influence is undermined."

Unexamined myths have affected many of the important events in my own life. Over the years, as I challenged myself with new goals and allowed myself to take risks, I have watched those same myths explode.

I grew up thinking I was pretty but not particularly intelligent. My looks, I was constantly told, were my greatest asset and one I should fully exploit. Naturally, I accepted that since I was a girl, I was not capable of doing math, much less science. When I went back to college for nutrition, my initial courses in chemistry were extremely difficult. At times my mind had to stretch so far I would almost cry. But I completed my program successfully and went on to a new career.

Another myth was the one about being alone. Terrified when I was first separated from my husband, I heard the voices of my family in my head: "What a terrible fate for a woman to be alone." Yet in those first few months on my own I found myself getting up early in the morning to read, something I had never done before in my life because I hadn't had the time. I actually felt great, and it dawned on me that while being alone might not be preferable in the long run, it was hardly terrible.

In my twenties I was newly married with young children, having achieved on schedule what I grew up expecting to do with my life. I was playing the part of an adult although, filled with uncertainty and insecurity, I really had no idea of who I was. In contrast, my forties and fifties have been an exciting time of self-awareness and growth. I have talked about this myth of the twenties being the prime of our lives, our great youth, lost and never to be regained, with dozens of the women I interviewed. Whether we made it through the decades married to the same man we started our adult lives with, whether we got divorced along the way, whether we're on a third career or never worked outside the home, we laughed together, recalling how unformed we were back then and what a limited idea of middle age we had.

All these myths remind me of stainless-steel sinks. When I was first married, everyone had to own a stainless-steel sink. Stainless-steel sinks never scratched. They were always clean, unlike those porcelain sinks, and you *had* to have one. So I had my stainless-steel sink and it scratched all the time and it always had spots and no matter how much I cleaned it and fixed it, it always looked awful, and what kind of stainless-steel sink was this? I was sure I had the one bad sink until one day I dared to imagine that we had all been misled.

Could the myths surrounding menopause and the accompanying associations with decline and middle age be akin to the truth about stainless-steel sinks? Have we, in believing the myths without examining their sources, been subjected to their "subterranean potency"? Despite our insistence that life gets better, we are confused and often fearful of menopause. Could we be fulfilling those myths by unconsciously slowing ourselves down and diminishing our expectations of ourselves in our middle years? It is time to replace those myths. We have a more exciting version of an old, old story to tell.

SECTION ONE

✼

The Myths

CHAPTER 2

Myth 1:
"No Longer a Woman"

Women was created for two things, making meals and babies.

—ARCHIE BUNKER

In the early 1970s, during the advent of the women's movement in the United States and after the well-publicized sexual revolution, David Reuben, in his book *Everything You Always Wanted to Know About Sex,* told us that during menopause:

As the estrogen is shut off, a woman comes as close as she can to being a man. Increased facial hair, deepened voice, obesity and the decline of breasts and female genitalia all contribute to a masculine appearance. Coarsened features, enlargement of the clitoris and gradual baldness complete the tragic picture. Not really a man but no longer a functional woman, these individuals live in the world of intersex.

Let's kill ourselves now, thank you. Death is preferable even to imagining the world of intersex—a long corridor lined with *Let's Make a Deal* doors Number 1, 2, and 3: male, female, hybrid. Or intersex—a tangled forest of body hair, decay, and the alternating falsetto and deep-throated tones of a human being who cannot determine who she/he is.

Granted, Reuben's description *was* criticized by

professionals and the public. He voiced his assumptions about women simply on the basis of the fact that we could no longer have children. He didn't pluck his ideas out of thin air, either. His assumptions were born in the silent, therefore unexamined, myths that shaped us.

NOT A COMPLICATED PROCESS

The word "menopause" comes from Greek. *Meno* refers to month and is used specifically to refer to events pertaining to menstruation. *Pausis* means cessation, or halt. Precisely, menopause is the cessation of a woman's menstrual cycle, the halt in menstrual bleeding. No more periods. The last one ever.

"Menopause" does not mean the physiological changes leading up to the final period, although that is the popular term for the process. Medically, those physiological signs—such as changing menstrual patterns, hot flashes, or night sweats—are known as the climacteric. The months or years before our final period during which we experience the climacteric are sometimes known as the perimenopause. The postmenopause refers to the years following menopause.

Not particularly complicated, right? While medically menopause and the climacteric are relatively straightforward occurrences, the word "menopause" is loaded. Beyond its actual meaning, menopause in our culture signifies a great deal.

BACK TO THE SOURCE

As women, our identities have traditionally been determined by our ability to get pregnant and have children. In early cultures, men and women alike were in awe of the processes of life and death. Such processes occurred daily as the sun rose and set, and seasonally as the weather changed and crops and game diminished or grew plentiful. The same kind of process was seen in the fertility of women, and for thirty thousand years humans worshipped fertility goddesses. The male gods who built the world as opposed to giving birth to it are a relatively contemporary trend in religious thought.

Ultimately, the biological fact of pregnancy determined how early communities, going back to cave dwellers, were organized. Men went out to hunt; women, pregnant and taking care of little children, tended the home fires. Certain ancient and primitive societies varied this theme somewhat, as can be seen in the tales of the Amazons and characters from Greek mythology such as Artemis, the huntress. But for the most part a woman's mobility was limited once she began having children.

Over time this division of labor came to mean something. It came to mean that men were strong, perhaps because they hunted and killed or because they roamed far from home. It came to mean that women were weak, perhaps because they were always surrounded by children, who were dependent, and dependence was associated with weakness. It came to mean that men, because of their physical separation from the immediate needs of little ones, had the time to make the laws, write the books, handle the money, dictate the religions, and indulge in their favorite pastimes, such as fighting wars. And that women had the babies and took care of what went on at home.

Myths developed around a woman's childbearing abilities. Over time and through the course of developing civilization, a woman's ability to carry and bear children became synonymous with who she was. From a biological fact came a definition of female fulfillment, self-expression, and destiny that is still with us today. Those of us currently in our forties and fifties who were simultaneously growing up and raising families in the 1950s and 1960s knew what was expected of us. Whether we were financially and socially privileged or struggling to make ends meet, many of us fashioned ourselves in relation to an ideal of femininity in which taking care of children, husband, and home was at the center of our world. The height of feminine achievement was giving birth. Our ability to give birth, however, was never meant to negate our need for other forms of fulfillment and accomplishment.

A LEGACY OF EMBARRASSMENT:
MENSTRUATION THROUGH MENOPAUSE

Along with the development of civilization as we know it came less and less respect for earth and fertility goddesses. Such goddesses were associated with mystery, magic, darkness, and confusion. Reproductive occurrences such as the shedding of menstrual blood were both revered and feared by men, who were afraid it would cast evil on their hunts. Later, Muslims, Hindus, and Jews required a woman to seclude herself while she was "unclean." Medieval Christians would not allow menstruating women into church.

Negative attitudes toward menstruation survive into our enlightened times. Some of our mothers and grandmothers slapped us when we naïvely announced the beginnings of our "womanhood." While *we* may have educated our daughters with training manuals and sanitary napkin starter kits, monthly bleeding is not an event that is announced in public. Women whisper to each other on the way to the rest room; men smirk when a woman is shrill. We call the menses "the Curse," "having our periods," "being unwell," "having our friend," "that time of the month," and the graphically descriptive "being on the rag." At all costs, menstrual blood must be hidden. Most of us follow the silent rules of not wearing white on those heavy-flow days; we take painkillers to mask cramps that might keep us from being active. For years, any pain or distress we might have felt when we were menstruating was dismissed as "in our heads." Only recently has premenstrual syndrome legitimized the discomfort many women feel.

This legacy of embarrassment about a natural part of the female reproductive process extends beyond menstruation into the menopausal years. As girls we knew from the first that our periods were private, slightly mystical, definitely messy, and perhaps unclean monthly events not to be referred to in mixed sexual company. In similar ways, as menopausal women coming to the end of our menstrual cycle we know that such an event is not to be the topic of public conversation. As Evelyn Glenn, fifty-eight, a mother of four, noted, "Whether it's part of being uncomfortable about the whole area of sex, you just don't talk about things like that. I wouldn't go to a cocktail party and announce to everybody, 'Guess what I'm going through.' "

THE BEGINNING AND END OF WOMANHOOD

For all its secrecy, however, most girls look forward to getting their period because of the underlying meaning attached to the event. Simply, the onset of the menses is the onset of womanhood. The girl who begins to menstruate is grown-up. She is now capable of getting pregnant and having a baby. She is a woman.

Mickie Kramer, the forty-eight-year-old entrepreneur who opened the first chapter of this book by saying her life is richer than ever before, remembers the anticipation with which she waited for her period to start. "There was a film put out by Disney that was shown in all the grammar schools. It was about getting your period. It went through what physiologically happens when you got it. But the bottom line was that when you started to menstruate you were a woman. You left your girlhood and this was your rite of passage into womanhood."

I sat in Mickie's suburban home on a closed-in porch among plants and wicker furniture. Mickie served tea from a perfectly arranged tray as she remembered back to her girlhood in southern California. "I guess because of the Disney picture I really looked forward to getting my period because then I was going to be a woman.'' She settled back with tea in hand. ''Once menopause started, *not* having my period initially felt funny. I noticed that my whole life cycle was actually based on my period. The times when I felt like Chicken Little, with the sky falling down on me, I could look to see when my period was due. Then, I had a reason for why I was feeling emotional or moody. Without my period I didn't have a guidepost or guideline to understand my emotional makeup.''

I had never considered the end of my monthly cycles in those terms. When we are used to gauging our emotional lives by an internal clock and that clock is taken away, we truly have to get to know ourselves all over again, which is what Mickie said she did.

''If I feel depressed now or anxious, I just notice that I'm depressed—or that I'm not if I'm not. Some days I wake up feeling I am of some intrinsic social value, and some days I wake up and I don't think I am. I'm learning to have an inner conversation with myself that I didn't have when I had the crutch of being able to say my feelings were due to my menstrual cycle.''

Hannah Simmons, in her early thirties, had not reached the stage Mickie had and understandably had not given the end of her period much thought. ''This might sound strange, but I love having it,'' she told me. ''It makes me feel very female.'' Hannah is an artist who supports herself as a paralegal. She lives in an inner-city neighborhood in Detroit. She is independent and feisty and wonders whether she will ever have children—but not because, like so many women in their early thirties, she is worried about meeting the right man. Instead she honestly questions whether or not she *wants* to have children. At the same time she said, ''Having my period makes me feel like a woman. Afterward I feel cleansed. I never thought about how it would feel when I didn't have it. I've taken it for granted that it will always be there. When it's not, will I feel less of a woman? I honestly don't know.'' Hannah voices the popular thought that once menstruation ends and menopause begins, so ends womanhood.

Nonsense, all of us who have been where Mickie is, or who are approaching that place, insist. I am still a woman. Look. Can't you see? And we pinch ourselves to make sure we're still here. But we are shouting into a long history.

CLAIMS TO CONCEPTION

By the time the Greeks came to power in the Western world, culture and nature had grown increasingly far apart. Women—and, by default, femininity—were associated with nature. Nature was the arena of intuition, emotions, unpredictability, the lunar, darkness, mystery, and magic. Culture became associated with logic, reason, control, the solar, light, freedom, and intellect—the male and, again by association, masculinity. In Athens during the fifth century B.C., when two of the great thinkers of Western civilization, Plato and Socrates, roamed the markets and plazas with their young disciples, Athenian women were confined to the home and not allowed to come out. The law said they couldn't walk the streets. Yet history books call this period the Golden Age of Athens.

Primitive societies did not understand the role a father played in conception. A woman became pregnant by ancestral spirits who somehow found their way into the womb. But this scenario changed once the man's role in conception was discovered. Simone de Beauvoir notes, in *The Second Sex*, that this discovery, coupled with laws that legalized private property, enabled men to lay claim to the children that would eventually be born. By legalizing attachment to their heirs, men gained control over reproduction, which meant they controlled their future to some extent. A woman was now merely a receptacle that sheltered the man's child.

Aristotle believed that the mingling of sperm and menstrual blood created the fetus. Women merely provided the "passive matter" that carried and nourished the masculine force of "activity, movement, life." And Hippocrates believed life arose from two seeds, the weak female and the strong male. In the 1600s people thought that a woman's body housed an already formed miniature adult, the homunculus. It wasn't until 1883 that current discoveries of the true nature of fertilization and fetal development were made.

So biology, culture, and justification for social and sexual roles were blurred over time into truths about female and male nature, traveling through the ages to haunt us today. In a lecture I attended at Clark University, Gloria Steinem quoted Thomas Jefferson as having written that in "our state of pure democracy there would still be excluded from our deliberations women who, to prevent deprivation of morals and ambiguity of issues, should not mix promiscuously in the gatherings of men." Steinem noted that even the "most radical of our founding fathers didn't perceive women as part of democracy."

THAT WAS THEN . . .

Out of the shadows of so much history arose the 1950s in America—a decade during which a good number of the women currently going through menopause were coming of age as girlfriends, wives, and mothers. Strides had been made over the centuries in science, technology, medicine, and consciousness. Yet, in post–World War II United States the suburban ideal was heralded as the dream existence. For women, the parameters of such an existence included charming a man, taking care of her own beauty, having babies, and making a home—this, in an era when women were free, because of birth control, to choose the number of children they would have, free of the threat of death by some of the diseases that took our ancestors, and free of the drudgery of household labor through the invention and marketing of modern labor-saving machines.

What has this to do with menopause? Although we have come a long way since the 1950s and 1960s, we were encouraged as girls to see ourselves in terms of bearing children, supporting and serving our men, and keeping warm, clean, and well stocked a safe and happy hearth. The financing of that well-stocked hearth was left up to the man (part of *his* socialization), which didn't leave us a lot of room for earning money on our own and having access to the power that money gives people in our world.

And then we arrive at midlife. For some of us, the children are launched. If we chose to have children in our thirties or forties, we are busy enjoying their early years. When we are physically unable to bear any more children, the desire, for many of us, is probably gone as well. Those of us who chose not to have children, or for whom conception was difficult, have most probably confronted that loss and grieved over it by this time, coming face to face with the "a woman without children is not really a woman" myth long before menopause. Now what?

None of this is a denial of the importance and value of raising children. Having my girls and watching them grow into young women has been the greatest of pleasures for me. And for the majority of women with children who speak in this book, raising children has been their greatest accomplishment and the most important job they have done in their lives.

At this stage, what we take issue with is the idea that we are useful to society and important as human beings *only* because we are able to have children.

. . . THIS IS NOW

We have outgrown the age-old images of successful womanhood available to us. They just don't make sense anymore. Yet, if we looked for fully realized public images of ourselves—in the media, in the workplace, in our families—until recently we would have found very few. When asked who they identified with in public life or in the media, most women drew a blank. It's not that role models are not out there. Many well-known women of strength, intellect, and beauty will be mentioned in these pages. But for the most part, since we have been underrepresented for such a long time, we are hard-pressed to come up with public images with whom we can readily identify. And we have no private images, either. Without inner and outer validation, no matter how rich in life experience we are, the desire to retire ourselves, to take ourselves out of the game, will be stronger than our determination to move forward. We must consciously rally against the perception that we are past our prime.

We need to replace old myths with new myths, with fresh concepts and ideals that emphasize our resources and our resourcefulness. Beginning by establishing a personal image of ourselves, we can individually determine our power and strength. We can develop these strengths in the ways we choose and project them into the world, so that others see us for who we are—experienced, loving, and capable people who have significant contributions to make.

Merlin Stone is the author of *When God Was a Woman*, one of the first books to examine ancient goddess-centered religions. I was intrigued with the idea suggested by her title and thought she might have an interesting perspective on this time of life. I called her and we met in a café in downtown Manhattan. She was slim, with wide flashing eyes and her hair in long white braids, and she wore several layers of black clothing. "My uniform," she informed me, with a grin. "I'm prepared for any temperature change," and indeed during our time together she peeled off a jacket and then a scarf.

Merlin wrote *When God Was a Woman*, the first of her books, in her forties. Her early training had been in sculpture and art history. She remembered being told when she was in her twenties that "visual artists don't do their mature work until their fifties." Therefore she has lived her life expecting her work to get better with the years. She continues to work freely and flexibly as a writer and artist at her current age of sixty, with no plans to retire. I am reminded of how our expectations of life are formed by what we hear about ourselves when we are young. Creativity, I had once been certain, was limited to adolescence. And I remember what I have just reread in Gail Sheehy's *Passages* about how people in their forties and fifties in East Asia are considered relatively young, since the most valued occupations in that part of the world, such as meditation and poetry, take years to master.

Ironically, biology, which has given us so many mixed messages and blessings up until now, has reared its head to spur us forward. Our function solely as childbearers is antiquated. The thirty years we can now expect to live past fifty allow us ample time to distinguish ourselves beyond that role. At the same time, we have no reason to give up the pleasures of being mothers, grandmothers, caretakers, and richly expressive, intelligent, emotional, and inventive individuals.

CHAPTER 3

Myth 2: Sex and the Nonfertile Woman

ARCHIE: *Wait a minute, Edith. Will you lay off that honeymoon stuff? Honeymoons is for kids, not for older people like you.*

EDITH: *Archie! Right now I am in the prime of my life and at the height of my sexual attractiveness.*

Our bodies, male and female, are sexual all our lives. There is a myth that insists, however, that as women we are no longer sexual once we are no longer fertile. Why that myth exists becomes clear when we look at its source. We were put on this earth to make babies. Once we can no longer do that, our function is null, void, our purpose used up. Menopause, therefore, spells disaster in terms of who we are and what we have left to accomplish and offer. And whoever heard of a sexually desirable or desiring disaster?

Stereotypes exist that reinforce the idea that postmenopausal women are not sexual, and enough images abound in the media to cement such stereotypes. The lack of positive images is a more abstract but perhaps more damaging influence. Remember the estrogen-deprived world of "intersex" in Dr. Reuben's popular book? Medical texts have called lack of estrogen "the loss of the woman in the woman."

Sexuality that is dependent on fertility is part of the same equation that says being young equals being hot. Teenagers, with their lively hormones, are expected to consider sex an immediate priority. And it follows, in popular thinking, that as hormones no longer rage, sex cools down. No one has done a study, but the number of lovemaking sessions in the back seats of cars probably does decrease between the ages of sixteen and sixty. But cars are no longer necessary when there is the safety of one's home and the comfort of one's bed—a much more encouraging environment for intimacy.

Let's put the popular ideas about hormones and sex to rest. Sexual activity in nonhuman animals is directly influenced by hormonal conditions. Testosterone in the male and estrogen in the female signal cells in the animal's brain that trigger sexual activity. Female animals will mate only when the ovum is ready for fertilization, during estrus. We human females, on the other hand, are willing and able to have sex at any time during our cycle. The androgenic hormones, *not estrogen,* are responsible for desire (libido). The point is, we are capable of being sexual and sexy way past middle age. Young, however, is definitely considered sexier.

THE MEDIA'S MESSAGE

How do we know? Commercials, movies, and television shows tell us so. Romance novels tell us, too. Designers and manufacturers who glut the market with clothing for young bodies give us the same message. And young models in magazines and print advertising scream it at us. Those of us with wrinkles, the slightest bit of weight or sag, or spots and blemishes are out of the picture.

In a scene in the popular movie *When Harry Met Sally . . . ,* pretty, blonde, late-twenties Sally proves to Harry that women can fake orgasms by doing just that, faking an orgasm as she sits across from him in a restaurant. Afterward, a middle-aged woman at the next table says, "I'll have whatever she's having." The middle-aged woman, as it happens, is played by the director's mother.

All of us *know* that our mothers can't tell the difference between an orgasm and a corned beef sandwich.

Advertisers and the entertainment industry can get away with ignoring the sexuality of older people because of the unexamined assumptions about sexuality during the later years of life:

Assumption 1.   "Older" people are not sexually attractive.

Assumption 2.   They are not sexually active.

Assumption 3.   They are not interested in sex anymore.

Assumption 4.   They don't *have* sex.

Assumption 5.   Sex doesn't really matter in old age.

Assumption 6.   Interest in sex after a certain age is not only distasteful but abnormal.

Men can experience the same sex and age prejudices against them as women. For example, doctors may assume that middle-aged couples are not interested in sex. Many doctors are unresponsive to questions about sexual activity after one partner has been ill or undergone surgery. Nursing homes are reluctant to allow male and female patients who may be elderly but who have sexual desires to sleep together. In popular thinking, though, older men are considered sexier than older women. Take a look at the different words we use to describe each.

OUR WORDS AND THE IMAGES THEY CREATE

Young men are studs who are restless and who roam. Older men are bulls, lions, and bears—large, powerful, leaders of the pack. Young women are kittens, birds, chicks, and lambs—cute, fluffy, cuddly, and acquiescent. Older women are shrews, hens, cows, sows—high-pitched, fat, and slothful. Women daring enough to be sexual at any age are vixens and vamps—conniving and slinky, *their* potency comes from an undermining trickiness that traps the roaring male by appealing to his concealed soft spot.

Unmarried men are awarded the status of bachelor, a word that brings to mind images of smoky bachelor pads equipped with leather furniture, black lacquer bathrooms, and two-seater sports cars. Bachelors as they grow older are distinguished, attractively gray-haired, their faces weathered and full of character, Henry Higginses ever ready to enlighten the unworldly young girl about the realities of womanhood. Above all, bachelors are free. Nowhere do we hear a joyous calling out of relationship statistics for men. You lucky Joes, there are so many remarkable women out there for you to choose from. Instead we are heartbrokenly informed that hordes of unmarried women are bound to a life of frustration, since there are so few men willing to commit to them.

The female equivalent to the bachelor is the spinster, alias the old maid, terms that do not conjure up a pretty picture. No high-tech spinster pad for her. Literature and history serve up images of the curmudgeonly schoolteacher who lives with an elderly parent, or the kindly aunt living off a married sibling in a back room populated with aging Raggedy Ann dolls and sticky sour candies for the occasional visiting niece or nephew. Then again there are the maiden ladies who have lived together all their lives. Everyone suspects that they may not have wanted a man in the first place. Either way, the myth of the old maid has her barren, lonely, frigid, and frustrated, a biddie, shrill, a dried-up prune. And no matter how much liberation we have cultivated, a woman who chooses a life alone has to contend with a lifetime of defending her choice.

Other caricatures that repeat themselves through literature, art, and the mass media include the matron. Unlike the spinster, the matron is married, yet she is no longer a blushing bride. She alternates between the battering ram, corseted to look like a tank, who intimidates the masses with her rolling pin raised overhead, and the sweet, loving grandmother. Grandma is a perennial mother with powder-white, poufy hair who wears cardigan sweaters and sensible shoes. This Lady of the Cookie Jar has no interest in sex and—in the eyes of her ever expanding clan, at least—never did. She bakes innumerable pies and crochets innumerable afghan squares until they overtake the house and bury her. Both she and the rolling pin wielder are the infamous old wives whose unscientific tales are considered interesting folklore.

To confuse us even more, however, let us not forget another image of the older woman—one that contradicts the images of the dried-up, frustrated old maid and the sexless grandmother. In this corner we have the insatiable, voracious, middle-aged dragon lady, devouring everything in her path. This lady is the she-devil, the queen bee, the black widow, the wicked stepmother, the bitch in heat who is overripe to the point of decay. In our lifetime we've known her as Mrs. Robinson. Who in America can forget Anne Bancroft, drink-ravaged, her eyes shadowed, leaning against the shuttered closet door in the upstairs hall? Exhausted by deception and frustration, her own life destroyed, she is hell-bent on destroying the young lives around her.

THE GOOD NEWS

According to the old images out there, we are a frustrated biddie, a doting grandma, or the Queen out to get Snow White. Granted, Susan Sarandon's characters in *White Palace* and *Bull Durham* have single-handedly done more to publicize the sexuality of women in their forties than decades of previous images. But how about in real life? Is there room for a vibrant, vital, sexual, lusty, experienced, loving, exciting woman? Move on over. There actually is good news.

If you happen to be in a good sexual relationship, if you happen to be having sex on a consistent basis, it is likely that in middle age your sex life will continue to thrive. Shere Hite, in her *Hite Report on Female Sexuality*, tells us that theoretically libido should *increase* at menopause, since a woman's androgens, the hormones influencing sexual desire, are not affected by a decrease in estrogen.

The *Starr-Weiner Report on Sex and Sexuality in the Mature Years* provides further evidence of Hite's assertion. The report concludes that certain physiological changes—such as an increase in the time it may take an older woman to become aroused compared with her younger self—do occur with age. Yet no evidence suggests that sensation or feeling is lost during sex. The clitoris continues to be the main organ for sexual stimuli and a woman of eighty has the same physical capacity to achieve orgasm as she did at twenty.

"SEX IS WASTED ON THE YOUNG"

Clearly, the capacity for orgasm and enjoyment continues for years past middle age. What, however, has been the actual experience after menopause? Many women report a renewed excitement in their sex lives at this point in time. The long conditioned fear of pregnancy is gone. Along with the end of that fear comes no longer having to bother with the awkwardness, messiness, and possible side effects of birth control. And women whose children are out of the house find themselves less inhibited with their partners as well as less tired after years of child rearing.

Carolyn Sutton, the fifty-nine-year-old actress and educator, who had early dreams of being a lawyer, told me, "When menopause ended it was a relief. We don't have to use birth control, and that is a plus!"

Francine Lewin, fifty-five, works part-time in a real estate office and has been married to Roger for thirty-four years. They have three children, who are in their twenties. Menopause has not made a difference in her sex life. "Sex is better at this time of my life than it ever was because Roger and I are very comfortable together and very, very pleased with our lives. We're even closer now than when we had all our children at home, because we were always busy with them and that was a distraction. We have more fun now than we ever had.'' Marriage to the same man for thirty-four years has not resulted in boredom or restlessness. Francine's only regret, if it can be called that, is that sex would have been better back then if only she knew in those years what she knows now.

Shirley Grant has been through menopause and at fifty-one years old describes her marriage as very loving. She and her husband have eight children. She obviously learned about sex quickly enough, yet she remembers that the subject was not something people talked about when she was growing up. ''So many taboos you never talked about. You didn't talk about anything below the waist. Even above the waist sometimes!''

She assumed that when she got close to menopause she would be less sexual. ''I know I went through a little period there where I think the adjustment to getting older made me think, I'm not the sexy little thing I used to be. I had the thought that maybe I'm not the same person I was. Does my husband still want me? Am I still desirable? I do have a little bit of weight on here or there.'' But she found that her husband didn't care about the extra pounds. ''He says the pounds aren't *me*. He doesn't even see them,'' and her sex life remained the same.

Mickie Kramer was divorced in her thirties. At forty-eight, she is not married to her boyfriend, who is ten years her junior, but they do live together, sharing a house. Mickie was candid with me about her frustrations with menopause. While intellectually she feels sharper and more flexible than ever before in her life, menopause brought on physical differences that left her feeling out of control, such as not being able to gauge her moods without the signposts of a menstrual cycle. She has also gained weight, which she finds increasingly hard to lose.

I wondered if the man she lived with shared her frustrations. Perhaps his criticism contributed to her dissatisfaction. But Mickie set the record straight. "He could care less. All of this makes no difference to him whatsoever. He thinks my body is perfect. The perfect body, just exactly what he wanted. My body is turning to freckles. He says he ordered someone with freckles."

Apparently menopausal changes have not affected Mickie's sex life. "Sex," she informed me, "is wasted on the young. Twenty years ago sex was something I performed at. I gave a good performance but it didn't mean much to me. Ten years later I was ready to give up the performance. I hadn't found satisfaction. Now it's perfect. The good news is that you have to have an orgasm at least once a week to keep the system running. Use it or lose it, as they say. Well, I think that's terrific. So it has given me permission to be playful. That's a little bit like saying you *have* to have candy."

CHANGES MAY OCCUR

Mickie's life is a testimony to discovering sex at middle age. Yet, other women, who *have* had satisfying sexual lives up until menopause, *do* experience changes in sexual patterns. Of the total number of women responding to the 1979 *Stanford Medical Study,* 48 percent noticed a decline in libido; for 29 percent sex remained the same, while 23 percent reported an increase in desire at this time in their lives.

Such statistics do not make it clear whether a decline in libido is caused by lack of estrogen. Desire may wane at midlife for a host of reasons. To begin with, we have been taught to expect a lessening of desire over time, so our expectations may become a self-fulfilling prophecy. Changes in circumstances that cause stress, such as a new job or the breakup of a relationship, also influence desire. And an ebb in desire could be part of the normal, natural evolution of a long-standing relationship in which the partners have developed interests together beyond sex. Decline in libido on the part of a woman may also have to do with her partner's lack of interest. And physical or emotional illness, unrelated to menopause, tends to dull sexual desire in the same way it dulls one's appetite for food. Yet, once recovery is under way, desire returns.

Despite our society's seemingly insatiable urge to classify and track libido, in general the desire for sex falls into a subjective gray area, at any age. A woman may report that her interest in sex has waned over time, but in her forties and fifties she still may be more sexual than another woman currently is in her twenties. And that younger woman would never claim to have low sexual desire, because her level of desire is "right" for her.

Julia Phillips is fifty-nine years old, has been married for thirty-six years, and has three children. She and her husband are contemplating retirement, although her career as an elementary school principal provides her with a great deal of satisfaction. She was forthcoming as she revealed, "My sex life was very good actually, but it's lessening. It's not like it was when we were younger. It's good when we do have sex. We don't have sex as often as we used to, but it's good. And I don't know if—I guess the fire isn't there, but it's very pleasant and very nice when we do have it. We both seem to be comfortable with not having sex as often. And of course, a sex life changes over the years. When you're very young, it's a constant thing. And then when you have children, it's not as constant. There has been a change recently, but I think we still have a good sexual rhythm."

Julia went through menopause at fifty-three and two years later had a partial hysterectomy in which her uterus was removed, a procedure that did not effect the production of hormones in her ovaries. I wondered if those events caused the new sexual rhythms, but Julia said, "I don't think so. I still do have a desire for sex. It's just not as frequent. But I can tell you I would be very unhappy if I didn't have it at all."

Susan Galway sees her lessening of sexual desire and interest as a particular phase in her self-growth. Susan is fifty-one years old and a lesbian, and has recently begun studying psychic healing. She has been in a committed relationship for the past five years and lives with her lover and her lover's three children. She noticed that her sex life has been affected in the past year or so but claimed the lessening of desire had more to do with upsetting memories she had been confronting during an intensive period of counseling than it had to do with menopause. And she added, "I'm not really concerned about it, because I have a full love life. The companionship and the love and the care is there. There are times that I miss when it was hot, but it's not a great concern. And I also believe it will come back, especially when I hear what I hear from a woman in her seventies." Susan's psychic-healing teacher is her mentor. "This woman is at least seventy-five and she may be older than that. She married a man of forty and she's wearing him out. Their sex life is an inspiration to me. She tells me that finally she's found someone who can keep up with her."

As with Julia and Susan, most of us have experienced the ebb and flow of sexual desire over the course of our lives. How many of us sustained much lovemaking between 2:00 A.M. and 6:00 A.M. feedings when our children were infants? Through any change it's important to be true to our own feelings about sex, instead of judging ourselves on how we think we should feel. Maybe less sex is a relief but we haven't let ourselves enjoy that because we think we should still be hot. Or maybe we crave sex and intimacy more now than we ever have but we push the notion aside because we think that at our age it is unseemly.

For some women, sex was never very important to begin with. Betty Rogers was born and raised in South Carolina but moved to New York in the late 1950s. She was not married when her first child was born, but a year later she met her husband, and they have had three children of their own. Of her marriage she said, "I've been very lucky because my husband—I can't even describe my husband. He is such a doll." But sex between Betty and her husband was never "what you hear people talk about. It was never like 'as soon as I see my husband, I'm ready.' I've never been that type of person. I still enjoy being with my husband and he enjoys being with me, but there are so many other things that sex is at the bottom of the list."

EFFECTS OF STRESS

A big factor in sexual difficulties and disappointments at all ages is stress, and the stresses that accompany midlife can inhibit sexual expression. Losing a partner, whether through death or a breakup, brings up fears of not meeting anyone or worries about what to do if one does. A woman may worry about changes such as slower arousal and dryness. She may have bought into the idea that she should no longer be sexual. If her partner is not as interested in sex because of his own midlife concerns or anxieties, the woman may feel it is because she is not attractive anymore even though it has nothing to do with her.

Gina Rollow was led to believe that women never had any interest in sex at all. In fact, no one ever talked about women and sex. "We didn't discuss that or know that women have orgasms and things like that. I had to read about these things," she said, sitting at a desk in a back office of a college admissions department, where she works as an administrative assistant. "I've tried hundreds of times to give these up," she continued, almost apologizing as she lit a cigarette and then let it rest against an ashtray. Gina is fifty-four years old, well dressed, and carefully groomed. She tells me that she and her husband, Will, met each other in high school. Will had owned a garage but now teaches auto mechanics at a vocational high school.

She began our talk by claiming that sex since menopause was "a problem, a big problem. Menopause has caused a dryness, which created a problem for me. And naturally for Will." Yet, as our conversation continued Gina confided that Will had difficulties as well. "I've never used birth control or the pill, only rhythm, and during the change of life, because of the fear of getting pregnant, I couldn't use rhythm anymore, since you're not sure when you're ovulating. He never liked contraceptives, so it created a problem. My not having anything to do with him in that sense could have frozen him. I mean, I kind of blame myself to some degree."

Since they had not been active for so long she finally convinced him to tell the doctor, even though he had been resistant to speaking with anyone about his not having erections. "The doctor said to him, 'It's all in your mind.' I don't know what that means. I have some ideas, though. Maybe it's revenge for when we were single and I really didn't enjoy sex or want sex as much as he did. I don't think he took the time to worry about me then. I don't know what guys thought, but the books I read said women weren't supposed to enjoy themselves. Today, it's so different. And then he started to work around young girls, and maybe his fear of getting older, being around young, solid bodies, made him more or less retreat from me and not think about sex. I have my theories. And we're trying to work it out, we really are. We sat down. We discussed it. And we're trying."

Gina paused to pick up the cigarette she had let smolder, then continued. "When I was young I didn't feel like it. Now I'm older and have no fear of getting pregnant or anything, I find myself hornier than I ever was. I mean than I ever was in my life. It's wild."

Gina was raised to think of sex as an obligation or a duty. As the culture changed its attitude toward a woman's enjoyment of sex and as Gina got to know herself better over the years, she began to fear sex less and desire the sexuality and intimacy that a marriage can bring. But

Gina's situation also exemplifies how men can be as confused as women can about the changes in women's expectations of sex. Yet, couples like Gina and Will who have been together for a long time share a trust that goes along with knowing someone well. Our early training not to discuss sex can make talking about the subject difficult, but patience and a commitment to talk things through, as Gina and Will have, can make a difference. It is possible to talk about what you want, to listen to what your partner wants, and even to share your fantasies with each other.

A TIME FOR FREEDOM AND CREATIVITY

Advertising, television, and the movies have not come up with a lot of images of sex lives in middle age. Of course, Susan Sarandon's roles come to mind again. In *White Palace* her Nora is forty-three to her boyfriend's twenty-seven. Barbara Hershey is the older woman in a relationship with the younger Keanu Reeves in *Tune in Tomorrow*. But there is a double standard at work here. Another movie that came out at the same time, *Russia House*, has Michelle Pfeiffer in a romance with Sean Connery, some thirty years her senior. Age is never mentioned between them, in contrast to the older woman/younger man scenarios, in which the age difference is the foundation of the story.

The double standard is not surprising considering the traditional attitudes toward older women and sex. What I find more interesting, and potentially rewarding, is that the lack of an authentic public image for sex in middle age and beyond can actually be good news. The absence of a public image of how to be sexy can mean a lot of freedom for partners. We are outside the hoopla and noise about quantity and performance, beyond the sexual depersonalization and marketing that snares the young. We know that sex and lovemaking are completely different for everyone. There are no right or wrong ways to be sexual. Individual desires and choices can be honored and satisfied with the right amount of patience and caring. For example, partners can personally rewrite the myth that sexual intercourse resulting in mutual orgasm is the only satisfying and acceptable sex and that all other activity is only foreplay and does not really count.

The focus on orgasm as the ultimate goal of making love is like rushing to close a business deal in bed. Orgasm becomes the thing to ''go for''—the raise, the promotion, a pot of gold, the ring on the merry-go-round, the prize in the Cracker Jack box, the measuring ourselves by an external result. Lovemaking, like anything worthwhile, takes time to nurture and cultivate. And allowing ourselves to remain sexual beings through middle age and beyond gives us more time than ever for such nurturing and cultivation. We would be foolish to judge ourselves by the sexual standards of the young. We are entering a new stage in our sexuality. We will be maintaining sexual relationships in first marriages over longer periods of time than ever before. And we will be entering second or third marriages that may last several decades and that will not produce children.

This new stage can be an exciting time of discovery. The more time that may be required for both men and women to be stimulated allows for cuddling, caressing, manual stimulation, or oral sex. Discomfort can be handled by water-based creams (oil-based can cause irritation), slow entry, soft entry—in which a man enters a woman before he gets completely hard, a method of intercourse favored for centuries by the Chinese—and masturbation for increased lubrication.

Ourselves, Growing Older, a book produced by the Boston Women's Health Collective, well known for the popular *Our Bodies, Ourselves,* uses the phrase ''pleasuring ourselves.'' The term is attributed to Eleanor Hamilton, a seventy-five-year-old pioneer in sex education. Hamilton objects to the word ''masturbation,'' which is derived from the Latin term meaning ''to pollute with the hand.'' Pleasuring ourselves can take many forms, including giving ourselves the sensual experience of a bath, a weekly massage, running, or swimming. Pleasuring ourselves can mean fantasizing or creating erotic images that aid in arousal.

ADDRESSING AUTHENTIC CONCERNS

Along with new sexual horizons come concerns about physical difficulties, concerns that are real and are not to be discounted. Linda Avery, the forty-five-year-old attorney who has two children still at home, has yet to go through menopause, but she is worried about at least one aspect of it. ''A friend of mine who is in her fifties confided in me a few months ago that she was having dryness in her genital area. She was starting some medication, but the dryness was uncomfortable and it did have an effect on her sexual activity and relations. I don't know if that is typical.'' The condition of dryness Linda referred to was the same condition Gina Rollow complained about earlier in the chapter. The different responses the body has to loss of estrogen will be discussed in greater detail in Chapter Seven, but in short, for some women, anywhere between two and ten years after their last period, the vaginal wall may begin to thin because of lack of estrogen, and can become irritated and cause discomfort during lovemaking. The dryness can safely be corrected with topical estrogen cream. The most frightening aspects of the condition are its medical names—''vaginal atrophy'' and ''senile vaginal syndrome.''

'' 'Vaginal atrophy.' No friend to woman invented that phrase!'' Irene Stocker, forty-seven, a professor of women's studies, has researched the medical and historical literature on menopause. She understands why women can be concerned about dryness: they learn the medical names, which suggest inevitable withering and disuse. Neither description is accurate, since dryness, if it occurs, can be eliminated through lubrication during lovemaking. Stocker concluded, ''Basically, such dryness sounds like the condition you're in when you're a teenager in the early stages of sexuality, but nobody ever points that out. And it's true that it's certainly not comfortable but you can do something about it. It's not an irreversible condition.''

KNOWING WHAT WE WANT, MAKING SURE WE GET IT

Sex is a healthy, natural extension of many sides of ourselves. Sex lets us express fantasies, relieves tension, and often helps us sleep. With a partner we trust, we feel loved and cared for and we get to love and care for someone back. Through sex we are intimately connected to both another person and ourselves at the same time. And sex can mean a great adventure.

Knowing what we want sexually and choosing how we want to express ourselves creates an exciting opportunity for the choice years. Studies show that one out of every five middle-aged women is single. Why does everyone assume that this is not by choice? Rather than panicking, we could interpret that statistic to mean that being single is what we want. Choosing to be single may be very liberating and even empowering. And choosing to be celibate is as valid a sexual choice as any.

This is the time of life to enjoy ourselves and to cultivate personal pleasures, including sex. Perhaps the most difficult step to take if you *do* want to be with someone is initiating the relationship. For women who have been raised to wait for the man to make the first move, this can be quite hard.

When I was divorced, at forty, I was surprised at the number of men around to date. Looking back, I can see that many of them had just gotten out of long-term marriages as well and we were all beginning to date again for the first time since we were teenagers. In the years that followed I had several long-term relationships as well as dating relationships. In the past two years I have found that I am dating less.

Sometimes not being involved with anyone in a committed way feels wrong to me. I often feel an invisible pressure to be married, as well as a not-so-invisible pressure from my family. I am no stranger, therefore, to the resignation, and that old feeling that I don't have a date on Saturday night, that women at midlife experience, particularly when it looks as if our options for mates grow slimmer and slimmer. Women outlive men, and the men who are around, everyone knows, go for younger women.

I have two things to say about that. One is that all men do not automatically find younger women more desirable than women their own age. My experience has been that men my age are looking for partners who share similar backgrounds and histories. Most of them do not want to date a woman who doesn't remember the Korean War.

Second, when I am honest with myself I admit that in the last two years I have not made dating a priority. I have put a lot of energy into a new career and I do not regret this for a moment. This is not to say that having a relationship is incompatible with a career, but I have not made it my business to have a social life. And when I do, I suspect I will.

Perhaps I sound too flippant, too facile, or lacking in compassion for the loneliness of single life. But I will never forget seeing sixty-three-year-old Mira Linder on a talk show. Linder was a lively, vivacious woman who opened her own beauty spa at the age of forty-seven. She was sharing with panel members and the audience what life for women in the middle years is *really* about. She was upbeat, funny, down-to-earth, and inspiring. When she relayed that her husband with whom she had been extremely close had died fourteen years ago, everyone was moved. Barely skipping a beat, however, she perked up and said, "So I found another!"

A CONFIDENT SENSE OF A SEXY SELF

Being sexy is not just about the act of sex. It is not just about estimated time of arousal or number of love-making sessions a week. It is about the way we hold ourselves and about our involvement in life. A woman who projects the pride of her many accomplishments, whether family or career, is sexy at midlife. So is a woman confident that her wisdom and experience make her better than she has ever been.

Janet Lowe explained the difference between who she was in her twenties and who she is now. "I have a lot more freedom with men than I ever had in my life. Freedom that I enjoy." She is currently in her forties; her husband was killed in Vietnam when she was twenty-five. She raised two daughters as a single parent, never remarrying. "I appreciate men more than I ever did before. Back then I was trying too hard. I was always trying to prove something. Now I have no need to prove anything."

Tanya Leroy, a forty-one-year-old health administrator, considers herself as attractive now as she was in her twenties. Menopause has not changed her level of desire, but time has changed the importance she once placed on sex. "Sex probably played too much of a major role in relationships in the past, because I felt that by putting the emphasis on that, any of the other problems in a relationship would automatically be solved. And that has proved to be wrong. Within my marriage we would have an argument and we would solve it by making love and not really addressing what the issue was. Now I don't like to whitewash problems by covering them over by fantastic love-making. That's not the issue. In my current relationship we really deal with the problems as they are and don't camouflage them by making it seem as if everything is wonderful."

Forty-eight-year-old Carrie Brouwer, a writer and an artist, has also been shifting emphasis from the purely sexual to something closer, perhaps more sustained and spiritual. "I want a deeper sexual experience. I feel as though my husband and I haven't even begun to explore that. I think we fell into a routine of sex when we first got married—how we did it together—and we tried to just continue, without going into more spiritual directions.''

Does she think this is possible? Carrie did not hesitate to say yes and referred to a book called *Cultivating Female Sexuality.* Her husband, she relayed, read parts of the book, they discussed her desires, and they have had ''really positive results.'' The book advocates developing sexuality within oneself, and as a result, Carrie says, ''you can experience sex with a partner much better, on a much deeper level. I want that in my marriage.''

The words of different women show how individuality and imagination can make for a rich sexual relationship and a confident sense of a sexy self. With the wisdom of years we have the patience and determination to work through difficult times, whether alone or with a partner, in order to discover what we really want. What I have seen through research and interviews is that if a woman has been sexually active throughout her life, this pattern is maintained through menopause and beyond. Estrogen production does not influence a woman's interest in sex. If genuine difficulties do exist, treatment, both physiological and psychological, is available. No woman has to give up on this part of her life.

''I sort of assumed that I was attractive sexually when I was younger,'' said Evelyn Glenn, the woman who couldn't imagine announcing her menopause in public. ''I guess I also assumed that I wouldn't be when I got older. And when I got divorced I was really quite pleased and surprised to find that I was still attractive.'' Evelyn, who was divorced at forty-eight, laughed. ''I guess I had thought that maybe I would just go to my rocking chair. Or that everyone else would expect me to go to my rocking chair. Now people say, 'How did you find your second husband?' Well, there must have been something about me that said that I was still available. Whatever it was, I wasn't ready to be put out to pasture. I still wanted to be a sexual person. I was glad to find that I could be and was.''

❦

CHAPTER 4

Myth 3:
Menopause as a Medical Disease:
"The Womb Is Part of Every Illness . . ."

EST FEMINEO GENERI PARS UNA UTERUS OMNIUM MORBORUM
The womb is part of every illness of the female sex.

Disease is defined, in the *Random House Dictionary of the English Language,* as "a condition of an organ, part, structure, or system of the body in which there is incorrect function resulting from the effect of heredity, infection, or environment." *Webster's* adds that disease is "a particular destructive process in the body, with a specific cause and characteristic symptoms."

A female child is born with approximately 500,000 eggs in her ovaries. The ovaries lose eggs throughout a woman's life, without the supply being replenished, until there are no more left. No more eggs means no more menstrual cycle; hormone production in the ovaries decreases as the menstrual phase of a woman's life ends, signaling menopause. The depletion of the supply of eggs and the decreased hormone levels are part of a normal biological process. The ovaries are not *functioning incorrectly,* nor is the end of available eggs due to a *particular destructive process.* Yet, the National Institute on Aging includes menopause along with senile dementia and cerebrovascular and cardiovascular diseases on its list of "diseases associated with aging."

Activity having to do with a woman's reproductive organs has long been associated with sickness. During menstruation, we are unwell; during pregnancy, indisposed; and during menopause, as a number of women have already noted, we might describe ourselves as sick, weak, or half the person we used to be. With menopause in particular, the medical language surrounding the event reinforces the idea of disease. The tendency of the vaginal wall to dry and thin is known as "vaginal atrophy" or "senile vaginal syndrome." Hot flashes, night sweats, and whatever else accompanies the loss of estrogen are known as "symptoms." Symptoms imply an illness or a disorder that needs to be cured. Since menopause is not a disease, throughout this book menopause-related effects will be referred to as signs or signals.

Liz Reynolds, a recently remarried journalist with grown children, is approaching fifty. Her thirty-year-old female doctor did not say, in so many words, that menopause was a debilitating disease, but her assessment of Liz's future left Liz feeling weak and susceptible. "I said, 'I think I'm in menopause.' And she said, 'Okay, be prepared. You are going to gain a lot of weight. It's going to be harder for you to keep the weight off. You're going to have hair on your face.' She went on with a list of really depressing things and she said, 'That's the way of it.' This thirty-year-old. It's not going to happen to her for a while. I looked at her and, you know, it was such a downer for her to say these things. Why prepare me for this next stage of life in that kind of way?"

THE MOST SIGNIFICANT PART OF OUR ANATOMY

A woman's place in society has been determined by her biological role. Even now that technology and progress have made it possible for women not to be tied solely to the home and taking care of others, the old social expectations live on.

Looking back on the nineteenth century in America, we can see that these expectations went beyond social ones. Not only were women identified by their reproductive role, but their reproductive *organs,* it was assumed, determined their physical health and psychological nature. If a woman's purpose on earth was to bear children, then her reproductive organs were the most significant part of her anatomy. The leap was not far for nineteenth-century American medicine men to make: any physical difficulties a woman experienced must be due to a disorder or dysfunction in her reproductive area. F. Hollick, in his 1849 book *The Diseases of Women,* wrote, "The Uterus, it must be remembered, is the controlling organ in the female body, being the most excitable of all, and so intimately connected by the ramifications of its numerous nerves, with every other part." Other medicine men also considered the ovaries to be the controlling organs. In 1870, W. Bliss wrote, "Accepting, then, these views of the gigantic power and influence of the ovaries over the whole animal economy of woman—they are the most powerful agents in all the commotions of her system—what must be their influence and power over the great vocation of woman and the august purposes of her existence when these organs have become compromised through disease!"

Any physical difficulty or complaint voiced by a woman, from headaches to backaches to indigestion to lethargy to constipation to sore throats, was regarded as a uterine or ovarian disorder. With this assumption widely accepted, the next medically logical step made perfect sense. A woman's reproductive system determined her personality as well. Historians Barbara Ehrenreich and Deirdre English vigorously document the nineteenth-century medical establishment's assumption of such a connection in *Complaints and Disorders: The Sexual Politics of Sickness.* They note that in the Victorian United States, a woman's nature was considered a direct extension of her reproductive functions. Thus, this "psychology of the ovary" allowed any trait a woman exhibited, from moodiness to boredom to restlessness to ambition, to be ascribed to an ovarian disease.

What better way to cope with the diseases caused by the ovaries than to strike the cause at its source? Ovariotomies were practiced throughout the second part of the nineteenth century and doctors boasted of having removed between 1,500 and 2,000 ovaries, passing "them around at medical society meetings like trophies." We now know that removal of the ovaries, "female castration," brings on a premature menopause with indications such as hot flashes coming fast and furious and with greater intensity than during spontaneous menopause. According to Dr. Robert Battey of Georgia, however, who is credited with the invention in the nineteenth century of the "normal ovariotomy," or removal of ovaries for nonovarian conditions, when wives were returned to their husbands "castrated" they were "tractable, orderly, industrious, and cleanly."

Normal female reproductive activity was thus seen as a physiological crisis, whether it was puberty, pregnancy, or menopause. And a high incidence of disease was particularly associated with menopause, with hot flashes, tumors, uterine and breast cancer, diarrhea, rheumatic pains, prolapse, erysipelas, and paralysis on the list of what to expect. Katherine I. MacPherson, in her article "Menopause as Disease: The Social Construction of a Metaphor," explains that according to medical science a woman's susceptibility to such diseases was heightened because of certain attitudes or actions. These included attempts at abortion or birth control, too much sex, excess education, support for women's suffrage, or not enough devotion to husband or children.

Sex during or after menopause was considered "morbid"; menopausal women who wanted to marry were advised to consult their doctors; depression was seen as inevitable, since women would no longer be attractive and young. Menopausal patients were often described by their doctors as "ludicrous or physically repulsive."

A NEW ERA OF TREATMENT

By the early 1900s, it seems, attitudes toward menopause had changed. A sociological study of articles in popular magazines from the first decades of the century reveals that menopause was viewed as a new phase in a woman's life, when she could find tranquillity and contentment. Between World War I and World War II, however, the medical profession discovered and isolated sexual hormones, ushering in a new era of treatment for menopause.

Glandular therapy has long been a form of treatment for increasing vitality and attempting to prolong life. Dr. Wulf H. Utian, founder of the North American Menopause Society and co-author, with Ruth Jacobowitz, of *Managing Your Menopause*, notes that the ancient Egyptians, Greeks, and Romans believed glandular remedies cured impotence. Powdered ovaries and powdered ovarian tablets were used at the turn of the century to counteract obesity, menstrual cramps, and, not surprisingly, symptoms of menopause.

The discovery of estrogen and progesterone as the hormones produced by the ovaries came in 1923, and by the 1930s synthetic estrogens were being produced. The 1920s and 1930s saw the beginnings of estrogen replacement as a possibility for postmenopausal women, who could now be treated for something they had lost. Rather than viewing such replacement as an extension of a normal function that had lived out its life course, doctors saw estrogen as necessary for menopausal women, who would suffer without it. A condition needing treatment and a woman needing a doctor to treat her defined menopause *itself* as a disease, and not just the cause of disease, which had been the nineteenth-century view. Medical literature began to include phrases such as ''bizarre set of symptoms'' and ''gynecological disorder'' to describe menopause. And in the 1960s, the medical term *estrogen deficiency* linked menopause in the popular mind with deficiency diseases such as diabetes, in which an individual was dependent on medication.

This examination of medical attitudes and terminology shows how the social and cultural life of a time and place can have as much to do with the determination of scientific fact as science itself does. In other words, myths that support particular cultural views are often developed in the name of science and rationality. Facts may be interpreted to support the accepted views of the times. Another example of this is a popular belief subscribed to by doctors in the nineteenth century, known as the "conservation of energy" law or "limited vital force." This law claimed that the body had only a certain amount of energy to direct to all its organs and functions. Too great an emphasis on one function drained the strength of another. Therefore, it was believed that women who focused on the development of their intellect used up energy that would otherwise be put into reproduction. Such women were in grave danger of threatening the health of their uterus and ovaries. This medical and scientific fact was a terrific rationale for women not to indulge in too many lively thoughts. And no institution had to enforce limited thinking: any woman who accepted the idea that intellectual activity would hurt her made certain that she keep such activity to a minimum.

Today we are certain that attitudes such as those are primitive and absurd. Yet most of us feared, at some point, that we *might* transform into a "ludicrous," "repulsive," "tragic," "no longer functional" woman—all descriptive phrases used at one time by the medical community. Only by knowing that "facts" can often be interpretations that support the current status quo can we be alert to possible misrepresentation, and guard ourselves against internalizing such misrepresentations. We are not sick. We are not stupid. We are not ruled by our wombs. We are healthy, vibrant individuals. *Those* are the facts.

CHAPTER 5

Myth 4:
Menopause as a
Psychological Crisis:
"The Depression Natural to the
Change of Life"

*When written in Chinese, the word "crisis" is composed
of two characters—one represents danger and one represents opportunity.*

—JOHN F. KENNEDY

The development of psychoanalysis by Sigmund Freud has been a major contribution to our understanding of ourselves over the last century. Freud wrote and spoke vividly of the human experience. He was, however, a product of a particular time and place in history—middle-class Vienna. As a man in Victorian Europe, he believed that women were inherently ruled by their biology and were on earth for the purpose of producing children. He did not invent the idea behind the often quoted phrase "anatomy is destiny." He just put it into words. Along with this assumption about women, he developed theories and drew conclusions that have profoundly influenced attitudes about women and mental health into our time. Much of his work was done with upper-middle-class female patients classified as "hysterics."

"Hysteria" is considered to be an emotional disorder. The word has its roots in the Greek *hystera*, meaning

49

"womb," and the Latin *hystericus,* meaning "disturbances of the womb." True to their era, medical men in the nineteenth century assumed that a woman's reproductive organs, including the uterus, had a controlling influence on her brain and personality. Ovariotomies, or ovariectomies, surgical removal of the ovaries, were thought to alleviate a range of diseases, including neurasthenia. Medical authorities found this abstract nervous disorder, which mysteriously afflicted women, difficult to define, although it was thought by some to be the mark of intellect and sensitivity. Hysterectomy, the surgical removal of the uterus, has replaced the ovariotomy as the popular reproductive surgery of our day.

NO LONGER GENTLE AND SWEET

Ironically, the normal, nonsurgical end to childbearing potential, menopause, was not viewed as a logical cure to emotional instability. Rather, natural menopause was seen as a psychological loss that left a woman full of despair and no longer gentle and solicitous. Back then, it appears you were damned if you did or damned if you didn't.

Freud did not hesitate to make authoritative pronouncements about women who were past the childbearing years. The changes in character women underwent when they "abandoned their genital functions" were well known. Once they were no longer in the womanly phase of their lives, they became "quarrelsome, peevish, and argumentative, petty and miserly." If that didn't make his point, he went on to say that sadistic and anal-erotic characteristics emerged in this person in whom sweetness and tenderness had deteriorated.

Helene Deutsch, a student of Freud's and a prominent psychoanalyst in her own right, wrote the influential two-volume *The Psychology of Women* in the 1940s, while she was in her sixties. In it she asserts that once through menopause a woman's purpose as the reproducer of a

new future has ended and with that end comes a certain
kind of death. Her beauty is lost, along with the warmth
of her emotional life, and her energy is consumed by
fighting against her total decline.

Deutsch, along with other women of the intelligentsia
who acted as social critics in the middle of this century,
such as Simone de Beauvoir and Margaret Mead, was
seen by society as extraordinary and exceptional. These
women often wrote about women in general in the third
person, as if they were not one of them. De Beauvoir
wrote that in middle age men gradually grow old but a
"woman is suddenly deprived of her femininity." She
speaks, in relation to that sudden deprivation, of the "depression natural to the change of life." In our current
world, women with as wide-ranging accomplishments and
influence as De Beauvoir, Deutsch, and Mead are less
the exception than the rule. Yet attitudes left over from
the middle of the century still exert an influence on us
today.

Freud's observation of a small sampling of Victorian
middle-class women influenced generations of psychoanalysts. One of the results of this influence was psychiatry's belief in the feminine ideal of homemaking and
childbearing as *the* path for American women in the late
1940s, the 1950s, and the early 1960s. For example, the
housewife of the 1950s who sought help with depression
was encouraged to see her "illness" as part of her refusal to fulfill her role as dutiful wife and mother. Often
this refusal was treated, in part, with antidepressants.
Psychiatry at the time did not take into account social,
political, and economic factors in the lives of wom-
en, such as the isolation of staying alone at home all day
or the lack of opportunity for such women to earn any
money.

By the early 1960s, gynecologists had joined forces
with psychoanalysts in a repeat of nineteenth-century
medical opinion. Physical health was interpreted by some

gynecologists as a barometer of how well a woman accepted her feminine role.

WHAT WE ALL SEEM TO FEAR

In the last three decades, the field of psychology has moved beyond the couch and the medicine cabinet. Expanded theories of human development, influenced in a large part by the work of Erik Erikson, have emerged and have had an impact on how we see ourselves. We are more likely to feel we have the potential for continued growth, change, and development throughout our lives and less likely to see ourselves as needing to fulfill a predetermined role, such as wife or mother, in order to be emotionally healthy. Menopause, however, remains a signpost that many of us suspect will bring a halt to our development. Over and over, the first association women I interviewed had with menopause was depression or craziness. We still seem to be gripped by a fear of irreversible mental and emotional upheavals, over which we will have no control, that are supposed to accompany "the change." And we are not alone in our fears.

Ned, a thirty-one-year-old engineer, recently married his girlfriend of three years. He is a man who grew up in the "feminist generation" and is accustomed to women speaking their minds, pursuing careers, and setting their own timetables for marriage and children. His wife has an M.B.A. degree and works in a high-level business position with a national bank. When asked what came to mind when he heard the word "menopause," Ned did not hesitate to react: "I think of very emotional, crazy women, emotions multiplied or magnified unbelievably and raging hormones attacking me. Similar to what I think of pregnancy. A woman who is extraordinarily demanding."

I wondered what a raging hormone looked like, but I didn't ask. Instead I asked if he had any firsthand experience with an overwrought woman at menopause that would have led to his expectations. Ned thought for a moment, then said, "Those images must have come from reading books. I don't remember when my mother went through menopause, although she must have—she's in her sixties. Maybe it was when I was a teenager, when I was reading all those books and was so crazy myself."

The idea of hormonal change brings up what he calls a "fear factor." "At this point in my life my expectations are for a woman to be sympathetic to my wants and needs so I can be babied. I'm worried that my wife will become more demanding and won't baby me. Playing around with hormones at menopause— How will I know, when she goes into an emotional crying period, whether it's hormonal changes or something else?"

Ned's fears seem ludicrous. First of all, to link neediness with hormonal states reduces a person's emotional complexities to the level of a gland. Second, even if our emotions do go up and down, don't we have enough life experience by the time menopause hits to handle those ups and downs? After all, moodiness ostensibly strikes many women once a month at menstruation. On the other hand, while Ned did seem to be overreacting, he voiced a fear many of us have about the depression expected at midlife. Whether such depression is psychological—based on being devastated that we can no longer have children and on the accompanying loss of identity—or whether it is biological, based on the loss of hormones, this depression is expected to alter our lives permanently and never go away.

REALITY DEBUNKS THE MYTH

In my interviews, I observed a completely different pattern, however. While woman after woman included depression, insanity, and hysteria in her previously held notions of menopause, none of these women attributed the remotest form of mental illness to their own experience. A significant number of women, including myself, did go through scary, hopeless, and lonely bouts with depression in their lives, but such episodes tended to occur at a younger age. This observation defies two myths—that of an all-encompassing middle-age depression and that of an irreversible depression. Based on my sampling of sixty women, the fact seems to be that depression came to the younger woman who was insecure, uncertain, and not yet comfortable with her own identity. And that kind of depression, with time and growth, can be overcome.

While I was in my twenties, I was depressed. I had two wonderful children, a beautiful home, and a successful and ambitious husband. I had everything I had been raised to aspire to, yet anyone can see in photographs of me at the time that I was suffering. Compounding my depression was the feeling that since I had everything in the world a person could possibly want and I was still miserable, somehow I had failed.

With the perspective of the years I can understand what I had no capacity to understand back then. My husband had achieved his dream, to become rich and have a beautiful home. But while he was out working and rarely at home, I was isolated with my daughters. I thought at the time that my misery was personal, although I have come to learn that many women felt just as cut off and isolated in similar situations. At the time, however, since my family had brought me up to be happy and it seemed as though I had everything, I could not understand why I felt so sick. I was numb. I felt as though I had polio and I just couldn't move. From the outside everything looked fine. I was taking care of business, cooking and cleaning, except that there was no time during the day when it all seemed to be worth the effort. I saw a psychiatrist who did not seem to think I was particularly ill but who gave me tranquilizers, which helped at times.

Finally, after several years of this, I found myself on what felt like a boundary line. I could see an abyss on the other side of this line that was horrifying and I knew if I crossed over into it I would not be able to find a way back. Somehow from somewhere inside me I reached down and made a conscious, true choice, perhaps the first I had ever made. I took charge in some small way and simply said, "I am not going there. I am going to live."

I had never viewed myself as a strong person. I had been a cheerleader type, pretty, but I had never considered that I had much substance. And yet, once I brought myself back from the darkest moments of a depression, I began to gather pockets of strength, finding myself stronger in ways I had never been before I had gotten sick. And I have just been getting stronger ever since.

Right before Sandra Littleton's fortieth birthday she gave birth to her third child. During that pregnancy she put on a tremendous amount of weight. The nurses at the hospital she visited joked that she looked as if she were going to have sextuplets. Her weight kept rising, but she assumed she would lose it after her child was born. Instead, while nursing her new daughter, she continued to gain more weight.

That summer her husband told her he was in love with someone else and wanted a divorce. "On my fortieth birthday I went to a psychiatrist and swept him out of his office in a river of tears. I faced forty feeling like I'd lost my youth, lost my good looks, and lost my husband. I was just so extremely depressed by the whole thing. And the following decade I just continued to be depressed. That's a whole decade. It was a long time before I began to recover from that. I separated from my husband the next summer, but I didn't divorce him for seven years. I couldn't bring myself to do it. All that time, I felt like my life really wasn't in my hands, because in a lot of ways I was leaving major decisions to him and living on very little money. But I was paralyzed in that situation. I finally divorced him because I wanted to take control over my share of the assets."

For Sandra, her extra weight and the loss of her husband precipitated depression. Menopause, when it finally came, was almost an afterthought. "I just had a terrible time the year I was forty, but this past year—I'm fifty-six—hasn't been any different from any other year, except I haven't had to bother fooling around with Tampax."

Major studies affirm the idea that depression is not simultaneous with menopause. In the 1970s, Myrna Weissman, then at Yale, and George Winokur, of the University of Iowa, were suggesting that the menopause blues were a myth. Their work has since been confirmed by studies in Europe and a major American study conducted in Massachusetts. A 1986 British study found a rise in the rate of depression for women between forty-five and forty-nine compared with women of other ages. This rise, however, was strongest among women who had yet to reach menopause.

The Massachusetts Women's Health Study, conducted by Sonja and John McKinlay, began in 1981–82 with a sampling of 8,050 women, out of which 2,500 were selected for the continuing work. The 2,500 women, between the ages of forty-five and fifty-five, were interviewed by telephone or by mail every nine months for nearly five years. The results of the study indicate that menopause does not cause depression. The majority of women surveyed were relieved not to worry about menstruation, contraception, or pregnancy any longer. Women who expressed concern going into menopause had lost that concern by the end of the six-year study. Menopausal women who did report depression had a history of the condition prior to menopause.

This study is unique among those of its kind because it sought, as subjects, women who had not come to a medical setting for care. Conclusions were drawn based on a sampling of average women instead of women already complaining of menopause or other health-related difficulties. The women in the study were dealing with the normal routines and stresses of daily life. And their lives also defied the myth of the middle-aged woman at home, moping in an empty nest. In fact, two thirds of the initial 8,050 women surveyed still had children living at home. Twenty-five percent were providing care for an elderly relative, while 6 percent had an elderly relative living with them. About three quarters of those surveyed held full-time or part-time jobs.

Research from Europe has further substantiated the claims of the McKinlay study. As reported in *The New York Times* in January 1990, findings in Europe, which have yet to receive widespread press in the United States, contradict accepted beliefs about a woman's risk of depression after menopause. Robert O. Pasnau, a psychiatrist at the University of California at Los Angeles Medical School, reviewed the studies in the *American Journal of Psychiatry* and saw them as significant in altering the myth of the inevitable "change-of-life emotional crisis." Pasnau contends that menopausal women have no more tendency toward depression than women, or men, of any age.

The case is clear—the physical changes of menopause do not bring on depression. The physical changes of menopause do not cause us to go crazy. The fears and worries the best of us harbor will not come true when our periods stop. That myth is dead. But, alas, there is another myth lurking around the corner. This one, formulating even as you read, says something to the effect of: Since it has been proved that menopause is not the traumatic event it was thought to be, it is now not an event at all. Midlife is effortless. Aches, pains, or feelings of loss are insignificant. Lady, it's all in your head.

COPING WITH LOSS AS PART OF OUR LIVES

Swinging with the pendulum in this other direction is as wrongheaded as typecasting menopausal women as mentally unstable. While the physical process of menopause is not a source of depression, menopause does constitute the end of a specific stage in a woman's life. As with all stages or changes, whatever our age, it is helpful and often necessary to take stock of where we have been and to make some choices about the direction in which we now want to proceed. And taking stock requires admitting that we have experienced loss.

The crucial word here is "loss." While any woman can have a meaningful, productive, and vital middle life—combining health, exercise, work that is purposeful, strong friendships and family—the forties and fifties are a time when many of us experience a sense of permanent loss for the first time.

Carolyn Sutton, fifty-nine, is the woman who did not become a lawyer in her twenties but did begin writing one-woman historical dramas while she was in her forties. Her first show was about slavery and Harriet Tubman, and she has continued writing, producing, and performing such plays as *Six Women of Courage* about nontraditional American women. While the past fifteen years have been her most creative professionally, they have also been a time during which she and her family lost a large number of people close to them. Carolyn found that the compounded losses altered and reshaped many different real-life roles that she has been called upon to play.

Carolyn and her husband were the caregivers for both her parents and his. Both sets of parents died in the past fifteen years. Important friends, including a woman Carolyn spoke of as "wonderful and darling," also died during this time. Perhaps most devastating was the death of her fifteen-month-old granddaughter. As a result Carolyn has seen herself move from being the child of her parents to being their caretaker, to being an orphan, and from proud grandmother to comforter to her son, a role she never expected she would be required to fulfill. She is acutely aware of the fragility of relationships, the nature of loss, and the need to grieve and mourn.

"My father died when I was forty-five and my mother died when I was fifty-one. The year my mother died we made a black comedy out of it. We called it the 'Death-of-the-Month' year, because I lost someone every month of that year. When your parents die you become an orphan, no matter how old you are. And you move up into a certain space in the world. When you become a grandparent, you also move in space. You're not just a parent, you're also a grandparent. So you have position, and it's a wonderful position, it's not something that you regret. Among my teaching friends I was the first grandmother and everybody envied me, that sort of thing. It is a marking, a very important benchmark. Just like marriage, having children. These things changed my life. They changed my life dramatically.''

During this period Carolyn went through menopause. She considered the event one of the losses among the many she was experiencing. ''Menopause does represent to me and I think to almost every woman, it has to mean, that my childbearing years are over. And with that, a loss of youth.

''Menopause definitely marks the end of—what is the word I'm looking for? I want the right word. *Create.* In the sense that you create another life. And even though there isn't a chance in hell that I ever would have had another child, the fact that I could not was an emotional thing. I don't mean that I sat and cried about it, I don't want you to think that. But in terms of loss, the loss of your procreative life makes you look at your own life and death. It is also a loss of a large part of what you were. You're a young person many years longer than you're an old person. In my case, anyway, I thought of myself as young until my mother died.''

Along with the death of parents, friends, and a grandchild, Carolyn faced a change in body image and the fact that she could no longer bear children. Within a hierarchy of losses, menopause was not the source of despair. Yet, as part of the grieving process she had come to know intimately over the past fifteen years, she seemed able to acknowledge the event of menopause and give it the time and attention it called for—time and attention someone denying the process might not afford herself.

The myths say that the loss of childbearing potential is devastating to a woman's concept of herself and her future. But I say such an idea is too large and too general. Carolyn's losses at midlife were impossible to ignore. For the most part, however, we do not suddenly arrive at midlife and begin to lose what we have accumulated over the years. Loss of childbearing potential is but one in a series of losses we have sustained over time. Is that loss greater or lesser on the scale of daily losses that seem to describe and qualify life? Where, for example, have my daughters gone? I do not have the daughters I used to have. The six-year-olds no longer exist. Neither do the sixteen-year-olds. We can get nostalgic and sentimental about the past, yet the change that comes with the passing of time is what life is about. We can feel despair. Some days I feel I have lost more over time than I have gained. Other days I know I have gained so much along the way. To begin with I have myself, more fully than ever before, and I believe with that, everything is possible.

What turns sentiment and nostalgia into misery and despair is denying change and loss. The woman who denies the change in her status as childbearer, who denies that her role as a mother to dependent children is transforming into the role of a mother to adult children, who denies that her marriage, relationships, and career are at new points may find herself confused and possibly unhappy. To deny the changes and loss is to push away the present and to prepare inadequately for the future.

Evidence shows that we will not go insane or become clinically depressed because of menopause. For most of us, in fact, our middle years have proved to be more productive, self-confident, and healthful than any other time of our lives. Coming face to face with our own vulnerability, however, as our bodies change and as our friends and family change, move away, or die is very sobering. As a way to understand such shifts, we might choose to look at the threshold we are on as a time to welcome crisis.

CRISIS AS AN OPPORTUNITY FOR CHANGE AND GROWTH

Who welcomes crisis? The word brings to mind opposing forces that will never be reconciled—between husband and wife, between parents and children, or within oneself. A financial crisis can spell ruin. And a tragic crisis such as the death of a loved one is so profound there seems to be little hope of recovery. Crisis means a point of no return, so we often find ourselves attempting to shield ourselves from such events. Everything, we insist, is okay, knowing all the while that something is brewing just below the surface.

The assumption is that women hit their biggest emotional roadblocks at middle age, particularly around menopause. This may be the case, as in Carolyn's situation, when one loses important people in one's life for the first time. But the event of menopause is not what precipitates crisis. And for many women, crisis points are encountered much earlier in life.

Tess Berkeley reached a crisis in her marriage while she was in her early thirties. At the time she felt she had hit an impenetrable wall, yet the actions she took helped her develop a strong sense of self-worth, which continues to fuel her life today. In her twenties Tess, currently forty-six, a nurse, a teacher, and a single parent, had an image of an ideal relationship. "I had a whole fantasy built up around that," she remembered. "I would be married and we would be saving the world together."

But she married a man who turned out not to conform to her ideal picture. He was an alcoholic and physically abused her. "I was not prepared for any of the valleys and the suffering that I encountered in my thirties. I never pictured that I would be in the marriage that I was in *ever* in a million years. I came to a point in the relationship where I realized I had to leave. But I was scared. And then I went into a strange mental and emotional state where I felt like I was falling over an abyss, like I was being pulled to it. And the only way I kept myself from going over the edge was to keep invoking my son's name. I stayed dissociated for a couple of days. I felt that my identity was being threatened, that's what was going to go. If I went over that abyss, the me I knew would never return. I guess it took coming to that breakdown point of knowing I might lose myself, not only physically but lose any ability to grow, for me to pick up my son and my life and leave.''

Tess was able to alter her situation and take charge of her life, to, in effect, break with her past and shape a new future. She had been terrified of losing her identity, but ironically she did lose her former, passive self when she acted with courage and determination.

In the past thirty years psychologists have evolved a view of human development that includes possibilities for growth during times of transition. Erik Erikson is a psychoanalyst whose work blends basic Freudian themes with the belief that human beings continue to grow all through their lives. Erikson, popularly known for his theory of the adolescent identity crisis, believes that people go through crises of identity at numerous stages in their lives. Each of these crises involves a confrontation between what we know ourselves to be and the new self the next stage of life demands us to create. According to Erikson, the identity confrontations of middle age involve developing personal creativity that extends beyond oneself to include work, concern for others, and community. Erikson defines the developmental task of middle age as ''fulfilling life goals that involve family, career and society; developing concerns that embrace future generations.'' The crisis point we reach at middle age involves a choice between productivity and stagnation.

Many psychotherapists have built on the work of Erikson.

Among them is Carol Gilligan, the Harvard psychologist who came out with *In a Different Voice: Psychological Theory and Women's Development,* in the early 1980s. Gilligan views crisis as a time of "heightened vulnerability" in one's life, which, instead of signaling depression or decline, can actually be used to encourage changes we might not otherwise have had the opportunity to make.

Welcoming periods of "heightened vulnerability" is easier to say than to do. During such periods we don't feel particularly strong. Usually, we feel in these periods as though our lives are doomed to continue forever in a state of confusion, uncertainty, helplessness, anger, and often pain. As we get older, we seem to have less resources with which to bounce back and a lot of evidence from the past that tells us in no uncertain terms that we've been down before and no matter how good it gets we'll eventually be down again. In such a vulnerable state, the addition of menopause, with its series of physical changes and psychological implications, may seem to contribute to confusion and despair. Or to be the only cause of such feelings.

Fifty-five-year-old Doris Lambert's story offers an example of a life that reached a crisis point at the same time that middle age and menopause occurred. Her family did not buckle under to the pressures, however, but instead took the opportunity these crises afforded to reshape their lives.

By the time Doris turned forty-five, her husband had been unemployed for a number of years because of a work-related injury, and she had developed debilitating pains in her neck and back. "My husband had been out of work for four and a half years. It's a wonder we even stayed together, things were so bad. Then my daughter became pregnant. She was an unwed mother. Between the stress of him being out of work, no money coming in, and problems with our daughter, everything just took a hold on me. My body reacted with a lot of neck and shoulder tension and low back problems."

Doris had never had physical problems like that before. She sought chiropractic help and then counseling, to no avail.

When she went to her family doctor, he put her on Valium, which she didn't take for long because she was concerned that it would cause other problems or have physical side effects. Finally, she noticed a brochure from a community college that advertised massage classes. She decided to try that, thinking it might be a cure for her. And that's how she started her career. Ten years later she has a thriving neural-muscular therapy practice and makes her living relieving other people of their stress.

Menopause came and went during those ten years, posing no threat to her newfound stability. Before her midlife success, Doris had worked full-time for only one year of her married life, as a fish packer. "What I think has helped me the most is being in my own business. Life didn't seem to have a purpose before my business and now it sure does."

As they were for Tess and Doris, times of vulnerability and crisis can be an opportunity to move through conflicts and actually arrive at satisfying resolutions. Recovery can follow loss, relief can follow pain. We can feel as though we have accomplished something by getting to this point in our lives instead of having failed. And by looking at our lives through the lens of accomplishment instead of failure, we can experience ourselves as creative instead of stagnant, resourceful instead of used up, productive instead of confused, supple instead of shriveled, enlivened and regenerated as opposed to withered and discarded, passionate, not lethargic, wise and not dulled, invigorated and not depressed. The natural crisis points of normal life, which in certain situations may be accompanied by menopause, can be thresholds to new landscapes and frontiers or passages to new shores instead of the same old journey down a dead end. The term for the process leading up to menopause, the "climacteric," comes from the Greek *klimakter,* meaning "the top step of a staircase or the top rung of a ladder"—a perfect point from which to launch ourselves.

CHAPTER 6

Myth 5: Menopause Signals the Onset of Old Age

What's the youngest you can die of old age?
—STEVE WRIGHT
Comedian

It's a terrible thing in women's culture that you're sup-posed to be dead after menopause.... You're not beau-tiful anymore, nothing. Since I was 60 I've written more and had better energy and more energy than I ever had in my life. I went to a doctor when I was about 70 and he said, "Oh, just take these tranquilizers." I said, "Are you kidding?" In three years he was dead.
—MERIDEL LE SUEUR
Novelist and poet, ninety-one years old

The generation of women between the ages of forty-five and sixty are redefining middle age. What used to conjure images of exhaustion, resignation, weight gain, and a point of no return has given way to confidence, vitality, and the possibility of an exciting future. Women know this is true because they feel better, look better, and are more active than their mothers—who were ''old'' at fifty— felt, looked, or acted.

Even for the most active of us, however, menopause is often feared as the boundary line that marks the begin-ning of old age. Although personal experience, demo-graphics, and statistics combine to assure us that we have lots of quality time ahead, we shiver inwardly with the suspicion of what old age, sparked by menopause, will bring. Carrie Brouwer, forty-eight, has yet to go through menopause, but in her early forties she experienced a change in her menstrual flow that made her consider the possibility for the first time. "There were some months when I had serious clotting, and cramps associated with that. I wondered what it was, and a physical therapist I was seeing suggested that maybe I was starting menopause. I was under a lot of stress, and when that changed the cramps and clotting went away. But it frightened me to think I might be at the age of menopause and I thought, No, this can't be, I'm not old enough for that and I don't expect that to happen until I am in my sixties. I felt that to go through menopause was an indication of being aged before my time."

It is easy to appreciate why menopause has for so long been linked to, even synonymous with, old age, considering average lifespans through history. A woman born during the Roman Empire could expect to live twenty-nine years. By 1900 average life expectancy for women in this country was 49.2 years. In contrast, the current average life span for women is seventy-eight, and that average is expected to rise into the eighties over the next decade, offering us a good thirty years of postchildbearing life. Yet the image of the dried-up, decaying, depressed menopausal victim does persist, and many of us still approach menopause with anxiety and concern.

NOT AN AGE-RELATED EVENT

As a physical event menopause has absolutely no relation to age. Menopause means the cessation of one's menses. In the average course of events in this country, menopause happens to women at midlife, between the ages of forty-five and fifty-five. Yet women have been known to go through natural menopause in their early thirties and in their early sixties. And menopause can be induced, through the surgical removal of the ovaries, at any time in a woman's life, from her teens through middle age.

Because the majority of women experience menopause during middle age, the event is linked with that era in our lives. And before our generation, middle age was not generally perceived as a time of renewal or opportunity. Instead, middle age was a time when women could no longer count on the status accorded them when they were young. With that loss of status came a loss of power as they knew it. No longer able to have children, they were unable to produce one of the chief products for which they were valued. And they were no longer supple, wrinkle-free, slim, and strong. Most of our mothers and grandmothers did not have access to the nutritional information we have, nor did they have the time for exercise other than housework or for the relaxation that makes our bodies less susceptible to the effects of estrogen loss. The older woman moved out of the spotlight to make way for the fertile and smooth-skinned younger girl.

A CONDITION OF SILENCE

Menopause happened in the vague realm of our mother's and grandmother's middle years. A condition of silence surrounded the event. We knew about it, not through explanation and a sharing of experience but through hushed and secret implication. Whomever we imagined we would be once we went through menopause was shaped not through direct communication but through inference.

Adrienne Garrity remembered her Aunt Ethel and Aunt Ethel's friends continually gathering together in someone's living room. "Those women were old and they would always say they were so hot or they were so uncomfortable. Everyone knew without their saying so that they were going through 'the change,' except the change seemed to be lasting for years. And they just looked so *antique*." At forty-six, Adrienne is in the process of menopause. She is slim, exercises regularly, and has a career as a psychotherapist. Yet the image she had for years of the menopausal woman, influenced by the women she remembered as a girl, was someone with "tons of wrinkles on the upper lip and moles with hairs growing out of them. Bad ankles, support hose, and a rayon dress with lint all over it."

Julia Phillips's mother was widowed in her early fifties and lived with her daughter, son-in-law, and grandchildren until she died at age seventy-five. "My father died at fifty-eight, my mother was fifty-two, and I always saw her as an old woman. She moaned and groaned about menopause, but that seemed tied up with terrible circulatory problems. She found walking very hard. Her feet hurt, her legs hurt her. She was very heavy and she had swollen legs. And I think because of her obesity her blood pressure was elevated and her arteries were clogged. She loved people, she loved to go out and do things and have a good time. Yet she always seemed old."

For the woman of today, going through menopause at the average age can mark the passing of youth. Unlike our mothers and grandmothers, however, because of improved health care and longer life spans, this passing of youth does not mark the beginning of being elderly. Instead, it signals a new era in our personal lives somewhere between youth and old age, one for which we are setting the first large-scale precedent. The lack of historical precedent makes this time particularly exciting, since we can create for ourselves as women a future that has never been created until now. Yet the lack of a precedent also makes us vulnerable to both our culture's fears of aging and our own fears. We may know we are not old, but attitudes about old age, as embodied in Adrienne Garrity's and Julia Phillips's caricatured images, are still very strong.

NOT A PRETTY PICTURE

Fear of aging, regrets about losing one's youth, and an almost unmentionable terror of death are not new dilemmas and are as real for men as for women. Literature and mythology are filled with an obsession with youth and the search for eternal life. Ponce de León searched for the Fountain of Youth; Faust sold his soul to Mephistopheles in exchange for eternal life; the dying Gustav von Aschenbach pursued the young Tadzio through alleys and canals, in *Death in Venice*.

The older woman is a particularly unsavory character in Western mythology. Remember Hera, wife of that irrepressible cad Zeus? Perpetually middle-aged, she was unable to control her husband's philanderings. Instead she vented her frustrations by taking sides in wars and disputes, at times wiping out entire battalions. Not to be forgotten either are the old bags, the hags, the witches, the wicked, wart-nosed spell casters guaranteed to spoil any princess's good time.

The archetypal older woman of fairy tales, incapable of eliciting anyone's sympathy, is the Queen in *Sleeping Beauty*. Poised to be dethroned by a bride's virginal purity and armed only with past-one's-prime rage, she consults that instrument of torture that never lies. The mirror tells her that indeed "though you are of beauty rare, the young bride Sleeping Beauty is a thousand times more fair." Folklorists don't actually attribute the queen's disappointment or her plot against Snow White to erratic hormones, of course. Popular opinion, however, might say she was "going through the change."

Except we've now seen evidence contrary to the fact. Menopause does not cause a woman's personality or gender to change. Menopause does not prevent us from being sexual. Menopause is not itself a disease nor does it for the most part instigate disease. Menopause is not the source of midlife depression or instability. For all of the above, however, menopause can serve as the reason, the crutch, the catch-all for crisis in any of those areas. In the same way, passing off anxiety about growing old (gerontophobia) onto menopause can be a way of avoiding a real terror.

Who can be blamed for such concerns? In the United States, youth and its alleged power, passion, and opportunity are celebrated, whereas being old is not at all fun. In fact, a general disgust with aspects of aging makes it seem as if growing older, with its losses and deficits, is really rather in poor taste. Elderly people's needs are not accommodated, almost as if ignoring them will make them go away. Social services and medical benefits for the elderly are consistently being cut; nursing homes and hospitals are overcrowded and understaffed. The majority of the elderly, who happen to be women, are not resting comfortably on nest eggs but must clamor to buy food and medication and pay heating and doctor bills on social security, pension, or insurance checks that do not expand with inflation. Opportunities to earn money are rare for most people once they've passed the age of retirement and particularly rare for today's and tomorrow's elderly women, who, unlike women currently in their twenties, thirties, and forties, have not made careers for themselves. Along with such material realities, we have few if any dignified cultural images of the aged. Of course there are the feisty *Golden Girls,* but it's easy for them. They're on TV.

Such grim realities do not read like an optimistic endorsement for the postmenopausal years. The realities, in fact, lend a certain appeal to the myths! But we are less likely to tackle the realities of aging if we succumb to images of ourselves as old before our time. Positive and rewarding postmenopausal years will be the result of our attitudes and actions during the years when menopause occurs. Will we succumb to pressures that we are less beautiful, less worthy, less marketable? Or will we provide dignified images of old age by beginning with dignified images of ourselves, now?

REVISIONING OLD IMAGES

A simultaneous loss of beauty and youth is considered an outcome of both menopause and middle age. For the many women who have measured their personal value by those standards, both menopause and middle age can mean a particularly early loss of value. Mickie Kramer, years after her mother's death, speculated on the cost of such a loss.

"My mother was very youth-oriented. She died when she was forty-seven. She was very beautiful and she never understood the value of her brilliance. She was actually a very bright woman and read all the time and was knowledgeable, but the only part of her that *she* knew was valuable was her beauty. The only part of her that she knew was worthy of love was that she was beautiful. And certainly not that she was bright. My mother died of cancer, a legitimate reason, but when I look at her psychological makeup I can see that for her to grow old might have been truly intolerable. I'm not even certain whether she had gone through menopause yet. But to see her beauty go would have been a devastating thing to happen to her."

Mickie's life has followed a different path. By her own choosing, she has cultivated numerous skills by which to measure her self-worth. Menopause and middle age have not been impediments to success or indications of old age. In her forties she has been successful as an entrepreneur and a consultant, in ways her mother never had a chance to be. She described herself, when I asked if *she* was beautiful, as a beautiful person who was sometimes physically attractive. Physical attractiveness, she maintained, was but one of the sources of a woman's beauty. Strength, curiosity, imagination were just as necessary to her in order to achieve what she was after in life. She has continued to grow in both her professional and personal lives past the age her mother was when she died. But she had a starkly different picture of her forties when she was younger.

"I thought being forty was old. I can't even imagine how foolish I was to think the way I did about what being in my forties would mean. I thought it meant I would be dowdy, boring, whatever the opposite of vital would be. Sexually done for, since sex was just something you fooled around with in your youth. Women in their forties were needy, maybe stupid, definitely not good. My mental picture was of a figureless, colorless, sensible person." With an image of the forties, I did not expect Mickie's picture of the fifties to fare very well. "If forty was dowdy, fifty was the frayed edges of that dowdiness. It was falling apart. Just falling apart."

Hard-to-dispel images of growing older make sense in a country that has barely made it to puberty. The United States is just over two hundred years old, an adolescent compared with the rest of the world. Our values are sometimes adolescent as well. We are consumers, trained to discard what is no longer useful (often the same as what no longer pleases) for a new, shinier rendition. Societies with longer histories have a less disposable perception of their elders.

Chinese culture is based on a respect for the wisdom and strength of the elderly. The older woman in traditional China was the head of her household, in a position of power over her sons and daughters-in-law who lived with her. In modern China, an older woman still holds a secure and respected position. Paula Weideger, in her book *Menstruation and Menopause*, makes note of a Western psychiatrist working in China who claimed never to have seen a "menopausal psychosis" in a Chinese woman. Other sources also report that menopausal problems are rare in China.

In many traditional societies, a woman's status rises after menopause. Older women are the midwives, the matchmakers, the healers. For Bengali women, the enforced separation of *purdah* ends when they finish menstruating; they can now hold the keys to the kitchen and the storeroom as a symbol of their authority. In certain African tribes, women who no longer menstruate become, finally, full-fledged members of their tribes, participating in decision making and sitting in on tribal councils. In Sri Lanka, elders are addressed by the term "intelligent one." And in Native American culture, the ninety-one-year-old poet Meridel Le Sueur asserts that once a woman contributes to her community by having children she can become a shaman, or holy person. Elders are considered assets to the nation because of their life experience.

Cultural assumptions and expectations of aging also influence the quality of menopause. Anthropologist Estelle Fuchs found that some Welsh women are embarrassed by *not* having hot flashes since flashes are a sign of a healthy and successful change of life.

MEDIA CONCESSIONS

A consumer culture may not respect age, but it does respect buying power. In terms of population strength and available cash, everyone else had better move on over, because middle age has arrived. "Between 1990 and 2000, consumers aged 45 to 64 will increase 31% to 61 million," reports *Advertising Age,* and then goes on to say that while 1 in 4 Americans today are over 50, 1 in 3 will be over 50 by the year 2010. *The Boston Herald* writes that the forty-five-to-sixty age group is a prime market, quoting a specialist in age-group marketing. "These are the people with the empty nests, they're well off financially, their children are grown, the house is paid for, they're beginning to make major purchases. They have the largest disposable income." A 1987 Census Bureau and Conference Board study confirms that an estimated 63 million older Americans who are "the 50-plus market controls the purse strings of $130 billion in discretionary income—one half of America's mad money."

Not only are the numbers strong, the over-fifty population is active—going to the movies, watching TV, reading magazines and newspapers. People over fifty represent 45 percent of all prime-time television viewers (approximately 1 out of 2), 37 percent of newspaper readers, and 33 percent of magazine readers. Advertisers are finding it difficult to ignore such a critical mass of audience, particularly an audience with money. In response, the advertising industry has awarded this age group the status of a serious market with nomenclature such as "golden-agers," "empty-nesters," "senior spenders," "fifty-plus," "the mature market," "the gray market," and "master consumers." This last category are individuals over fifty with high levels of spendable income and the time and inclination to indulge themselves. The large numbers of potential middle-aged consumers have given rise to consultancies called Mature Market Institute, LifeSpan Communications, Age Wave, Inc., and PrimeLife. Market studies have determined that the over-fifty market represents an estimated combined annual income of $865 billion. Consumers over fifty have a mean household income of $29,000, which is higher than the national average. Eighty-eight percent own their own homes, which have an average market value of $94,000. Two thirds have paid off their mortgages, and almost one in ten owns a vacation home.

The rising demographics for women are also nothing to be sneered at by marketers, as they well know. The 47 million women over the age of forty in 1984 rose to approximately 52 million in 1990. Clairol, famous in the early 1960s for its hair-dye double entendre "Does she or doesn't she?" and its assertion that "If I only have one life to live, let me live it as a blonde," now promotes its Silk & Silver hair coloring with the tag line "Free, Gray and 51." Lena Horne (looking fabulous) "gets the best out of life" as she eats *Post* natural bran flakes. Ad copy attempts to sell products with such accommodating phrases as "grown-up fit" and "maturing with individuality and style" while appealing to one's "buying wisdom" and experienced "common sense." Advertising portrays us as attractive, well-groomed, in relationships, even in love.

Does advertising such as this reflect how we feel about ourselves—bold, confident, embracing the aging process with dignity, and retaining our sexiness at the same time? Unfortunately, advertising has a longer history of fueling dissatisfaction and craving, and plenty of us are still on the run to the makeup counter. Ida George, in her seventies, works as a Revlon saleswoman in Bloomingdale's. I asked if women of any age are content to grow old gracefully. Ida emphatically responded, "No. Women tell me, 'I can't stand these wrinkles. Give me something to get rid of them!' "

The fact that women in middle age, many of whom are going through menopause, are appearing with more frequency in advertising means we are being noticed and counted in ways we haven't been before. At the same time, if we rely on advertising to reflect our experiences, we will get only a surface interpretation. We can get a better picture by talking among ourselves.

SEEKING AND PROVIDING POWERFUL ROLE MODELS

"Who, when you're in your late forties or early fifties, can you talk with about the changes your body might be undergoing in the next five years?" asked attorney Linda Avery. "Who are our mentors?" she wanted to know, searching at the same time for her generation as a whole and for herself personally. "Our mothers, our aunts are perhaps elderly and do not come from a generation where they feel free to discuss these kinds of things. We all have to do it among ourselves."

And what is it that we have to say? Regarding menopause, women who have not yet been through it naturally tend to have more concerns, questions, and fears about the process and the changes it will bring than the women who have already gone through the event. Women who have been through it are more philosophical, seeing menopause as one in a series of changes that come along at this time in life. Yet, whether in menopause or anticipating it, women between forty and sixty claimed to be happier and more productive than ever before. All of them were more self-aware now than when they were in their twenties and thirties—and more self-aware than their mothers were at middle age. Some even said they felt younger now than they did when they were starting out in the adult world.

As a member of the current generation of middle-agers I would like to think we are the role models for our daughters and other younger women of today. We are showing them that midlife does not mean being old, that menopause does not mean a loss of beauty, vitality, sexuality, or mental health. Of course, there is Liz Reynolds's situation. Her thirty-year-old woman doctor presented Liz with a frightening image of a menopause-induced future. A recent study conducted by the Center for Research on Women at Wellesley College led me to believe that Reynolds's doctor was not the exception.

Eighty college women, with an average age of 19.3 years, responded to a questionnaire regarding their knowledge of menstruation, ovulation, and menopause. The majority of young women answering held "predominantly negative beliefs about the physical and emotional changes associated with menopause."

Those responding considered symptoms to be associated with menopause unpleasant and these included hot flashes, weight gain, unwanted hair growth, dry skin, and dry vaginas. A majority also linked negative emotional changes with menopause, including depression, irritability, mood swings, and feelings of worthlessness. One quarter of the young women surveyed expected a loss of some kind—such as the loss of femininity, sex drive, or youth—to go hand in hand with menopause.

Despite our discovery of a new middle age, the same old silences around menopause apparently persist. In general, breaking the silence regarding other areas of reproduction has always been a challenge. Widespread discussion and education about menstruation and pregnancy are relatively new phenomena. Astonishingly, birth-control education and the issue of whether to dispense birth control to teenagers continues to be furiously debated. Yet those events receive much more attention than the natural evolutionary end to the female reproductive cycle.

Ignorance regarding menopause is beginning to be addressed. The rest of the decade will see a swelling of the population into the ages when menopause occurs. We already see the repercussions of that trend, as national studies on menopause are introduced by the National Institutes of Health and the National Institute of Mental Health. We can influence the breaking of the silence around menopause and we can shatter negative attitudes, stereotypes, and misconceptions by speaking freely of the event, not just to our peers but to our daughters and to younger friends as well. We can encourage younger women to have a complete view of their reproductive cycle. We can dispel fears about growing old before our time.

Linda Avery spoke with some regret about the older women—her mother, her aunts, friends of the family—with whom she was close who didn't communicate what they were going through at midlife. She is determined to fill in that gap for her daughter. "Menopause was considered a family secret of some sort. I don't know if they felt it was shameful or if they somehow wanted to protect a younger woman or what it was, but no one opened up to me about it. That deprived me of the opportunity to learn earlier in life about maturing as a woman. I want to make sure that with my daughter I do share with her as I grow older. I'm starting to feel that I want to make connections with women of other ages, to be a role model or a mentor. Somebody younger women can communicate with.''

We have come a long way in claiming ourselves as whole women entitled to the fullness of life. And we are being represented in media beyond advertising. Where before it was difficult to find role models or even peers to identify with, women over forty are becoming increasingly more visible as characters on television shows, in the movies, on stage, and as subjects of studies in newspapers and magazines. Angela Lansbury's over-fifty Jessica Fletcher has been joined by over-forty Murphy Brown; Wendy Wasserstein brought single, over-forty art historian Heidi of *The Heidi Chronicles* to the stage, and the middle-age adventurers and friends of *Shirley Valentine* and *Steel Magnolias* made it to Broadway and Hollywood. And there's a roll call of women past and present who have made and continue to make important contributions to society during their middle years. This list is a mere sampling: Doris Lessing, Anne Bancroft, Gena Rowlands, Joan Baez, Madeline Kunin, Rachel Carson, Connie Chung, Diane Feinstein, Jane Fonda, Carolyn Heilbrun, the model Carmen, Kaylan Pickford, Shirley MacLaine, Lithuanian Prime Minister Kazimiera Prunskiene, Cicely Tyson, Gloria Steinem, Toni Morrison, Helen Caldicott, Geraldine Ferraro, Emma Goldman, Adrienne Rich, Maxine Kumin, Isadora Duncan, Audrey Hepburn, Carly Simon, Carol Burnett, Barbara Walters, Edith Wharton, Colette, Harriet Tubman, Mae West, Elizabeth Cady Stanton, Raisa Gorbachev, Susan B. Anthony, Sojourner Truth, Margaret Fuller, Joni Mitchell, Rosalind Russell, Ingrid Bergman, Katharine Hepburn, Judy Collins, Maya Angelou, Ellen Burstyn, Erica Jong, Angela Lansbury, Pauline Collins, Margaret Sanger, Willa Cather, Marie Curie, Cherokee Chief Wilma Mankiller, marathon runner Joyce Smith, Shirley Jones, Raquel Welch, Congresswoman Pat Schroeder, Joanne Woodward, Mathilde Krim, Elizabeth Dole, Eleanor Roosevelt.

One of the most public forums for midlife women has been new magazines. The most ambitious and successful is *Lear's*, published by Frances Lear, who put up $25 million of her own money to finance the magazine for the woman who wasn't born yesterday. Lear said her vision for the magazine came from "being tired of seeing seventeen-year-old models and reading stories for young marrieds. We have been shut out of the media for so long that we have not seen ourselves in positive images anywhere." Coming up for a title for the magazine proved a challenge. Lear experimented with dozens of names, and finding that "the only nouns for women over forty were 'crone' and 'hag,' " decided to go with her own last name. Other magazines include *Mirabella, Prime-Time,* and *New Choices for the Best Years. Harper's Bazaar*'s August issue has, for a number of years, been dedicated to women over forty, and *McCall's* has started what they call their "Silver" issue. Even magazines whose advertising and editorial slants are blatantly geared to single or newly married career women between the ages of twenty-five and forty have responded to the times. *New Woman* sports the tag line "A new woman is an attitude, not an age."

"Now my daughters keep asking when you are going to grow up?" said writer Merlin Stone. "I felt like an old lady at thirty-two. . . . I guess it's like the Bob Dylan song: 'I was so much older then. I'm younger than that now.' "

"I had this vision that as you get older things got harder, that you felt worse, or whatever," said Evelyn Glenn. "I really have found the reverse to be true."

"I'm doing away with the word 'age,' " ninety-one-year-old Meridel Le Sueur is quoted as having said. Le Sueur was born in Iowa in 1900. She has written fiction, poetry, history, autobiography, and biography for more than sixty years, often about the struggles of working-class people. "You never hear of anything in nature aging, or a sunflower saying, 'Well, I'm growing old,' and leaning over and vomiting. You know, it ripens, it drops its seed, and the cycle goes on. I'm not aging, I'm ripening.''

On the threshold of what the French call the ''third stage,'' we could easily be undermined by attitudes toward menopause and aging and toward ourselves as aged, which are deeply embedded in the culture's psyche. But we've lived too fully not to reap the rewards that are our due. We respect ourselves more than ever before and therefore command more respect. The depth of our experience and our perspectives on life afford us better judgment and greater wisdom. We speak our minds and find ourselves listened to. As we reach our middle years, our experience contradicts popular concepts. And wherever women speak of true experience, the old ideas, perpetuated in silence, come tumbling down.

SECTION TWO

The Facts

CHAPTER 7

What Happens

There is nothing either good or bad, but thinking makes it so.

—HAMLET

The myths surrounding menopause form a legacy of assumptions, hearsay, and preconceived notions that only now are beginning to be challenged by the voices of real experience. And the strongest feeling that emerged from the experiences of the women interviewed for this book is that menopause cannot be categorized. The process is different for every woman. Menstrual history, pregnancy history, genetics—none of those factors are final predictors of our own menopausal process. One thing is certain: physical signs and changes do occur, in varying degrees. This chapter is a guide to identifying these signs and responding to them.

At some point, usually during a woman's forties, her menstrual periods become irregular and eventually stop. The "climacteric" may last as long as seven years and is the natural result of age-related changes in the ovaries. Since menstruation still occurs, pregnancy is possible. "Menopause" refers to a woman's final menstrual cycle, her last period, usually considered final after twelve consecutive cycles have been missed. Women in North America popularly refer to the combined events as menopause.

Because of these age-related changes, the body's estrogen level is reduced by 75 percent. A woman's ovaries remain viable, however, and continue to produce two androgens (male hormones)—androstenedione and testosterone. The body's fat cells now act as "estrogen factories," converting androstenedione to estrone, a weak estrogen, which is then converted to estrodial. Overall estrogen levels vary enormously among menopausal women, but since fat becomes the major producer of the body's estrogen after menopause, the more fat a woman has, the more estrogen she will have.

On the average, women go through menopause between the ages of forty-five and fifty-five, although 8 percent experience the event naturally before the age of forty-five. Less than 8 percent menstruate into their late fifties and still less into their early sixties. For some women, however, menopause does not happen spontaneously and gradually. Instead, the end of menstruation is an abrupt event initiated by surgical removal of the ovaries, usually because of a significant medical threat. In such cases, the onset of signs such as hot flashes and the end of menstruation occur immediately. Menopause due to surgical removal of the ovaries can happen to a woman at any age after she begins to menstruate.

If the doctor tells me, "Your throat looks red," I start coughing. If someone says, "You look tired," everything immediately hurts. So I wasn't surprised that, when researching the changes that could accompany menopause, I was convinced I had gone through or would go through them all! I have included all those signs in the following pages. While they are very real physical events for the women who experience them, by no means does each event occur for everyone.

The experience of physical changes and discomfort directly related to menopause should not be minimized. Three hundred kinds of tissue in a woman's body are affected by estrogen. Yet, in a subject so rife with myth, even plain facts are hard to decipher. A hot flash, decidedly uncomfortable and often embarrassing, is a simple direct event that can be seen, touched, measured, and felt. While it is the most frequent sign reported by American women, Japanese women never even mention hot flashes as a problem. Instead they report headaches, shoulder stiffness, ringing in the ears, and aching joints as their most prominent signs. Obviously, cultural perceptions can influence a physical experience.

The women with whom I spoke reported a variety of effects. Some women claimed to have no physical signs other than the end of their menstrual periods, while others experienced a wide range of changes. The severity of signs also varied. Some women reported hot flashes severe enough to send them home from work soaking wet, while others merely wondered if someone had turned the thermostat up that afternoon. The majority of women spoke of experiencing between one and three signs of menopause. In general, the most common complaints women bring to physicians are irregular periods, hot flashes, and vaginal dryness.

Although discussion of the details of pregnancy and menstruation have become less taboo in recent generations, there is still a reluctance among women to speak about the physical nature of their menopause. No doubt this reluctance is due to the many stigmas attached to the process, as well as a fear that too much discussion will brand them as complainers—or worse, neurotic. Many active and happy women sometimes suffer severe physical discomfort due to menopause, discounting the notion that physical difficulties at menopause are connected to depression or emotional problems. I did observe, however, that in instances where many other life crises or problems occurred at the same time as menopause, women tended to have a stronger reaction to the physical events. Yet, in the majority of women such effects, even when severe, did not impact the overall quality of their lives.

Cynthia Richards, fifty-three, a community coordinator for a government agency, arrived on her bicycle after work for our meeting over dinner. She is married, with three children in their twenties, and her healthy look and her evident vitality belied the physical problems she described having experienced in the last year.

During a happy and satisfying time in her life, with grown children, a fulfilling marriage, and a job she loved, menopause hit her hard. She had had regular, symptom-free periods since the age of eleven, and now she was suddenly deluged with hot flashes day and night. "I was totally unprepared," she said, shaking her head, her natural enthusiasm evident even as she related what had been a difficult time for her. "I actually timed the flashes. I didn't think anybody could live through such things. My clothes would be soaking and I'd have to go home and change. I started bringing extra clothes to work. I thought I had malaria."

Her physician prescribed estrogen, which she found caused migraine headaches and which also caused her periods to resume. When she complained to her doctor about getting her period again, he claimed she should have known that would occur when she began taking hormones. She decided to discontinue the estrogen and has had severe hot flashes for the last year and a half.

Her family's reaction to her discontinuing estrogen was not sympathetic. "They thought I was stubborn. My husband said, 'Oh, Cynthia, no one has to go through this.' But the flashes were natural, and that was a consolation to me. Now I don't have as many as I used to. Maybe I have four a night and six or eight during the day. Today I was at a meeting and I felt something on the back of my ankles. Somehow you just get used to it. You can get used to anything. And now I don't see it as having made any long-term difference in my life."

THE SIGNS

Hot Flashes

Sudden increased body heat, starting at the chest and rising up to the neck and face. Accompanied by an outbreak of sweat, varying in intensity with the individual.

Eighty-five percent of menopausal women in America report hot flashes, which tend to be the hallmark of menopause, with images of huffing and puffing women frantically fanning themselves. Each flash lasts about 3½ minutes. During the flash there is a sudden rise of 1 to 4 degrees Fahrenheit in skin temperature. At the beginning of the flash, the heart suddenly beats much faster, and as the flash progresses the heart rate returns to normal. The heated skin begins to perspire, and evaporation then cools the body down. About 1 teaspoon of water is lost from each flash episode, and they can occur at the rate of a few mild flashes a week to six or seven an hour. Women can experience flashes for periods of five to ten years, and the flashes may come and go in stop-and-start patterns.

In Cynthia's case, for at least a year the flashes were severe and disruptive. Mickie Kramer, forty-eight, claimed they intruded into her life. Other women hardly noticed them. Some were so surprised it was happening, they found it funny. "I would laugh and say, 'This can't be happening to me,' " said Julia Phillips, fifty-nine. " 'Are you hot, do you feel warm?' I'd ask my husband and he'd tease me by saying, 'I think it's finally starting, Julia.' "

Irregular Bleeding

Changes in amount of menstrual flow, length of cycle, and overall cycle pattern. Always consult your physician, since menstrual changes may also indicate difficulties not related to menopause.

Dr. Lois Goodman, a menopause specialist at the Newton-Wellesley Hospital in Massachusetts, says that irregular bleeding is the most common indication of menopause presented by her patients. Cycles may be longer or shorter. Flow may be very heavy or scant. Ovulation may not occur on day 14 of the cycle as it had in the past. Several cycles will be missed, and then menstruation will return. Women who have relied on the rhythm method of birth control need to be particularly careful at this time. Dr. Goodman advises continued use of other birth control methods until twelve consecutive cycles are missed.

While some women, like Cynthia, reported an abrupt stop to their menstrual cycle, most reported a stop-start pattern, like Mickie, who remembered, ''All of a sudden the whole thing was a jumble. I would have a period, then it would stop again and I wouldn't have a period for three or four months, and then it would start up again.''

Altered Sleep Patterns

Interrupted sleep due to hot flashes and hormonal changes.

Hot flashes that occur once or several times throughout the night are known as night sweats. Night sweats disrupt the quality of sleep and are therefore a disruption to the waking hours as well. Julia thought her daytime flashes were amusing but she also claimed, ''There really has been a change in me. The night flashes changed my sleeping pattern. I used to be a wonderful sleeper.''

During a night sweat the body breaks into a sweat that wets nightclothes and linens. You may have to change yourself and your bed once or perhaps several times during the night. Such occurrences obviously disrupt one's usual sleep pattern and can contribute to irritability, sluggishness, and the lack of concentration that accompanies little sleep.

Studies at the Brigham and Women's Hospital in Boston also suggest that there is a fall in dream-rich sleep as estrogen levels drop, which may cause a less restful night. Several factors can account for this, but it is thought to be a dysfunction of the sleep center in the brain due to lack of estrogen. As time passes, sleep disruption becomes less of a problem and tends to disappear altogether after the last menstrual cycle.

Cynthia told me, "I had a terrible time with sleeping. I was waking up several times during the night. I got used to it, but the first few months were terrible. I'd go to work and be tired because I hadn't slept."

Carolyn Sutton added, "I never slept for about three or four years. I changed doctors three times because none of them would put me on hormones. I finally found a doctor who did, and that's when the night sweats stopped. As soon as I started taking the hormones I was able to sleep, and that was marvelous."

While night sweats are an easily identified cause of altered sleep patterns, changes in sleep may not necessarily be related to the sweats. Anxiety, stress, moodiness, or irritability about other aspects of life may cause disruption and should be discussed with your physician.

Depression

Low moods; despair; lethargy; feelings of purposelessness. Often diagnosed clinically.

Many people still think that women at menopause are crazy. You can't live with them and you can't live without them, so what are you going to do? Send them to the doctor!

Sonja and John McKinlay are the husband-and-wife team who conducted the *Massachusetts Women's Health Study* discussed in Chapter Five. The McKinlays' organization, the New England Research Institute, Inc., surveyed 2,500 women who were selected at random and were premenopausal at the start of the study. The women were followed for almost five years to see what effects menopause had on their lives. What made this sample of women particularly interesting and relevant was that they were chosen at random, whereas most studies about menopausal women originate among patients seeking help in a medical setting. Thus, the women studied, like the majority of the population, had not reported any medical problems before the study began. The McKinlays found that menstrual changes associated with menopause appear to have no effect on depression. Women experiencing menopause were not any more depressed than at other times of their lives and were not depressed compared with the general population. Those women who reported depression ascribed it to "someone causing worry" in their lives and not to menopause.

Further surveys support these conclusions. A North American study involving 460 women found menopausal women were not more depressed than the general population. In fact, the study found postmenopausal women to be the *least* depressed of the groups they surveyed.

A ten-year study in Sweden showed no increase in psychological disorders at menopause. This study found, in fact, that psychological problems among women were at their peak between ages thirty-five and forty-four. Another study out of New Haven, Connecticut, also showed no increase in depression at menopause. The highest rate of depression occurred in women under thirty-five years old.

Such a sampling of research indicates what studies worldwide continue to claim: the depression so many women expect to be their lot at menopause does not exist. Instead, all the studies unanimously show that women during the menopausal years have less of a tendency to be depressed than any other segment of the population.

Skin Changes

Increased tendency toward dryness of the skin as well as lining, loosening, and changes in color and texture, associated with age and with loss of estrogen.

Many doctors report that skin aging is not caused by estrogen loss. In addition, the *Physician's Desk Refer-*

ence states that estrogen replacement will not prevent wrinkles. But I have found that it does.

The scientific method evaluates the proof before recommending the pudding. While this is valid and necessary in many situations, the vitamin E controversy comes to mind. Impressive studies by respected researchers say vitamin E applied to the skin doesn't do anything for it. When I used vitamin E cream, however, among the several methods I have tried for skin care, my skin looked great. Vitamin E seemed to stimulate the skin so there was color where it had been pale.

Many women noticed rapid skin aging at the same time as menopause occurred. We know that men age, too, but their necks do not collapse into their chests at age fifty.

Drs. Cutler, García, and Edwards, in *Menopause,* report that skin does tend to age more rapidly at menopause. It gradually loses its thickness and some of its fluid as estrogen decreases. A 1972 report from Scandinavia found that lack of estrogen had a thinning effect on the epidermis (the outer layer of skin, the layer that is seen) and that adding estrogen therapy thickened the epidermis. They also noted in animal studies that estrogen cream applied to the skin helped to hydrate the skin. Local estrogen therapy also increased the number of skin capillaries and corrected some fragmentation of skin collagen. A 1977 report from Finland showed the skin to be an important target organ for estrogens. It further reported that estrogen therapy appeared to prevent epidermal thinning and diminishing. Dr. Wulf H. Utian reports that estrogen keeps the skin smoother, thicker, and softer.

Fifty-three-year-old fashion model Helena noticed that her skin had a different quality since menopause. "My skin seems to be less taut, as if it were getting thinner. The texture has changed, as if the elasticity has gone out." Pauline Worlen, at fifty-seven, did not experience a loss in elasticity as much as dryness that had not been there before. "I never used moisturizer through all those years. Now I cream my hands and face all the time."

Loss of Libido

Decreased interest in having sex.

The Stanford Menopause Study (1979), involving several hundred women, surveyed attitudes on sex. Seventy-one percent of the women questioned commented about their interest in sex since menopause. Of these 71 percent, 48 percent reported a noticeable decline in sexual interest, 29 percent reported that sex was the same, and 23 percent noted an increase in sexual interest.

Sex is hardly the unmentionable subject it was for many of us when we were growing up, but it's not easy to go against years of training. During the interviews, some women responded to questions about their sex lives with the answer, ''Fine, thank you,'' a subjective assessment I found challenging to interpret. Other responses ranged from, ''I don't care if I ever get laid again,'' to, ''My sex life is better than it's ever been. I'm not young anymore, but if I knew then what I know now . . .''

Overall, many women reported a slight decline in their interest in sex. Are hormones behind this? Although a lot has been written about the hormonal basis for sexual desire, many factors beyond hormones influence sexual interest. Perhaps with so many women describing their lives as fuller and richer than ever, sex just seems less central.

Helena is a beautiful fashion model in her fifties who has worked successfully in the field for more than twenty years. After a long and disastrous first marriage, she has been happily remarried for the past year and a half. Turning fifty terrified her because it meant she was getting old and losing her youthful looks. ''I lived on what I looked like, most of my life. Menopause meant I would not be as attractive, physically and sexually. I was afraid of not wanting to have sex at all, or much.'' Yet, not only does she feel more attractive now than she has ever felt in her life, the quality of her sex life has not changed significantly either.

"I'll say this. Sometimes I might want sex a little bit less than I used to. I don't feel the physical need for sex as much as I did when I was younger, but I have enough sex to be able to satisfy my husband and to satisfy myself. There's no pressure about it. I figure once or twice a week is plenty for me, you know. I mean, that's plenty for a lot of people who are twenty."

For the women who *have* reported decreased desire for sex, the possible effects of estrogen lack need to be considered. The chain of sensations leading to orgasm involves a series of estrogen-sensitive cells. A study at Yale University on sexual problems during menopause involves ninety-three women to date. The women report a range of difficulties, including vaginal dryness, a decrease in clitoral sensitivity, decrease in orgasmic frequency and intensity, and a decrease in sexual desire.

The researchers noted a direct relation between the sexual difficulties of these women and their blood levels of estrogen. Sexual responses improved markedly after hormonal treatment. The most dramatic response was in the 77 percent of women who reported lack of desire. Ninety percent of them reported an increase in desire after three to six months of treatment. None of these women were given male sex hormones. Does this indicate that menopausal women who do not report a lessening of desire lose less estrogen? Does estrogen affect some women's sexuality more than others'? While the one study doesn't answer these larger questions, it does point to a relationship between estrogen and sexual response in certain cases.

Other researchers have found that adding a small dose of the male hormone testosterone to estrogen has improved the sex drive in women who have an otherwise satisfying relationship with their partners. Some researchers are using a combination estrogen-testosterone preparation for all postmenopausal women, producing a stronger sex drive and more energy.

This is not to say that all changes in desire are directly

due to estrogen lack or that women who do not use estrogen-replacement therapy experience decreased libido. Mickie Kramer chose not to take estrogen because of a family history of cancer. Her sex life is better now than when she was in her twenties.

If you are experiencing any changes in your sex life and in desire, it is important to discuss such changes with your physician. Early treatment can avoid a break in an otherwise satisfactory sex life and can avoid the psychological and emotional fallout that may result if physical changes are not helped medically.

Vaginal Changes

A thinning of the lining of the vaginal wall.

Some of the last menopausal signs to appear, often anywhere between two and ten years after menstruation ends, are physical changes in the vagina. The sensitive membranes along the vaginal walls thin, irritate easily, and are prone to a greater number of infections. Along with the possibility of painful intercourse, there is a resulting tendency toward urinary tract infection and an increase in urinary incontinence.

Dr. Goodman comments, "A lot of women don't want to think about it. They don't bring it up to a doctor. What happens is that intercourse becomes uncomfortable, and then they find a million reasons why they don't want to do it. They avoid it, and then the next time they have it, it's much worse. Now they *really* want to avoid it and then it's darn near impossible. They come to my office and they say, 'I didn't think this part of my life would be finished at this time.' It's a wonderful problem for the physician because it can be cured. A little bit of estrogen cream treatment once or twice a week and it's 100 percent reversed. People come back relieved. It also can improve the urinary leaking, although not 100 percent, because those tissues are estrogen-sensitive."

Related uterine changes due to hormonal loss may

cause the uterus to become smaller and its lining thinner; external genitalia may shrink somewhat, and a certain amount of pubic hair may be lost. None of these changes need affect one's sex life or life in general.

Not only are "senile vagina syndrome" and "vaginal atrophy" unsexy terms, senility and atrophy of our genital areas are not inevitabilities. Sexual activity keeps us supple and functioning for many long years. Recent research has found that remaining sexually active throughout life helps prevent vaginal thinning. For example, a study of fifty-two postmenopausal women found that women who had intercourse three or more times a month were less likely to suffer from the "syndrome" than those who had intercourse less than ten times a year. Other studies show that orgasm, rather than intercourse, makes the difference, and a woman who achieves orgasm at least once a week, whether with a partner or alone, significantly reduces her level of vaginal thinning.

Carolyn Sutton, fifty-nine, found the genital dryness caused by menopause to be maddening. Her sex life, she claimed, was not tremendous, but she and her husband were being sexual and that was satisfying to both of them. Dryness took the pleasure away. "Sex was not fun anymore. It was painful. Once I started taking hormones, it made an enormous difference almost from the beginning."

Warm baths can soothe pain, itching, and dryness. Experts also suggest drinking adequate fluids daily to keep from getting dry; add moisture to the air in your house; avoid antihistamines, douches, sprays, perfumed toilet paper, and perfumed soaps.

Weight Gain

A tendency toward increased weight gain, often reported at menopause.

While numerous women report weight gain during the middle years of their lives, there has been no proven association between menopause and weight gain.

Not everyone gains weight at this time, but almost everyone says they have to work harder at maintaining a proper weight. Mickie is twenty pounds heavier than she was four years ago, yet she said she had not changed the way she ate. "I am eating on a consistent basis what I used to eat to lose weight. The things I knew about controlling my body do not work anymore. I knew that if I did this and that I could knock off five or six pounds, or if I did this little bit of exercise I'd lose. I knew how to control my body. And it's not true anymore. My body has a separate, opposite agenda."

Dr. Goodman reports that her patients say, "Well, maybe if I go on estrogen I'll lose weight." They go on estrogen and gain weight, and when people come off estrogen they gain weight. It seems that no matter what they do, they gain weight.

No studies substantiate a link between loss of estrogen and weight gain. So why *do* so many women report putting on extra pounds at midlife? The basic measure of how many calories a woman needs to maintain her weight is the amount of muscle on her body. A number of factors contribute to the loss of muscle as we age, among them less physical activity and a decrease in muscle mass due to years of dieting. You may, therefore, be eating the same number of calories you have always eaten, but because of loss of muscle, weight is gained.

The immediate response to such an equation is to eat less in order to compensate for less muscle. Here we get into a catch-22. Cutting down on calories actually promotes muscle loss, encourages weight gain, and perpetuates the cycle. Cutting calories is not the solution. Exercise is, and the case for this will be made in detail in Chapters Nine and Eleven.

A lot of the concern around weight stems from cultural pressure, and a tendency to confuse issues of weight and self-esteem. Advertising, television, and movies encourage us to crave looking bone thin. Women of all ages dread gaining even a pound, and most of us think we are heavier than we are. Studies have shown that we want to be thinner than men want us to be and that twice as many women as men, ages thirty to sixty-four, think they are overweight. A recent University of California study reported that 58 percent of seventeen-year-old girls claimed they were overweight. Only 17 percent actually were.

Julie Hatfield, the fashion editor for *The Boston Globe*, noted, "I'm exercising now more than I ever have, and I am just maintaining my weight. But more than that, I wonder how long can I keep this up? When I'm seventy will I be keeping the weight off, pretending to be twenty? Isn't it natural for a fifty-year-old to look a little pudgy in the middle? I'm always saying, 'When will I be able to relax, when can I eat a cream puff and not feel guilty?' "

Cardiovascular Effects

Changes in blood vessels and blood fats that increase the risk of heart disease.

Blood vessels become less flexible and cholesterol and triglyceride levels rise in response to lowered estrogen levels. Isaac Schiff, chief of the Department of Gynecology at Massachusetts General Hospital, reports, "Cardiovascular disease is the leading cause of death among postmenopausal women in the United States. A growing body of evidence suggests that estrogen deficiency may be the primary cause." This is related to the rise in LDL (bad) cholesterol and the lowering of HDL (good) cholesterol. The ratio of LDL to HDL cholesterol is considered to be a more important risk factor in predicting arteriosclerosis, coronary artery disease, and stroke than the cholesterol level alone.

Since estrogen deficiency is a major risk factor in heart disease, it is best to keep your ovaries if possible when undergoing surgery. Hormone-replacement therapy appears to be associated with a reduction in heart disease risk. In addition, a review of your lifestyle can point to risks that we now know how to prevent. Smoking is a major contributor to coronary disease. It not only affects the heart directly but actually can bring on an earlier menopause.

Osteoporosis

Porousness of the bones, due to less calcium content. Common in older women, and accelerated by decreased estrogen.

By the 1940s, medical literature was reporting that bones started to thin after menopause. By the age of sixty, at least one half of the women in every country studied showed a degree of osteoporosis when X-rayed. The frightening ramifications of osteoporosis led to a media scare several years ago. Books were published on the subject, and for a time it seemed impossible to open a magazine without seeing a dreadful photograph of a woman shrinking away to nothing. A result of the influx of information on osteoporosis is the popularity of calcium, the chief bone mineral. Getting enough of this mineral is important, yet there is more to bone health than taking calcium supplements (see Chapters Nine and Ten).

The first noticeable sign of osteoporosis is backache in the lower spine, becoming noticeable approximately 9½ years after menopause. Hip fractures due to osteoporosis happen to 30 percent of all women over sixty-five. Caucasian women, whose bones are thinner, have a 50 percent rate for fracture. Of the women with hip fractures, 17 percent will die within three months, 40 percent within six months. Among survivors, 75 percent will lose their independence and 25 percent will require skilled nursing care. Because of bone loss, a woman may lose between one and five inches in height after age fifty. Bone loss can cause the vertebrae to collapse and is the cause of the commonly noticed dowager's hump. For a population living many years past midlife, this is a serious problem.

Estrogen facilitates the uptake of calcium by the bones. Winnifred Cutler, who is actively engaged in research about healthy menopausal women, reports in *Menopause* that most studies show women who take estrogen do not lose bone mass. Another factor in maintaining bone mass is calcium intake, with 1,000 milligrams the recommended dosage for menopausal women. The average woman, however, consumes 500 milligrams per day, or one half the advised intake. Along with the calcium, experts recommend taking 400 I.U. (international units) of vitamin D, since the mineral and the vitamin work together.

Women with a family history of osteoporosis and women who have never been pregnant have an increased risk for the condition. Also, smoking and alcohol consumption decrease calcium deposits in the bones. A regular regimen of exercise is an important factor in bone health, because the bone most readily absorbs calcium under stress. Testing your bone density is now possible, through your physician. Some doctors are using this test as a guide in prescribing hormones.

The most effective treatment for osteoporosis is a combination of exercise, diet, and estrogen-replacement therapy. The nutrition and exercise programs in Chapters Nine through Eleven provide working systems for increased health in this area.

SURGERY OF THE REPRODUCTIVE ORGANS

TOTAL HYSTERECTOMY: *surgical removal of the uterus and cervix.*
SUBTOTAL HYSTERECTOMY: *surgical removal of the uterus only.*
TOTAL HYSTERECTOMY AND BILATERAL SALPINGO

OVARIECTOMY: *surgical removal of the uterus, tubes, and ovaries.*

OVARIOTOMY, OVARIECTOMY, OR OOPHORECTOMY: *surgical removal of the ovaries (female "castration").*

The surgical removal of the uterus is called a hysterectomy and is the most commonly performed operation in the United States. In fact, women in the U.S will have hysterectomies at the rate of 21 percent by the age of forty-four. This rate is five times higher than that of European women of the same age, whose rate is 4 percent. Hysterectomies in the U.S. rose between 1962 and 1978. By 1978 the rate leveled off and has remained at a point where a woman's chance of having a hysterectomy in her lifetime is over 50 percent (compared to a 10 percent chance for women in Sweden). Only 10 to 20 percent of these operations are performed in response to a life-threatening condition. Given that statistic, I cannot help wondering if the over-50-percent rate of surgery is necessary.

Doctors have different opinions regarding the importance of the uterus and its use in a woman's body after her childbearing years are over. Obviously, if a doctor believes the only function of a uterus is to carry a fetus, surgical removal for women who have been through menopause may appear on a par with removing an appendix. But available evidence now shows that the uterus does have other functions. It is a living muscular and glandular organ that responds to certain important hormones. And it has a role in a woman's sex life, since many women experience uterine contractions during orgasm.

While 40 percent of hysterectomies conducted in this country are estimated to be medically unnecessary, about three times as many psychiatric referrals are reported after hysterectomies, in comparison with referrals after other kinds of surgery. Why such a high rate of psychiatric referrals? One interpretation is that, influenced by the myth, women are conflicted about a loss of woman-hood. But my feeling, after speaking with dozens of women who have had hysterectomies, is that doctors may consider the procedure routine, but women are not pre-pared for it adequately and often feel they have had no choice in a matter they do not understand.

Margery O'Connell, a fifty-five-year-old divorced mother of two grown children, works as an administra-tive assistant. She recalled her hysterectomy at forty. "I felt very angry at the way I thought my rights about mak-ing a decision were treated. The way I was told matter-of-factly that I would be having my uterus removed made me think, Son of a bitch, what if a woman doctor was saying that to a man: 'You will be having your testicles removed'? I felt like the doctor was saying, 'Let's have another cup of coffee. We do this all the time and it's nothing.' "

Nancy Ryan, forty-one, vice president of a marketing company, believed her hysterectomy was necessary, but looking back she wished she had seen another doctor to confirm it. "I'm not angry that I didn't get a second opinion," she insisted, "but I do think now it was thoughtless on my part. I just didn't put a lot of thought into it and just went ahead and did it."

Hysterectomies involve the removal of the uterus or the uterus and cervix but they do not involve the removal of the ovaries, which continue to produce hormones after the uterus is taken out. Premenopausal women who have hysterectomies often continue to have normal hormonal cycles because their ovaries still function, although they do not menstruate. Their cycles can include such indi-cations as mood swings and breast swelling, which con-tinue until the age of natural, spontaneous menopause. Even after menopause the ovaries continue to produce important hormones.

Surgical removal of the ovaries is known as bilateral oophorectomy, ovariotomy, or ovariectomy, and is usu-ally performed at the time of a hysterectomy, although partial or whole removal can occur because of a ruptured ovarian cyst. Removal of the ovaries, whether diseased or not, was common practice in the nineteenth century and into the twentieth century. In modern times the ovaries are sometimes removed because of a concern for later development of cancer in the ovaries or to avoid possible later surgery for removal of ovarian cysts. Some doctors routinely remove the ovaries when they remove the uterus, but cancer or cysts may in fact never occur. Current statistics show that half of the women over forty who have their uterus removed also have their ovaries removed. This is an outrageous statistic that should not go unnoticed. Our ovaries are important no matter what our age, and they should not be removed unless they are diseased. The loss of ovarian hormones may effect changes in other organs; production of ovarian hormones prevents osteoporosis and earlier onset of heart attacks. And removal of the ovaries before menopause causes sudden, premature menopause.

Removal of the uterus and ovaries together causes an immediate, substantial drop in hormonal levels. Pronounced premature menopausal signs occur, compounded with the effects of surgery, and it may be a year before a woman feels like herself again. Certain women report experiencing hot flashes as they come out of anesthesia. Bladder discomfort and sexual discomfort may continue for three to four months. Women who have had both uterus and ovaries removed tend to report a higher rate of depression and decreased libido.

Roberta Evans, now in her seventies, had her uterus and ovaries removed because of peritonitis. She woke up from the operation in "instant menopause" to soaking-wet bed sheets. She also found herself terribly depressed, but eventually found relief with estrogen therapy.

Lena Small, seventy-six, remembered back to having both her uterus and ovaries removed at age forty-two. "I woke up from the operation and I had a hot flash. I thought I would die. The minute I opened my eyes, my whole body, my whole system changed, right away." She remembered on the other hand her friends who went through natural menopause. "I think they took it in stride."

In contrast, Louisa Curran, a fifty-four-year-old house-cleaner, found that other than the actual effects of surgery, the immediate menopause that followed was easy. She had her operation in her thirties because of a tumor. Afterward, "I was fine. I took estrogen in the beginning for a short while." She credited her easy time to her husband's support and encouragement, which helped her self-esteem and confidence.

The tendency to remove a woman's ovaries along with her uterus stems from an outdated medical attitude that women who already have children or women past age forty no longer need their ovaries. Every woman should know that this is not true, since the ovaries continue to produce necessary hormones past menopause. Going to a doctor who is trustworthy and who will answer any question at all is crucial. Too often I have heard that a woman has been made to feel like an untrained layperson who has nothing to say about ensuing medical procedures. A woman must make her doctor aware that her ovaries are important to her and that they should not be removed without consultation and agreement. It's important before having surgery to make sure all your questions are answered and that you are clear that the surgery you are to have is necessary, that there are no other nonsurgical alternatives to treating your condition, and that the type of surgery you are going to have is appropriate to your condition.

Eighty-five to 90 percent of all surgery performed in the United States is elective, reports Eugene McCarthy, director of the Health Benefits Research Unit at New York Hospital–Cornell Medical Center. Therefore, the patient has the final vote. A second opinion, which is required by many insurance companies, can be a very valuable resource in helping to make a decision about reproductive surgery.

LESS COMMON SIGNS OF MENOPAUSE

While the explanations up to this point cover the most widely recognized signs related to the climacteric and menopause, the following signs have also been reported by women during this time and are considered to be linked to hormonal changes:

Urinary Tract Problems

The urinary tract is lined with epithelial cells that are estrogen sensitive. With a decrease in epithelial tissue and a decrease in muscle tone, some loss of bladder control occurs. Stress incontinence, which is the loss of urine when under stress, can be inconvenient and annoying, especially when it happens in an everyday situation such as when you are laughing, coughing, jogging, or doing aerobics. The sensation of having to urinate when the bladder is actually empty may also occur. An exercise system called Kegel exercises has been shown to be effective in strengthening pelvic muscles and preventing incontinence. (See the Appendix for a complete explanation of this system.) If the problem is severe, consult your physician. Conditions that are the result of childbirth-related weaknesses may call for corrective surgery. Also note that bladder infections can occur more frequently at this time.

Prolapse

The other term for prolapse is "a dropped uterus." Loss of estrogen contributes to lessened muscle tone. The uterus, bladder, and vagina can drop to varying degrees. If the bladder descends during prolapse, the condition is called a cystocele. If the rectum prolapses into the vagina, it is called a rectocele. As a result of prolapse, a woman feels as if something is about to come out of her or has a feeling of heaviness in her genital area. In *Managing Your Menopause*, Dr. Wulf H. Utian outlines four successful treatments: pelvic exercises (see the Appendix, p. 316, for Kegel exercises) for mild cases, estrogen-replacement therapy, also for mild cases, plastic devices inserted by the gynecologist that can delay surgery, or surgery, which is the most effective of the treatments. Consult your physician for recommendations.

Hair Changes

As estrogen decreases, the male hormones produced by the ovaries have more effect on the female body than before, which can result in added hair on the face, chest, or abdomen. Hair increase can vary from occasional single hairs to a fuller growth and can be upsetting to many women. "I never had a hot flash," said Renata Gurvey, a retired hospital worker who found menopause to be no trouble at all except for seeing hair on her chin. "Wrinkles were bad enough," she recalled, acknowledging the inevitable, "but I don't want to look like an old man."

Estrogen therapy tends to decrease the growth of new hairs, but hair that has already grown needs to be removed, if desired. Many methods are available to remove unwanted hair. Shaving is effective on the body and the face, although regrowth occurs within one or two days. Shaving will not cause more hair to grow or make the hair that grows back coarser, as is commonly believed. Tweezing and a sharp scissors are effective, although the process is more time-consuming than shaving. Since tweezing removes hair below the skin line, regrowth is slower. There are also many hair removal products on the market that tend to produce a softer regrowth of hair. Before using any depilatory product, be sure to check your skin for sensitivity. Waxing, which can be done at home or at a salon, lasts longer than any of the above-mentioned methods.

The most permanent method of hair removal is electrolysis, the removal of hair by an electrically driven needle. Sessions last anywhere from fifteen minutes to one hour, and the cost varies according to the practitioner. While the method may be uncomfortable at times, many women find it worthwhile because once the hair is removed it is gone for good. Total removal of hair may take repeated sessions. Be sure to use a reputable and licensed practitioner, and in states where licensing of electrologists is not required, consult the state's Board of Cosmetology.

A product on the market since 1987 has been touted as an alternative to electrolysis. Finally Free is a machine, offered through magazines and mail-order catalogs for approximately $99.00, that can be used at home. The machine reportedly allows you to remove one hair at a time, permanently, without burning or scarring. While this method is attractive cost-wise, learning how to use the machine effectively and comfortably takes practice and can be time consuming.

Breast Changes

Menopause causes the glandular tissue of the breasts to shrink. The breasts become smaller and flatter. Loss of elasticity in the underlying ligaments also contribute to drooping. Nipples may be smaller and flatter and lose their erectile properties. Such a description recalls Gypsy Rose Lee's assertion "I have everything I ever had, except that it's a few inches lower." Women who take hormones will experience some return of their breast fullness, with this restoration lasting as long as the hormones are used. A good supportive bra can prevent some sagging and will hold the shape of the breasts. Bras with a strong underwire are supportive and vary in the shape they produce. Try bras on in the dressing room to see which shape is most flattering under clothing. Also, be sure to replace your bras often, before the shoulder straps stretch.

Formication

This is a tingling sensation all over the skin or the feeling that unseen insects are crawling across the skin. Though not a very common sign of menopause, it does feel strange to the women experiencing it and it can be very annoying. The exact cause is not known, but it is related to lack of estrogen. Formication is reported by 20 percent of women, with one study of 5,000 women showing the greatest incidence within twelve to twenty-four months after the last menstrual period. About ten percent of these women continued to experience the tingling for more than twelve years. Eventually it disappears. Formication is what Cynthia reported when she said that on top of constant hot flashes and night sweats, she was at a meeting and "felt something on the back of my ankles." Another woman reported a tingling sensation in her arms and hands. None of the other women mentioned this sign at first, although when I told some of them about it, they said, "Oh yes, I've had that." This may be a sign that often goes unreported, because it is not easily identifiable and therefore may not even be associated with menopause.

LESS COMMON SIGNS NOT NECESSARILY LINKED TO HORMONAL CHANGE

The following signs are also reported by women, although a link to these signs and hormonal change has not been substantiated:

Change in Vaginal Odor

Some women in the Stanford Menopause Study that surveyed attitudes toward sex described this as a problem they had never had before. The phenomenon has not been studied very much and is not well understood. One woman I interviewed said, "I didn't smell the same in the most personal part of myself and I hated that." She reported that her usual body odor returned after she started hormone-replacement therapy.

Memory Loss

Some women have reported loss of short-term memory, evidenced in such particulars as forgetting appointments or where they left their keys. Recently, this has been associated with decreasing estrogen levels and may be an early indicator of the onset of menopause. No links have been firmly substantiated between memory loss and lowered estrogen, however.

Visual Deficits

Whether this is a direct effect of menopause or part of the aging process is not clear but many women have reported a change in their eyesight along with changes in their menstrual cycles. In either case, women should have a full eye exam yearly with an ophthalmologist, starting at age thirty-five.

Backache

This common complaint may be the first sign of osteoporosis. While osteoporosis does not start to appear until nine and a half years after menopause, the condition is the direct result of bone loss due to decreasing levels of estrogen.

Palpitations

Fluttering sensations in the heart are reported by 44 percent of menopausal women. Fluttering may be related to the vasomotor instability that causes hot flashes. Report any palpitations to your physician, because they may be as easily related to heart disease as to menopause.

Other signs reported by women are dizziness, numbness or tingling in the arms or legs, and headaches. Such signs may or may not be related to menopause but could be caused by the same nerve and blood-vessel changes that cause hot flashes.

RECOGNIZING YOUR OWN MENOPAUSAL SIGNALS

The range of signs outlined in this chapter should not be taken as a formula for what to expect during your climacteric and menopause. In fact, only one third of all women seek medical help for menopause-related conditions. This percentage has risen since 1980, a fact that at first glance might seem to indicate an increased need in the last ten years for medical care at this time in our lives. The rise in the number of women seeking care is due to an increased awareness of our bodies, however, and of what to expect as we age, coupled with an openness in our society in speaking about menopause and aging in general. Many women are now seeking medical opinions to ensure preventive care and not necessarily to report debilitating symptoms.

Menopause is an individual process, unique to each and every woman who experiences it. Outdated assumptions held that a history of menstrual trouble, childbearing complications, or an early or late onset of the menses were gauges for measuring when a woman would go through menopause and how she would react to the process. In reality, clinical methods for knowing who will have extreme difficulties during the process, who will experience discomfort, and who will breeze through these years and when have yet to be refined. Lifestyle habits, however—such as lack of exercise, poor nutrition, heavy alcohol consumption, or smoking—do seem to exacerbate conditions like osteoporosis and poor skin quality.

A final point to consider is that the quality of one's menopausal experience is not a measure of whether we are good or bad, healthy or unwell, balanced or unstable. Women who go through menopause without a heavy spate of sensations are not morally, physically, or psychologically stronger than women who find the series of changes more difficult. The responses of the body merely vary from individual to individual.

The signs of menopause can be successfully treated and often reversed through estrogen therapy. Yet the decision to take estrogen remains an unresolved question for women who are not sure whether hormones will help them or harm them. Although the taking of hormones is not recommended for everyone, the controversy surrounding the issue has confused the pros and cons for many who could benefit from them. To clear up the confusion, the facts about estrogen merit a discussion all their own.

CHAPTER 8

The Estrogen Controversy

Each patient carries his own doctor inside him. We are at our best when we give the doctor who resides within each patient a chance to go to work.

—ALBERT SCHWEITZER

During the mid-1960s post–*Feminine Mystique* years, gynecologist Robert Wilson published an infamous book about the horrors of estrogen decline that tapped into our deepest female fears. In *Feminine Forever,* Wilson wrote that the loss of estrogen at menopause would cause a woman to "shrivel up." The only way to escape the horror of this "living decay," he insisted, was through estrogen-replacement therapy. Reports in the mass media followed, proclaiming the hormone's glorious fountain-of-youth qualities. Estrogen could stop aging, prevent cancer, and retain sexuality. This heralded the availability of estrogen-replacement therapy (ERT), in which the hormone was prescribed to women in large doses, to be taken every day of the month without interruption, a regimen very different from the current one. Within a decade, the 8.5 million American women taking estrogen had more than tripled to 26.7 million.

In 1975, however, reports appeared linking estrogen use to endometrial cancer (cancer of the lining of the uterus). In 1976, studies associated estrogen with breast cancer in animals, and in 1980 studies established the link between estrogen and cancer in humans.

111

WELL-FOUNDED SKEPTICISM REGARDING MEDICATION

If Dr. Wilson provoked our deepest fears, reports of breast and uterine cancer tapped into a waiting suspicion—collusion between the medical profession and the pharmaceutical industry to manipulate women's bodies for their own gain.

"I hadn't had a period for four months, so I went to the doctor, and he said it might stop completely or it might suddenly come back and be erratic," reported Francine Lewin, the fifty-five-year-old part-time real estate assistant whose long-standing marriage to her husband, Roger, is still going strong. "I never discussed hormones with the doctor because I hadn't had a lot of hot flashes. But even if I did, I'm not sure that I would take hormones, because I took stilbestrol and I'm afraid of the effects of these things."

Francine's suspicion was well founded. Stilbestrol, otherwise known as DES, is an estrogen-containing drug used experimentally in the 1960s for women with fertility problems. Doctors did not advise their patients of the known risks involved. Later, daughters of DES mothers were found to carry an increased risk of cancer.

Nonreproductive-related drugs have been prescribed freely to women over the years as well. Marsha Reeves, fifty-five, a homemaker with four grown sons, recalled her experiences with Librium. "I had glaucoma operations at age thirty-seven, and the doctor, with my husband's full agreement, thought I was too energetic. He wanted me to stay quiet between these two operations, so he gave me Librium." This led to a ten-year period of taking that prescription drug, which did keep her quiet, until she decided to discontinue its use. Her feelings were blunted during the years she was on the pills, but when she finally went off the drug her emotions erupted and she has been dealing with her anger over the incident ever since. Understandably, she is now wary of taking drugs.

"Since the Librium, I want to take as little medication as possible, even those having to do with menopause, so I try to look good and really work hard at diet and exercise." Many women share Marsha's skepticism about agreeing to take medication at times in their lives when they may be vulnerable and not as likely to speak up for themselves.

Have there been efforts on the part of doctors, psychiatric workers, and drug companies to "keep us quiet"? After the initial reports linking estrogen to uterine cancer, the drug companies continued to market estrogen aggressively, joined by some medical groups. When the U.S. Food and Drug Administration required a patient package insert describing the risks and benefits of ERT, the Pharmaceutical Manufacturers Association filed suit challenging the FDA's authority. The American College of Obstetricians and Gynecologists and the American Society of Internal Medicine joined the PMA in the suit. One physician stated in his affidavit, "It is hard to imagine a class of patients more susceptible to adverse psychological reaction from the patient package insert than the menopausal female."

A SECOND LOOK AT HORMONES

Founded as these fears are, it would be a shame to allow past ghosts to prevent us from looking at our medical options freshly. Hormone therapy does offer advantages well worth considering.

Plenty of women go through menopause without the aid of prescription hormones. "I had menopause naturally," said fifty-nine-year-old Grace Devereaux. "I asked the doctor about the hot flashes because my cousin told me she had awful hot flashes. She had to take these pills. You know, I told the doctor about it, but I didn't care about the hot flashes, and he told me he'd rather have me stay natural. That was fine with me. I just did it naturally and I told my cousins to do the same thing and they've gone through it.''

Taking the natural route is a valid choice for people, whether it concerns hot flashes, childbirth, or breakfast cereal. I wonder, however, if anything is really natural anymore. The late movie director John Huston made a well-taken point about the options for longevity in our times. At the Academy Awards he was asked to what he attributed his long life. He paused for a moment and then answered, ''Surgery.''

Technology has evolved so rapidly, it surrounds us in ways that are invisible. During my dietary internship in 1978 at the Brigham and Women's Hospital in Boston, there was one floor for diabetic pregnant women nearing delivery. During labor, the women were monitored by a machine that detected changes in blood sugar so that insulin could be adjusted in an ongoing manner. The machine was enormous, which is why it was used only at crucial times. Less than twelve years later, athletes were riding bicycles across the country wearing the updated version of this machine, which is now the size of a small transistor radio. Nobody is crying ''unnatural.''

When penicillin was discovered, nobody thought it was unnatural. If our lives are progressing normally, most of us need not concern ourselves with unnecessary discomfort during menopause. We have at our disposal the gifts of a technologically created future. Why not take full advantage of them?

A GREATER DEGREE OF CHOICE

Technology has provided us with many choices in our approach to menopause. Nonhormonal methods to diminish signs are available, and I have listed those later in this chapter. In addition, since the early days when estrogen was administered in large dosages continuously throughout the month, diverse methods of treatment have been developed, allowing for a greater degree of choice in planning treatment.

In the natural course of events for a premenopausal woman, the ovaries produce estrogen during the first part of the menstrual cycle. The hormone's job is to thicken the lining of the uterus (the endometrium) in preparation for a pregnancy. In the second half of the cycle, the ovaries produce a second hormone, progesterone, which further works to thicken the uterine wall. If no pregnancy occurs, hormone production stops and menstruation starts, as the lining of the uterus sheds, bringing the cycle full circle.

Large doses of estrogen prescribed in an unbroken daily regimen without the hormone progesterone did not allow the uterus to shed its thickened lining, as it does monthly in a menstrual cycle. Today, estrogen is almost always prescribed along with progestin, a synthetic form of progesterone, a combination that causes the thickened uterine lining to shed. The prescription of estrogen and progestin is commonly known as hormone-replacement therapy, or HRT.

The most common regimen prescribed in this country consists of one pill of conjugated estrogen (a mixture of natural estrogens), taken in a dosage ranging from 0.3 milligrams to 1.25 milligrams for the first twenty-five days of the month. A pill of progestin, in doses ranging from 2.5 milligrams to 10 milligrams, is added to the estrogen for days 16 to 25. The estrogen is started again at the beginning of the next month. This cycle mimics the menstrual cycle and allows the uterus to shed its lining monthly. Premarin and Ogen are the most widely prescribed brands of estrogen; Provera is the most popular brand of progestin.

Approximately three quarters of the women on this interrupted cycle of therapy experience a simulated period. Known as "withdrawal bleeding," it tends to decrease over time and often stops completely. A variation on the popular interrupted regimen is to combine continuous use, taking daily estrogen along with low doses of daily progestin. This avoids withdrawal bleeding but may cause irregular bleeding in the first six months of treatment.

Along with a wide range of possible dosages for both estrogen and progestin, the choice of two different monthly cycles for taking the hormones, and choices of brands, there are also several ways to administer HRT. Taking hormones orally, in pill form, is the most popular method in this country. Hormones are also available through injections, as skin patches, and as creams. Implants have been developed, although they are not being used at this time, since they were found to be difficult to insert and to remove.

Every woman's medical history is unique, as is her experience of menopause. Therefore the decision to take hormones is a personal one and involves a well-informed weighing of the pros and cons, in conjunction with a physician. If the decision to take hormones is made, the correct HRT method and dosage is also highly individualized. Many women try two or more methods and vary dosages until they find the comfortable regimen for their particular body.

Despite the variety of methods available, options seem to be falling on deaf ears. Dr. Wulf H. Utian reports that up to 70 percent of menopausal women can get relief with hormone supplements within a couple of months, but only about 10 percent take them. The reason is fear. When Utian recommended hormones to one of his patients, for instance, she heard "estrogen," thought "cancer," and turned the suggestion down.

A survey of attitudes toward estrogen published in the *Archives of Internal Medicine* showed that many women are reluctant to take estrogen even when the benefits are carefully explained. In fact, the survey reports, during a recent study in which women were prescribed estrogen after careful explanation of its benefits, half of the women stopped taking it before the study was completed. In addition, another survey found that while most physicians

acknowledged the benefits of estrogen therapy, their prescribing habits did not correspond with these beliefs. I
am reminded of Cynthia Richards, whose husband ac-
cused her of being stubborn, saying, "Cynthia, no one
has to go through this." Her justification and consolation
for putting up with excessive hot flashes was that "it was
natural."

Renata Gurvey is now retired after twenty years in the
Dietary Department of St. Elizabeth's Hospital in Brigh-
ton, Massachusetts. I worked with Renata at St. E's, as
it is called, and we were certain the hospital was the
model for the television series *St. Elsewhere.* What I always loved about Renata was her clarity and ability to
see straight through problems that everyone else treated
as complicated. This clarity was still evident as we spoke
about estrogen. "I really dreaded menopause as I ap-
proached it," she recalled. Her fears were relieved when
she heard about a new treatment, estrogen-replacement
therapy, which would relieve all such awful symptoms.
But her relief turned to dismay when she heard that the
new treatment caused cancer. As a result, she never used
it. Several years later she read an opposite report—
estrogen not only does not cause cancer, it may prevent
it. She shook her head at the difficulties involved in making well-informed personal-health decisions. "It's a big
nuisance, if you ask me. Everything causes cancer. Just
look at the diet soda controversy." (The cancer-causing
properties of saccharin have been debated for decades,
based on studies in which animals consume the equivalent of eight hundred glasses of diet soft drinks a day.)

Along with the cancer fear is the concern women have
that since hormone therapy is so recent a phenomenon,
the consequences of its use over time have not been adequately documented. Even women who have decided to
take estrogen wonder about its properties because of the
lack of long-term research. Julia Phillips remarked that
she took hormones "because doctors universally seem to

approve of it, but I'm not thrilled that no one is certain of what the future effects may be.''

ESTROGEN AND CANCER

Uterine Cancer

The early method of taking high doses of estrogen in an unbroken regimen caused the lining of the uterine wall to thicken. Without the addition of a second hormone, the uterus never shed this thickened lining. The ongoing accumulation of the uterine wall set the climate for increased cancer risk. The current pattern of HRT, which parallels the menstrual cycle, prevents the buildup of the uterine wall.

Three other risk factors for cancer of the uterus, besides an accumulation of the uterine wall, are obesity, never having had a baby, and high blood pressure. Of all the risks, obesity (weighing 30 percent over an individual's ideal weight), not estrogen, is the greatest. Estrogen therapy, however, has gotten the most publicity.

The usual risk for uterine cancer is 1 in 1,000. High doses of unopposed estrogen (estrogen prescribed without the progestin that is used in current HRT) raise the incidence of uterine cancer from 1 in 1,000 to 8 in 1,000. The incidence of stroke for women is 14 in 1,000. One of the benefits of taking estrogen is that it lowers the rate of stroke incidence. Therefore, depending on your medical history, even using the old regimen, estrogen can still be a health advantage.

In fact, estrogen—as it is now used, in combination with progestin—seems to *decrease* the risk of endometrial cancer. R. Don Gambrell, Jr., reports in *Menopause Management*, the journal of the newly formed North American Menopause Society, that more than a decade of investigations shows that the addition of progestin to HRT decreases the incidence of endometrial-cell overgrowth for women on HRT. The incidence of cell overgrowth is *markedly* lower in women on HRT. Women taking unopposed estrogen have a higher incidence of cell overgrowth than both HRT users and untreated women.

EFFECT OF HRT ON UTERINE CANCER

245.5 in 100,000 in untreated women
390.6 in 100,000 in unopposed estrogen users
49 in 100,000 in estrogen/progestin users

Certain progestins, in fact, have been shown to reverse cancerous growth in the uterus. And other cancer-reducing effects of estrogen were shown in a study conducted at the Epidemiology-Biometry Program at the University of Illinois. In this study menopausal estrogen was found to reduce the additional development of bowel cancer, supporting a theory that estrogen use may reduce the risk of large-bowel cancer in women.

Menopause Management reports that one particular research group has attempted to calculate the overall risk/benefit ratio of estrogen use. They took into consideration the increased risk of major illness caused by *not* using estrogen. They concluded that estrogen, even when taken alone, without progestin, and therefore posing an increased cancer risk, provides a significant gain in life expectancy. Dr. Gambrell's report states, "All post-menopausal women should be made aware of the consequences of untreated menopause and should be offered the opportunity to receive estrogen." The literature is consistent. High doses of estrogen may be harmful. Low doses are usually not harmful.

Menopause Management is a highly readable magazine that can be subscribed to through the North American Menopause Society (see Resources at the back of this book, page 317). The following chart from the publication compares the increased risk of uterine cancer to the decreased risk of bone and heart disease. (Note that the conjugated estrogens are also called "natural" estrogens, because they have been treated in a way that allows them to be handled more easily by the body. This is the type of estrogen prescribed for menopause. Unconjugated estrogens, otherwise known as synthetic estrogens, are used in the majority of oral contraceptives. It should be noted that many of the studies pointing to the risks of HRT have been based on studies monitoring the use of synthetic estrogens. Such data has been used because as of yet it is the only data available.)

ERT AND THE RELATIVE RISKS FOR CANCER, OSTEOPOROSIS, AND HEART DISEASE

Condition	Relative Risk	Cumulative Change in Mortality/100,000
Endometrial cancer	2.0	+63
Osteoporotic fracture	0.4	−563
Ischemic heart disease	0.5	−5,250

Estimated changes in mortality induced by 0.625 mg/day oral conjugated estrogens in women aged fifty to seventy-five years. Any adverse association of ERT with endometrial cancer is outweighed by reducing death from osteoporotic fracture, and far outweighed by the benefit of ERT on death from ischemic heart disease. *(Adapted from Henderson et al.)*

Dr. Lois Goodman states, "Once they added progesterone, it brought the risk of endometrial cancer right back to the normal level. There's always a risk of endometrial cancer, but they say that if you increase the progesterone dose to longer than the usual 10 to 12 days, you can reduce the risk of endometrial cancer to lower than the normal risk."

Breast Cancer

The issue of breast cancer is not as clear cut. The suspicion that estrogen might be an agent in promoting breast cancer comes from the association between our body's natural estrogen and higher incidences of breast cancer. Early menarche, late menopause, and obesity contribute to high estrogen levels. Women in any or all of these situations and conditions are at a higher than average risk for such cancer. Women who go through early surgical menopause, on the other hand, tend to be protected from breast cancer. Certain doctors contend that taking estrogen may promote existing growths but is not likely to *cause* growths. Overall, evidence on whether taking estrogen increases the risk of breast cancer has been difficult to obtain. The expected association has not been conclusively demonstrated, despite more than twenty-six studies on the subject. Dr. Isaac Schiff, gynecologist at Massachusetts General Hospital, and other experts discounted the infamous Swedish study which suggested that long-term treatment with estrogens can raise a woman's risk of breast cancer. Since the Swedish study showed an increased incidence of breast cancer after six years of use, it may be that women on hormone therapy had a better survival rate than nonusers. In addition, the women in this study used a synthetic form of estrogen, not the natural conjugated estrogens that most American women use. The study also specifically states that an increased incidence of breast cancer was *not* found in users of natural estrogens.

Studies that do not indicate a connection between taking estrogen and the risk of cancer do not make it into the news. The average woman, therefore, hears only alarming information. A November 1990 study out of Harvard Medical School received a great deal of media coverage. The study showed an increased risk of breast cancer for current users of estrogen over the long term. The study, however, was based on women using estrogen only, and did not include women on the estrogen-progestin combination. In the words of the study, "though this increase in risk will be counterbalanced by the cardiovascular benefits, these data suggest the need for caution in the use of estrogens."

Allan G. Charles, Professor of Clinical Obstetrics and Gynecology, Northwestern University Medical School, reports that estrogens were previously thought to increase the risk of breast cancer but that almost all recent studies show no relationship. An editorial in *Maturitas,* a medical journal dedicated to the subject of menopause, reports research from the Menopause Clinic in Melbourne, Australia. On the basis of an analysis of twenty-three studies, the results of the report are unequivocal: estrogen therapy does not alter the risk of breast cancer by any measurable amount.

Dr. Mark Weinstein, a breast surgeon at the Beth Israel Hospital in Boston, says, "The preponderance of evidence is that there is no risk of breast cancer caused by estrogen." Raymond Burnett, in *Menopause: All Your Questions Answered,* reports that multiple, large, long-term studies conclusively show that the rate of breast cancer is not greater for women using birth-control pills or postmenopausal hormones. He further cites a 1984 study which showed that estrogen, used with progestin, actually lowers breast cancer risk. In this report estrogen-progestin users showed a breast cancer rate of 67 in 100,000. The National Cancer Institute reports a breast cancer rate of 229 in 100,000 for the general population.

Dr. Goodman notes, "There are so many variables. It's such a hard subject to tackle because so many people are getting breast cancer and frankly the majority of them aren't on any hormones. They're just coming down with breast cancer."

Dr. Schiff wonders if we'll ever get a definitive answer. The estrogen-progesterone combination has not been around long enough to be tested accurately. He carefully explains the risks and benefits of HRT to his patients, both those who have histories of cancer and those who do not.

The American Cancer Society recommends a mammogram for women at around age thirty-five, regular mammograms every one or two years starting at age forty, and annually after fifty.

THE BENEFITS OF ESTROGEN THERAPY

Hot Flashes

A large number of studies indicate that estrogen use stops hot flashes. Also effective in monitoring "flashing" are two prescription medications, Clonidine, a medication for high blood pressure, and Bellergal, a sedative. As with most medications, there can be side effects, and usage merits discussion with your physician. Most of the women I interviewed who took estrogen reported an immediate halt to their hot flashes upon starting the treatment.

Sleep

HRT improves the quality of sleep. Studies in sleep laboratories in England showed that estrogen increased the proportion of sleep time spent in the rapid-eye-movement (dream) stage of sleep, thus enhancing a night's rest. *Also*, the elimination of night sweats promotes uninterrupted sleep.

Emotions

Estrogen has a reputation as a "mood elevator" and can improve your sense of well-being. The actual reasons for this are not clearly understood, although estrogen is known to have numerous effects on the brain and nervous system. Loss of sleep and physical changes caused by a decrease in circulating estrogen can be stressful, which may be the basis of this reported benefit. Shirley Grant, fifty-one, who had wondered if she'd still be sexy after menopause, reported, "Since taking estrogen I've gotten a little bit of pep back and I don't have the hot flashes the way I was having them."

Skin

Not many studies have been conducted investigating the effects of estrogen on skin changes. Generally, attention paid to a woman's skin is considered cosmetic instead of medical. Perhaps the lack of research in this area stems from an ingrained assumption that health concerns as we age are appropriate, whereas a concern for beauty is vanity. Better to grow old gracefully, as they say.

Maybe in some other culture, thank you.

Several studies on estrogen and the skin come from Scandinavia in the 1970s. A report from Finland tells us that skin changes associated with aging, wrinkling, dryness, and diminishing include thinning of the epidermis (the outer layer of skin). These changes were found to be prevented or delayed by six months of oral estrogen treatment. A review of the literature published in Scandinavia in 1972 reports: "Atrophy of the epidermis can be prevented by oral estrogen treatment, and atrophy that has already happened can be eliminated." According to this report, the epidermis begins to atrophy after a woman's thirtieth year, and this atrophy is intensified between forty and fifty. A relationship between skin changes and ovarian insufficiency was first noted as early as 1937. A 1949 report noted decreased skin circulation in women after the removal of ovaries, or female "castration." When estrogens were administered the circulation increased. More recent work (1987) shows that collagen, the major structural protein in the body, decreases approximately 2 percent per year up to fifteen years after menopause. This loss can be prevented by estrogen therapy, which gives the skin increased tone, glow, and thickness.

Libido

Evidence regarding the effect of HRT on any decline in libido experienced at menopause is inconclusive. Dr. Goodman has found in her clinical practice that alleviation through HRT of menopausal signs can positively affect one's sex life. It has also been shown that estrogen increases the sensitivity to touch.

Vaginal Changes

Vaginal changes refer to the thinning and drying of the vaginal wall that causes pain and irritation during intercourse. If you are suffering from vaginal dryness, estrogen will probably solve the problem entirely. Even small amounts of topical estrogen cream have been shown to alleviate the problem.

The vaginal changes we are discussing here do not include the general relaxation of muscle tone common among women who have had several children. If your pelvic muscles could use toning, doing daily Kegel exercises can help (page 316).

Heart Disease

Women taking estrogen have a lower rate of heart disease. Except in rare instances, taking estrogen does not increase blood pressure and can even decrease it. Since blood pressure goes up with age, this is a benefit.

Women with severe hypertension should think carefully about whether they should have HRT, although they can partake of its benefits with competent medical care. The reason is that in a small number of cases, estrogen raises blood pressure. These findings stem from studies conducted with users of birth-control pills. Oral contraceptives are a different product and involve a different dosage of estrogen than the dosage used for women in menopause, so the studies may or may not apply to HRT.

HRT lowers the levels of LDL cholesterol (the "bad" cholesterol), while HDL cholesterol, the cholesterol that is protective in coronary heart disease, increases.

Since estrogen is now usually prescribed along with progestin, however, new evidence should be noted. Progestins appear to interfere with the cardiovascular benefit

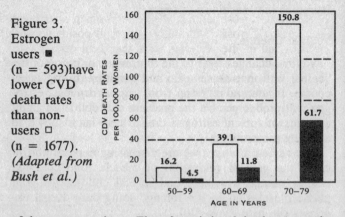

CARDIOPROTECTIVE EFFECT OF HRT

Figure 3. Estrogen users ■ (n = 593) have lower CVD death rates than non-users □ (n = 1677). *(Adapted from Bush et al.)*

of the estrogen alone. Therefore, it is advised to use only the lowest dose of progestin required.

In addition to the evidence of the cardioprotective effect of estrogen, through its influence on blood cholesterol levels, evidence exists that estrogen has a direct effect on the inside of the blood vessel walls of the heart. Estrogen receptors have been found in the heart vessels, and it is known that estrogen increases blood flow. To date there are no long-term studies to substantiate the cardioprotective effect of HRT. Isaac Schiff reports available evidence in *Menopause Management*, Summer 1989 (see table above).

Immunity

Estrogen may help stimulate the immune system. Experiments with guinea pigs at Stanford University revealed that estrogens increase the speed at which antibodies are produced and lower the rate at which they decay. This positive effect on the immune response may account for the longer life spans and better health reported by women who take postmenopausal hormones.

Osteoporosis

The single most serious disease for women after menopause, osteoporosis, will affect half of all postmenopausal women and is often referred to as the silent disease, with fracture often the first sign. Osteoporosis, or porousness of the bones, comes about not only with changes due to age but is directly affected by estrogen loss. A woman may lose between 1 and 2 percent of bone per year following menopause, with the rate of bone loss decreasing at about age sixty-five, returning to the same rate as that for men. It is not unusual for a woman to lose from 30 to 50 percent of her bone mass by age seventy-five.

ESTROGEN AND THE BONES

The skeleton is uniquely sensitive to estrogen, and estrogen therapy will prevent bone loss in the early stages of menopause, when the greatest amount of loss occurs. Most bone is lost in the three to seven years immediately following menopause. At this time bone loss in the spine, which is especially sensitive to estrogen, may be as high as 5 to 15 percent a year. Other bones may lose 1 to 4 percent a year in the initial postmenopausal period. HRT will be effective in protecting against further bone loss at any time and can be beneficial at any age. Evidence for this is conclusive.

Often physicians will recommend and insist on HRT for this reason alone. At a time when an eighty-year life span is not unusual, this disease poses a risk that outweighs any other supposed risk. While a bone fracture may not sound serious, the fact is women are *250 times* more likely to die of complications from bone fractures than of cancer of the uterus.

PREVENTION OF BONE LOSS

Osteoporosis can be diagnosed by a bone reading. The several available methods are painless and fast and can be done by a physician.

The best treatment for osteoporosis is prevention, with diet and exercise important preventive factors. Adequate calcium is essential, with 1,000 to 1,500 milligrams recommended for postmenopausal women. Since the average intake of calcium is 500 milligrams, supplements may be needed. Calcium carbonate is suggested, along with 400 I.U. of vitamin D daily. The bones best absorb calcium under physical stress. Exercise, particularly weight-bearing exercise, such as walking, provide the stress necessary to enable the bones to absorb the calcium that is available.

Research continues on other hormones that may be used in the treatment of osteoporosis. These include parathyroid hormone, calcitonin, and stanozolol, which is a male hormone. Thiazide diuretics, used to control high blood pressure, have been shown to reduce calcium loss. Use of sodium fluoride, which has been added to the water supply in many communities to prevent tooth decay, was once thought to be effective since it can stimulate bone growth, but updated research shows that the newly stimulated bone is more crystalline and therefore more easily fractured. To date, estrogen therapy is the single most useful agent in preventing postmenopausal osteoporosis. (See pages 152 and 222 for more details on bone health.)

Other factors that contribute to bone loss are smoking, caffeine consumption, alcohol consumption, and a high protein diet. The strongest prevention for this condition is a combination of diet, exercise, and estrogen therapy.

Added Benefits

Finally, estrogen has been associated with a lower incidence of Alzheimer's disease in one study. It can also reduce rheumatoid arthritis. It is the only available treatment for formication, the maddening skin sensation that can occur after menopause. And estrogen has been effective in stopping urinary stress incontinence.

The Risk of Not Taking Estrogen

Considering the benefits of estrogen therapy, there is a risk factor in not taking it. This risk has been put into numbers by some researchers.

Trudy L. Bush, of Johns Hopkins University, reports in *The New York Times* that heart disease, not cancer, is far and away the leading killer of women after menopause. For women over fifty, heart disease takes an average of 12 lives per 2,000 yearly, as compared with 2 deaths per 2,000 yearly from breast cancer.

At a conference in September 1989, the first meeting of the North American Menopause Society, Rogerio Lobo, an obstetrician-gynecologist at the University of Southern California, presented even more dramatic statistics. He calculated that each year, among 100,000 women fifty to seventy-five years old, HRT would save 5,561 lives, 5,250 of them from averted heart attacks.

Studies of many thousands of women followed for a decade or more indicate the overall cardiovascular benefit to women taking postmenopausal estrogens, which halve their risk of dying of a heart attack, compared with other women their age who do not take the hormones.

In 1983 the *Journal of the American Medical Association* compared causes of death of 2,269 women followed for six years. Estrogen users were found to have an overall lower death rate than nonusers.

With so many women standing to benefit from the taking of hormones, it is exciting to note that the first major government-funded study on the effects of various hormone treatments on menopausal women is under way. This three-year, $10 million study conducted by the National Institutes of Health is called the Postmenopausal Estrogen-Progestin Intervention Trial.

Yet, HRT is not indicated for every woman. Dr. Utian says, "HRT needs to be looked at for every individual. Women want to be more selective. They should use their doctor as one of several instruments or agents at their disposal, along with nutrition, exercise, and self-care in working on the quality of their lives.''

Risks and Contraindications

Estrogen can increase your risk of gallstones. Other risk factors for gallstones are obesity and cholesterol intake.

Some investigators believe that estrogens may increase the risk of intravascular coagulation. Physiologic doses of estrogens used for contraception have shown this increase, although the doses used after menopause have not.

Certain breast cancers are estrogen-sensitive, and HRT could promote the growth of a cancer that has not yet been detected. The combination therapy of estrogen-progesterone has been used only since the 1980s, and the long-term effects are not known. The decision for hormone therapy is a personal one and must be made by each woman for herself.

Elaine Cannon, a fifty-two-year-old realtor, told me, ''I feel so much better with the estrogen that I just decided I wanted to keep taking it. I know it's a risk, since I have a family history of breast cancer, but I'm going to take it. That's a decision I made.''

A number of women, after consultation with their doctors, determine that estrogen therapy is *not* for them.

MEDICAL HISTORIES NOT CONDUCIVE TO TAKING HRT:

- Deep vein thrombophlebitis in the legs or any thrombophlebitis.
- A history of blood clots.
- A stroke, even a mild one.
- A personal history of cancer—breast or otherwise.
- Pelvic disease.
- Gallbladder disease.
- Hypertension.
- Diabetes. (Progestins are responsible for the decrease in glu-

cose tolerance. Estrogens alone may improve glucose tolerance.)
• Varicose veins.
• Heavy smoking.
• Thirty percent overweight.
• Recurrent cysts.
• Kidney or liver disease.
• Enlargement of the lining of the uterus.
• A history of endometriosis or fibroids.

SIDE EFFECTS OF ESTROGEN THERAPY

Even the women who respond well to HRT show some side effects. For the most part, minor side effects will disappear within a few months of treatment.

Monthly bleeding occurs when the estrogen-progestin combination is taken. The bleeding starts when you stop taking the hormones, from day 26 to the end of the month. Research is under way to find a regimen that will reduce or eliminate this bleeding.

Breast pain similar to that experienced during the menstrual cycle may occur, although it is rarely severe. Relief is available by avoiding caffeine and salt, or by taking small doses of vitamin B_6. Other PMS-like symptoms, such as water retention and moodiness, may occur. Moodiness is linked more closely to the progestin use than to the estrogen.

HRT can contribute to migraine headaches, although there are some people whose migraines get better on estrogen. In most cases changing the type of medication and/or adjusting the dose has proved successful in eliminating this side effect.

Choosing HRT involves making an informed decision with the support of your physician. If your personal or family medical history precludes hormone treatment, or if you decide that HRT is not for you, the following chart provides nonhormonal alternatives to HRT. In all cases, yearly medical checkups and an open and honest relationship with your doctor are important.

NONHORMONAL ALTERNATIVES TO HRT

IRREGULAR BLEEDING	• See your physician to rule out disease.
HOT FLASHES	• Bellergal, a prescription drug
	• Clonidine, a high blood pressure medicine
	• Vitamin E (Available in foods such as dark green leafy vegetables, milk, eggs, meats, and cereals. Avoid high doses of vitamin E in pill form.)
	• Cool water splashed on face
	• Layered cotton clothing
SLEEP PROBLEMS	• Avoid polyester and nylon bed linens and clothing; wear cotton nightclothes, and use cotton linens.
	• Avoid caffeine and alcohol after 6:00 P.M.
SKIN CHANGES	• See Chapter 13.
LOSS OF LIBIDO	• Continued sexual activity, one or two times a week
	• Communication and sharing with partner; exploration of slower, non-traditional sex
	• Kegel exercises (see page 316)
PAINFUL INTERCOURSE	• Vaginal lubricant (e.g., K-Y jelly) (*Avoid* Vaseline.)
	• Continued sexual activity
	• Orgasm
	• Estrogen cream
	• Coconut oil
	• Warm baths
	• Drink plenty of liquids
	• Keep air in house moist
WEIGHT GAIN	• Aerobic exercise such as walking (see page 241)
OSTEOPOROSIS	• Exercise, either weight-bearing, such as walking or running or non-weight-bearing, such as swimming or bicycling.

NONHORMONAL ALTERNATIVES TO HRT (*continued*)

- 1,000 milligrams calcium per day (food plus 600 milligrams calcium supplement such as calcium carbonate)
- 400 I.U. vitamin D per day
- A new class of drugs known as diphosphonates are being tested in the United States and are currently being used in Europe. Sources claim they have "exactly the same effect on bone as estrogen, but without stimulatory effects on the reproductive system."

THE FUTURE

The health concerns of our next thirty years are concerns bred by progress. Until this century, most women did not have the privilege of living much beyond menopause. We are the first generation for whom the discomforts associated with the loss of estrogen are being alleviated medically. Hormone-replacement therapy may or may not prove to be the answer for future generations, but the field offers tremendous opportunity for study, which will affect the quality of postmenopausal life for generations to come.

Long before obvious symptoms of menopause occur, there are many subtle body messages heralding its onset. Can subtle hormonal changes be medically detected and estrogen therapy administered so that hormone levels remain relatively even through life? Dr. Bruce Ettinger reports, in *Menopause Management*, that a few years before menopause, the ovaries begin to show signs of tiring. In some women early signs—such as menstrual irregularity, hot flashes, sleep problems, and certain behavioral changes—may begin up to five years before the actual cessation of periods. A diagnosis of menopause can be made by a physical exam and certain laboratory tests.

Dr. Morris Notelovitz, a gynecologist specializing in what he calls "adult women's medicine," founded one of the first menopause clinics to include premenopausal women: the Women's Medical and Diagnostic Center in Gainesville, Florida. Ideally, he believes a woman should have a thorough medical evaluation at thirty-five, including screening for cardiovascular disease, instruction in breast self-examination, and a baseline mammogram.

Dr. Ettinger concludes that early identification of the risk for osteoporosis and cardiovascular disease in a woman can prevent the long-term consequences of estrogen loss. He feels that as soon as a woman shows vasomotor symptoms or urogenital changes, the early and continued use of HRT may provide maximum beneficial effect.

The decision to take hormones is not a moral or a political issue. The decision remains a personal one, based on your individual medical history weighed against an informed awareness of the pros and cons. The question of greatest significance is, will you benefit from HRT? Making the right choice may seem difficult since patients often feel uncomfortable broaching complicated medical questions with their physicians. To overcome this, I suggest making a list of questions before going to the doctor. In considering HRT, the questions you may want to ask include:

1. What are the advantages of HRT?
2. What are the disadvantages (or risks) of HRT?
3. What side effects should I expect from this treatment?
4. What are the risks of *not* taking any hormones?
5. What are the advantages of not taking any hormones?
6. What different methods of treatment are available?
7. How does the above information apply to my personal and family medical history?

Do not discount your own personal philosophy regarding your health and the medical approach you wish to take to insure your well-being. You want to feel good about your decision.

The number of women living years beyond menopause is currently gaining critical mass. As one of those women, I have found that HRT is helping to make those postmenopausal years relatively effortless. Yet I do not want to forget the numerous women who have lived full lives past menopause without ever hearing about estrogen. Such a woman is ninety-nine-year-old Helen Grout.

Remembering menopause, she said, "I hardly noticed it. I stopped flowing. I knew it was menopause because I didn't flow anymore. I didn't have any pain or anything. I was about—I was going to say fifty-eight, but I don't know if that's just right. But I think I was fifty-eight. I didn't see much change. I just lived."

Helen just lived, and so do we, with or without estrogen. The more we take our lives into our own hands, by staying informed about our bodies and by keeping our minds open to the possibilities of the next thirty years, the richer our lives will be. The health and beauty section of this book, which begins with the next chapter, discusses nonmedical self-care and outlines nutrition, exercise, and beauty programs so we can stay in top-notch condition—not out of drudgery, obligation, or duty but in order, as Helen said, to live.

SECTION THREE

The One-Hour-a-Day Guide to Self-Care

The good news about reaching middle age and going through menopause is that we are smarter, wiser, richer in experience and humor, less likely to conform to external expectations of who we are supposed to be, and more likely to express our unique selves freely. In other words, our minds and spirits are in top form. The not-so-good news is that our bodies sometimes seem to go in the opposite direction. In fact, anyone over forty who kneels down and tries to jump up as quickly as they did at twenty might dispute the idea that menopause and old age are *not* one and the same.

There is more good news, though. Paying attention to our bodies through good food, exercise, and beauty routines can increase the physical stamina and self-esteem that sometimes seem diminished with age. Of course, eating well, exercising, and paying attention to our looks take time and effort, and many women are at a loss as to where such routines can fit into their lives.

Last year I bought a power nozzle, an attachment to my Electrolux vacuum cleaner. The power nozzle has its own motor, which lets me vacuum my rugs with the power of two motors rather than one. "After all," the saleswoman told me, "time is money." I look around my house and see a myriad of time-saving devices. Amazingly, there *still* seems to be no time.

As true as that may be in modern life, women in the menopausal years cannot afford to use lack of time as a reason to deny themselves care. At middle age, self-care is not a luxury to be indulged in only when other business is finished. Nor is it frivolous or selfish. It is a necessity if we are to take full advantage of the years ahead. If spending time on yourself in the form of the right diet, a daily workout, and attention to beauty is foreign to you, assume it with a vengeance. No matter how spirited we may be, in the natural course of events we can expect medical problems once we hit midlife. We can, however, profoundly affect the condition of our own health through assuming the right habits. I, for one, will do whatever I can not to spend my next thirty years going to the doctor.

Although I was somewhat athletic as a girl, I never worked out according to any routine. In my late twenties, after the birth of my second daughter, I found it difficult to get up one afternoon after lying on the floor. My body, it seemed, was beginning to require attention from me in order to remain strong and in shape. Soon after that I was introduced to yoga, a wonderful system, which I outline in Chapter Eleven. I began to do yoga regularly and eventually became a yoga teacher. It was the first of many workout systems I have come to know and rely on to keep me in shape over the years.

I became aware of the science of nutrition in my thirties and went on to become a dietitian. The combination of a balanced diet with daily exercise has proved to be the best beauty program I could have found. When I became a model in my forties, my past habits stood me in good stead. I brought my health and well-being to modeling at age forty-seven, and it was reflected in the camera. Of course, adding a little makeup doesn't hurt at all, and although I tended to avoid makeup when I was younger, I have learned many tips through modeling and now make them part of my daily routine.

The following chapters on nutrition, exercise, and beauty are a synthesis of my experience and knowledge in those areas. The information and programs I offer take into consideration three aspects of the menopausal years.

The first is that, with the physical changes our bodies are undergoing, tips and tricks and beauty regimens we have relied on for years may no longer provide us with what we need. In many cases, we have had to get to know our physical selves all over again. This health and beauty guide is directed at those new selves.

The second consideration is effort. Many women find it hard to change old habits and establish new ones, since the new ones seem to intrude on or even assault the routines of their busy lives. In this guide, you will find a variety of suggestions on how to fit different aspects of health and beauty care into a hectic schedule. The flexibility of options allows you to mix and match a little exercise here, some food preparation there. Once you feel comfortable with the new program, in the way that you have designed it to fit your lifestyle, it will feel effortless.

Finally, these programs take into consideration that old demon time. In its entirety, the combined food, exercise, and beauty program, including food preparation and cooking, can be done in *under an hour a day*.

According to my vacuum cleaner saleswoman, I bought about half that time last year for $110.

CHAPTER 9

Eat Hearty, Stay Healthy

There is moderation even in excess.
—BENJAMIN DISRAELI

Food and sex are life's two renewable pleasures. The thousandth time can be as good as the first, although it may depend on what's happened in between. The two barriers to full dining pleasure are weight and time. This sounds like an Einsteinian equation but is really a social phenomenon.

THIN IS NO LONGER IN

Trends in body shapes change. Images of Marilyn Monroe and Jane Russell suggest that in the old days a little flesh to grab hold of was considered sexy. Betty Grable and Ava Gardner reigned as beauty queens with bodies that today could be called full. Women portrayed by the painters Botticelli, Titian, and Renoir were ample, curvaceous, and shapely. The various fertility goddesses of ancient civilizations represent women as symbols of plenitude.

In recent decades being thin has been the rage. The fashion of thinness reached its quintessence in the sixties with Twiggy, who started what I call the cadaver look. Women featured in fashion magazines have now come back to looking healthy, with fuller faces and much better color. We are even seeing a little flesh again, but I've been told this is the result of breast implants rather than a change in eating habits.

The pendulum has swung from cadaver to the at-least-alive look, but the reign of thinness perseveres. In order to get or remain thin people make a big mistake. They diet. This takes away one of the two renewable pleasures. As a registered dietitian, I have counseled thousands of people on weight control. Clients have told me, ''I stayed home all weekend because I was afraid of being around food.'' Since food is everywhere, to diet successfully in our culture you may have to be locked in a closet. Besides, dieting doesn't work. That's why you always see fat people eating salads. The success rate for weight-loss diets is 5 percent and I suspect that this percentage succeeded only because they exercised.

JUDY'S CHOICE-YEARS NUTRITION PLAN

Any discussion of the special nutritional needs of the woman in her menopausal years must take into account weight, heart disease, cancer, osteoporosis, and the skin. Specific nutrients that are key at this time—such as calcium, sodium, water, fiber, and vitamin and mineral supplements—will be reviewed. The next chapter provides a month of menus that incorporate all these factors. Although many of the physical changes that occur during this time of life are inevitable, a closer look links a significant number of them to bad habits that, without change, will rob us of our health.

WEIGHT

Menopause is a time when many women report weight gain. Although no biological basis for this has been identified, it is so widely claimed that it needs to be acknowledged. Many factors contribute to this phenomenon.

First, what is your ideal weight? This can be calculated by allowing 100 pounds for the first 5 feet of height and adding 5 pounds for every added inch. For example, a 5'5" tall woman with a medium frame will have an ideal weight of 125 pounds.

Add or subtract 10 percent of that total for a large or small frame, which can be determined by calculating your elbow breadth. To do this, place your thumb and first finger on the two bones on either side of your elbow. Move your fingers away from your elbow and measure the distance between them. (See table below.)

If a woman has "yo-yo" dieted all her life, and her weight has gone up and down frequently, she now finds that the only way she can maintain her weight is by taking in very few calories. Therefore, despite careful vigilance, any little slip results in weight gain. As times goes on, weight creeps up, despite close attention to calories and portions.

FRAME SIZE BY ELBOW BREADTH FOR WOMEN AGES THIRTY-FIVE TO SEVENTY-FOUR:

Small Frame	Medium Frame	Large Frame
less than 2.2"	between 2.3–2.8"	over 2.8"

Adapted from: Shils and Young.

Other women pick up a few pounds a year over time. After a number of years, they will notice this gradual gain has accumulated to twenty or thirty extra pounds. Every body has a point at which it cannot tolerate added weight. For most bodies this point starts at 20 percent over the ideal weight. Once that is surpassed, health problems directly related to weight can set in, such as high blood pressure, high cholesterol, and high blood sugar. The probability of these conditions increases after age forty.

Still other women gain and lose the same ten pounds every year according to the season. Again, this becomes harder to control as the years go by.

My menus will reverse the direction of these events. The combination of foods (carbohydrates, protein, and fats) balances the number of calories eaten in a day, the times at which meals are eaten, and the number of times a day to eat. Following these menus, along with doing the exercise program in Chapter Eleven, will produce a weight loss of a half pound per week.

Many people are impatient with this rate of weight loss and prefer instead to jump into very low-calorie diets in order to see results sooner. But over time, eating in the balanced way promoted by the menus and combining that eating with exercise will enable your body to return to the more active metabolism of earlier years. An active metabolism means that you will burn energy faster, require more food, and have much more leeway in what you can eat. In contrast, a very low-calorie diet or following the "yo-yo" diet pattern is equivalent to a life sentence of deprivation and mincing calories.

A small minority of women are either thin with no weight problems or unconcerned about being overweight. Choosing to remain fat may be a sensible choice, since constantly losing and gaining may be more of a health hazard than maintaining a steady weight, even if it is a hefty one. A decision to lose weight needs to be made carefully, as it is a lifelong project. Should you choose to participate in one of the 400- to 500-calorie diets that have been offered by several companies in the past few years, be certain that such a program is medically supervised.

WHY WEIGHT GAIN?

Pounds accumulated over the years are usually said to be due to age. But are such gains biological or lifestyle-related?

Although many women with young families prepare home-cooked meals, in general women are cooking less and less. Eating on the run usually means eating food with a high fat content. Surveys show that fast-food or sit-down restaurant meals contain more fat than food prepared at home. Also, a woman who works while still caring for a family struggles to find time to take care of herself, and exercise often falls by the wayside.

Women need 2 to 3 percent fewer calories per decade of age. This decrease is due to lowered amounts of body muscle and a general decrease in physical activity. Eighty percent of the calories we burn daily are used for basal metabolism, which are basic body functions, such as breathing, digestion, and cell activity. Since muscle tissue uses the most energy, the more muscle you have, the more calories you need. Men, for instance, have an innate higher muscle-to-fat ratio than women, which makes weight control an easier matter. My overweight clients always seem to be married to skinny guys who eat like horses.

Cross-section X rays of the thighs of older and younger women show smaller muscles and more fat in the older women. Not only has the muscle mass shrunk considerably, but fat has also infiltrated the muscle, further decreasing its overall amount. When muscle is replaced by fat, we need fewer calories to maintain weight. Since exercise done at any age, even ninety, has been shown to reverse this process, our need for fewer calories every decade has more to do with lack of exercise than the number of years we have lived.

On the other hand, never-ending dieting over the years actually causes weight gain. When calories are decreased, the body senses that there is a shortage of food. In response, body chemistry changes in order to preserve the fat we have, using available food to build added fat for protection and burning muscle for energy. Therefore, whenever you diet without exercise, you may lose some weight, but the body you end up with has less muscle and more fat than the one you started with. That's why at the end of each diet, as soon as you start to eat normally, pounds pile on fast. "It takes months to lose it and a few days to gain it all back," clients lament. As though this isn't enough, the body also slows down to adjust to the lower calorie intake. No wonder diets don't work!

A good way to understand this is to imagine the body as a calorie-burning machine. Are we encouraging our bodies to be low-calorie-burning machines or high-calorie-burning machines?

Longtime dieters have been known to maintain their weight at 800 calories a day and remain fat. On the other hand, eating plentifully, combined with exercise, encourages muscle to build up and fat to burn. My program readjusts the body chemistry to hold its ideal weight, while allowing you to eat well.

EAT MORE, WEIGH LESS

From every point of view it is not healthy to eat fewer than 1,500 calories a day. If you are now maintaining at less than 1,000 calories, you may want to increase your food intake gradually, in 200-calorie increments per week. Clients scream, "You don't understand my body. I'll gain weight on that much food!" If you've been dieting all your life and don't exercise, that is probably true. I, for one, think this is no way to live. Maybe exercise is like getting old—it's not so bad considering the alternative. Since dieting itself plus lack of exercise is the main cause of weight gain over time, "middle-age spread" is reversed by exercise plus meals plans of no fewer than 1,500 calories a day.

DO CALORIES COUNT?

Calories do count, but they are not all created equal. The type of calorie it is and how it is eaten contribute to how it ends up on your body. High-fat foods will cause more weight gain than other foods, *even when the calories are the same*. Recent studies from China, for example, show that the Chinese eat 20 percent more calories than people in the United States. Fat is minimal in that high-calorie diet, however, and obesity in China is rare.

The same amounts of food also act differently depending on the time of day they are consumed and how often. Most people eat very little during the day and have one big meal in the evening, but food eaten earlier in the day is efficiently burned, since we are active during that time. The same food consumed in the evening will probably not be used as efficiently, since we are less active at night. In addition, excess calories from any one meal at any time are stored as fat in our bodies. Our bodies are not as efficient at breaking down our own fat for energy as they are at using currently available (just eaten) energy. Therefore, having one main meal and eating late in the day are less efficient ways of eating, ultimately demanding that the body run on less fuel. As a result, we experience a lag in energy. This explains the great difference we feel when we eat three meals a day as opposed to less than three, which forces us to wait for fat to turn into energy.

My program provides the amounts of food, types of food, meal spacing, and meal timing to maximize calorie use. You can lose weight on these menus or add food for weight maintenance. To sum up, for weight control:

- Eat more calories in the earlier part of the day.
- Eat often (three to five small meals, as opposed to one big meal).
- Eat foods low in fat.

Calorie Needs

Since we are all so geared toward calorie counting, here is how to calculate calorie needs. The greatest majority of women can assume they need 11 calories per pound of body weight, plus exercise calories. Therefore, if you weigh 130 pounds, your daily calorie need is 1,430 calories, plus your exercise calories. Add two miles of walking (200 calories) to bring your calorie need to 1,630 in order to maintain your weight. If you want to lose weight, subtract 250 calories a day from your total calories, including walking. By these calculations, you will lose a half pound per week (or fifty pounds in two years) *as long as you continue to exercise.* Slow weight loss such as this is safer than a lose-it-quick method and easier to keep off in the long term, since time allows our bodies to adjust to new weight both physically and psychologically.

SPECIAL HEALTH CONCERNS

The three leading causes of death in American women between the ages of forty and sixty-five are heart disease, cancer, and stroke. Are these diseases due to age or lifestyle?

Heart Disease

Heart disease and stroke have the same cause—arteriosclerosis, or clogged arteries. In primitive cultures today, where the lifestyle resembles that of our ancestors, arteriosclerosis and cancer are uncommon. Granted, these societies don't enjoy the long life spans we do in modern society. But studies of individuals who have lived into their sixties in these cultures still show minimal heart disease or cancer. In contrast, autopsies during World War II on children growing up in Western society have identified arteriosclerotic lesions in ten-year-olds.

Heart disease is the leading killer of American women, primarily women over fifty, and one in seven women between the ages of forty-five and sixty-four already has some form of heart disease. Every American woman has a one-in-two chance of developing the disease, according to the American Heart Association. In contrast, her risk of getting breast cancer is one in eleven. Women usually do not have heart disease before menopause. After menopause, it takes us only six to ten years to catch up to men in heart attack risk because we have smaller arteries. The reason for this increased risk is estrogen loss.

GOOD AND BAD CHOLESTEROL

Estrogen affects cholesterol levels, which rise after menopause. In fact, there has been some therapeutic use of estrogens for certain types of inherited conditions of very high cholesterol. The three important numbers to know are total cholesterol, LDL cholesterol, and HDL cholesterol. The LDL cholesterol, known as the "bad" cholesterol, carries cholesterol in the bloodstream to deposit it where it is needed in the body. The HDL cholesterol, or "good" cholesterol, carries cholesterol to the liver, where it is broken down for elimination.

William Castelli has directed the Framingham Heart Study for more than a decade. This massive government-sponsored project has monitored 5,200 residents of Framingham, Massachusetts, since 1948 to identify risk factors for heart disease. Dr. Castelli says that the best predictor of heart attack in postmenopausal women is their LDL/HDL ratio. Over one half of all adult Americans have blood cholesterol levels of over 200, which puts them at increased risk for coronary disease. Dr. Castelli also points to another important blood fat, triglycerides, which start to rise in the middle years because of extra fat around the middle. Cholesterol and triglyceride levels can be determined by a blood test. If you do not know your values, consult your physician.

Dr. Castelli prescribes the right diet plus 200 calories of exercise a day (two miles) as the best protection against heart disease. Of the 5 billion people who live on the planet, more than 4 billion will never get heart attacks. Lifestyle changes can wipe out the risk of heart attacks for the rest of us.

Cancer

Scientists link 40 to 50 percent of all cancers to the foods we eat, indicating that those cancers are preventable. In 1982, the National Academy of Sciences issued a landmark study known as *Diet, Nutrition and Cancer*. This study was the first to identify clearly the relationship between reduced cancer risks and the low-fat, high-carbohydrate diet that had been recommended by nutritionists for years.

The most clearly established cancer promoter is dietary fat. High-fat diets (40 percent of calories from fat) stimulate the development of mammary tumors, while low-fat diets (10 percent of calories from fat) do not. The most recent dietary recommendations of the American Institute of Cancer Research are:

1. Reduce the intake of total dietary fat from the current average of approximately 37 percent to a level of no more than 30 percent of total calories and, in particular, reduce the intake of saturated fat. At least 10 percent of total fat intake should be polyunsaturated.
2. Increase the consumption of fruits, vegetables, and whole grains.
3. Consume salt-cured, salt-pickled, and smoked foods only in moderation.
4. Drink alcoholic beverages only in moderation, if at all.

Cruciferous vegetables (see vegetable list), so called because their leaves cross over each other, have been identified as preventive of cancer. A recent study suggests why: certain chemicals found in these vegetables were found to convert estrogen to inactive breakdown products rather than the active breakdown products that promote breast tumors.

Osteoporosis

Osteoporosis, the disease of thinning bones, has received a lot of attention in recent years, since, because of longer life spans, we are outliving our bones (see Chapter Seven). Calcium is the main material of bones, which start to thin after age thirty-five, with calcium loss accelerating after menopause. The biological basis of bone loss is undeniable, with estrogen loss being the key factor, but bone health is also determined by diet, exercise, alcohol consumption, and smoking. Nutritional advice on calcium and bone health will be provided later in this chapter.

The diseases that are assumed to be due to age are really the result of age compounded by lifetime habits the body will no longer tolerate. The yogis say that the body ages but the mind does not. The wisdom, creativity, and spirit we have achieved require a healthy body for their expression, and we now know enough about prevention to have both.

We may ask ourselves, "How long do we want to live anyway?" So far, the longest known life span is about 150 years. Whether we want to go that far is a question the philosophers can argue. I'll settle for quality rather than quantity.

Nutrition and the Skin

The skin is a mirror of human health reflecting most nutritional deficiencies. In fact, the discovery of vitamins and their effect on skin began in the 1700s, when English sailors cured skin lesions by eating limes, to this day tagging the English as "limeys." Today we know that the curative substance in the limes was vitamin C.

The discovery of the thirteen vitamins and fourteen minerals we now know to be necessary to human life took another two hundred years, and many of these discoveries came by observing the skin. Clinical dietitians in hospital settings assume that the condition of the skin is mimicked by the organs inside, and they will use skin's appearance as an assessment tool when actual laboratory data is not available.

Since 1950 there has been little research done in the area of nutrient effect on skin health. Overall, malnutrition became rare in industrialized society; a proper diet, combined with supplements when needed, seemed to have eliminated the common skin diseases of an earlier time. The subject, therefore, seems not to warrant research, since no pressing medical conditions are rampant. Yet in my clinical experience, I have found that eating healthful amounts of the right foods can improve the quality of our skin.

VITAMIN AND MINERALS FOR THE SKIN

The recommended dietary allowances (RDAs) for vitamins and minerals are based on the basic amounts needed to avoid deficiency disease, with a safety factor built in to the allowances. Because of lack of research, information is not available on what RDAs are required for optimum health, but it seems that our food intake is not even up to basic RDAs. Nutritional surveys have shown that women's diets do not meet the RDAs for some nutrients necessary to healthy skin.

The first thing a nutrition counselor does is take what is called a diet history. For the experienced counselor, the diet history is often a formality. The appearance of a client's skin gives rise to suspicions about her eating habits, which the diet history often confirms. Although this is not an exact science and no signs of actual deficiency disease can be seen, the texture and color of the skin reveal a person's daily habits.

Collagen, as stated earlier, is the major structural protein in the body, representing 75 percent of the skin protein. Collagen and elastin, another skin protein, are made of long chains that are held together by a cross-linked web. Certain important nutrients are involved in the building process of this structural web, which provides the skin with its structure and form. They are riboflavin (vitamin B_2), pyridoxine (vitamin B_6), ascorbic acid (vitamin C), copper, and zinc. As you will see later in this chapter, I recommend a daily vitamin-and-mineral supplement to cover the daily needs for all nutrients.

I must interject a point here that I cannot make too strongly. By all means do not run out and buy "skin vitamins." Supplements are no substitute for the balance provided by foods and should not be relied on as a substitute for the nutrients provided through food. For one thing, the vitamins and minerals found in supplements are not absorbed by the body as well as the nutrients found in food. And an overdose of many of these supplements will cause problems. For example, an overdose of B_6 can cause irreversible neurological damage. An overdose of ascorbic acid can lead to kidney stones and kidney failure. Selenium was the supplement of the year a number of years ago, when it was publicized to have cancer-preventing qualities. Yet, it caused neurological damage and tremors in people who took too much. Why recommend supplements at all? A balanced diet provides all the nutrients our bodies need, but it is the rare person in today's world who eats a truly balanced diet. Supplements act as insurance, to round out what we may be missing. In short, they act just like their names, to supplement what has been left out. But they are not to be relied on instead of food.

The following chart is based on studies reviewed by the National Academy of Science:

RECOMMENDED DAILY ALLOWANCES FOR VITAMINS & MINERALS

Nutrient	Usual Intake for Women in the United States, in Milligrams	RDA, in Milligrams	Food Sources
Riboflavin (vitamin B_2)	1.34	1.2	Dairy, all animal protein, green vegetables

Pyridoxine (vitamin B$_6$)	1.16	1.6	Chicken, fish, liver, pork, eggs, unmilled rice, soy, oats, whole wheat, peanuts, walnuts
Ascorbic acid (vitamin C)	77.0	60.0	Citrus fruits, greens, broccoli, potato, vegetables
Copper	0.9	1.5–3.0*	Organ meats, seafood, nuts, seeds
Zinc	6.6	12.0	Meat, eggs, seafood (Whole grains and legumes are a less rich source of zinc, but are still good.)

*Safe and adequate amount.

The above table suggests that many women do not get enough vitamin B$_6$, copper, or zinc in their diets, with vegetarians at possible risk for copper and zinc deficiencies. Vegetarians need to plan meals that include generous portions of legumes, nuts, and seeds. While most Americans need to cut down on fatty meats, I recommend including low-fat animal protein such as fish, chicken without skin, lean beef, lean pork, and veal, in appropriate portions (approximately 3 ounces), several times a week. Animal proteins are rich sources of most of the important skin nutrients, except vitamin C, which can be added with potatoes and vegetables. I have included many old-fashioned meat-and-potato meals in my menus, updated to be heart-healthy.

To assure healthy, radiant skin:

1. Eat a wide variety of foods.
2. Include low-fat animal proteins several times a week.
3. If you prefer a vegetarian diet, use generous amounts of

legumes—such as kidney beans, chickpeas, and navy beans—nuts, seeds, and whole grains in your diet.
4. Have at least one serving of a low-fat or nonfat dairy product daily.

The menus include all these components. I have also noted any recipes that are particularly good for the skin.

THE RIGHT THING TO DO

The oat bran controversy suggests that nutrition research leaves something to be desired. After so many years of extolling the cholesterol-lowering benefits of oat bran, in 1990 one study came out that said cream of wheat, or any starch for that matter, could lower cholesterol in the same way. Not only do scientific studies often contradict one another, but the advertising industry and the media are always willing to confuse issues even further. Oat bran does help in lowering cholesterol. Yet, I strongly suspect that from the beginning to the end of the oat bran rage, the numbers that were seen changing the most were those affecting the business profits of companies involved, as opposed to anyone's cholesterol count.

The problem with any popular nutrition study, or mass media excitement about one product, such as oat bran, is that the overwhelming attention given to one purportedly miracle food seems to get people focused on a single tiny detail of their health. The idea that any one food will greatly effect your health is, well, silly.

However, there is at this time a tried-and-true consensus on healthy eating, which can be summed up as high carbohydrate and low fat. The carbohydrates should be complex (grains, fruits, vegetables) versus simple (candies, cakes). Such a consensus is good news because the high-carbohydrate food plan is plentiful and appetizing. The villain, fat, is not only twice as caloric ounce for ounce as other foods but a health risk for many diseases. Remember the high-calorie Chinese diet? Its low-fat and high-carbohydrate nature keeps the risk of obesity to a minimum.

The diet prescription for most of the major diseases that currently plague us is almost always the same. Physicians have sent me patients with gallbladder disease, diverticulosis, coronary artery disease, cancer, high blood pressure, obesity, and even diabetes. The most beneficial diet is always high carbohydrate, low fat.

NOBODY IS PERFECT

In the early days of nutrition education, nutritionists were taught to tell someone who wanted ice cream to fill up on carrots and celery. We actually considered such substitution a brilliant solution. Devoted to my new profession, I tried it many times myself. I discovered what has now become common knowledge—if one wants ice cream, after filling up with carrots and celery one still wants ice cream. Nutritionists have developed a new approach. If you want ice cream, have it, and leave off the guilt. I like this much better.

Do-or-die eating usually dies, which is why certain foods in my program include some salt and some sugar, which most people can handle very well. And a few high-fat items have been chosen for their nutritional wealth. Food is fuel, and it is also pleasure and taste, giving us feelings of satisfaction.

FIBER

Many of the health benefits of the high-carbohydrate diet are due to its high fiber content. Whole grains are the chief source of fiber in the diet. Some of my clients have said, "I eat plenty of fiber—I have salad every day." Some vegetables, however, such as iceberg lettuce, have very little fiber. In order to meet the recommended amount of daily fiber (25 to 35 grams), include plenty of whole-grain cereals and breads, brown rice, whole-grain pastas, legumes, and fruits and vegetables. The more a food is processed, the more fiber is lost, which is why eating foods as close to their original form as possible is desirable. The following chart shows that fruits and vegetables vary greatly in their fiber content. A little arithmetic will also show that in order to get adequate fiber, almost all of your breads and other starches need to be made of whole (unmilled) grains.

FIBER CONTENT OF VARIOUS FOODS

Product	Dietary Fiber, in Grams
Cereals	
All-Bran, ⅓ cup	8.5
40% Bran Flakes, 1 cup	5.0
Raisin bran, Kellogg's, 1 cup	5.0
Fruit & Fibre, ⅔ cup	5.0
Bran 100%, ¼ cup	4.2
Nutri-Grain, rye and wheat, 1 cup	2.4
Shredded Wheat, 1 biscuit	2.2
Oatmeal, cooked, 1 cup	2.0
Total, 1 cup	2.0
Wheaties, 1 cup	2.0
Grape-Nuts, ¼ cup	1.4
Cheerios, 1¼ cups	1.1
Granola, Nature Valley, ⅓ cup	1.0
Legumes, ½ cup (cooked)	
Kidney beans	6.0
Split peas	5.0
Lima beans	5.0
Peanuts, 1 ounce	2.8
Peanut butter, 2 tablespoons	2.4

FIBER CONTENT OF VARIOUS FOODS (CONTINUED)

Product	Dietary Fiber, in Grams
Vegetables	
Avocado, 1 medium	4.7
Peas, ½ cup	4.0
Brussels sprouts, ½ cup	4.0
Corn, ½ cup	4.0
Potato, ½ cup	4.0
Broccoli, ½ cup	3.5
Eggplant, ½ cup	2.5
Carrots, ½ cup	2.4
Green beans, ½ cup	2.1
Beets, ½ cup	2.1
Cabbage, ½ cup	2.1
Zucchini, ½ cup	2.0
Cauliflower, ½ cup	1.6
Tomato, 1 small	1.5
Cucumber, ½ cup	1.1
Mushrooms, ½ cup	1.0
Spinach, 1 cup fresh	0.2
Lettuce, 1 cup	trace
Grains	
Brown rice, cooked, ½ cup	2.5
Pumpernickel bread, 1 slice	1.9
Whole-wheat bread, 1 slice	1.5
Graham crackers, 2 squares	1.4
Matzo, 1 ounce	1.2
Spaghetti, white, cooked, ½ cup	1.0
White bread, 1 slice	0.5
White rice, ½ cup	0.1
Fruit	
Blueberries, raw, 1 cup	4.4
Pear, raw, 1 medium	4.1
Prunes, dried, 3	4.0
Strawberries, raw, 1 cup	2.8
Apple with skin, 1 medium	2.5

FIBER CONTENT OF VARIOUS FOODS (CONTINUED)

Product	Dietary Fiber, in Grams
Pineapple, raw, 1 cup	2.4
Banana, 1 medium	2.0
Orange, 1 small	1.6
Peach, 1 medium	1.5
Applesauce, ½ cup	1.4
Apricots, raw, 3 medium	1.4
Raisins, 2 tablespoons	1.3
Cherries, raw, 10	1.1
Grapefruit, half	0.8
Cantaloupe, 1 cup	0.5
Grapes, 12	0.5

What does a high-carbohydrate diet look like? A lot of food, which may be what causes some people to be wary. Feeling full is associated with getting fat, but they are *not* the same! A high-carbohydrate daily intake of approximately 1,500 calories includes:

- 4 or more servings of fruit or vegetables
- 7 servings of starch (bread, rice, cereal, pasta) (I recommend whole grains)
- 2–3 servings of low-fat dairy products
- 5 ounces of protein-rich food
- 4 teaspoons vegetable oil (mono- or polyunsaturated)

Fruits and Vegetables (4 or more servings a day)

Because the sugar content of fruits varies, their serving size varies. All servings are approximately 60 calories, although 60 calories of strawberries is a large portion while 60 calories of figs, you will see, is small. Four servings of fruit or vegetables a day may mean that in one day you could have a half banana, an apple, ½ cup cooked broccoli, plus a mixed salad.

FRUITS
(4 OR MORE SERVINGS A DAY)

Fruit	Serving Size
Apple	1 medium
Applesauce, unsweetened	½ cup
Apricots, raw	4 medium
Banana	½ medium
Blueberries, raw	¾ cup
Cantaloupe, medium	⅓ melon
Cherries, raw, large	12 cherries
Figs, raw	2 figs
Fruit cocktail (canned)	½ cup
Grapefruit, medium	½ grapefruit
Grapes, small	15 grapes
Honeydew melon, medium	⅛ melon
Kiwi, large	1 kiwi
Mango, small	½ mango
Nectarine, medium	1 nectarine
Orange, medium	1 orange
Peach, medium	1 peach
Pineapple, raw	¾ cup
Plums	2 small
Raspberries, raw	1 cup
Strawberries, raw, whole	1¼ cups
Watermelon (cubes)	1¼ cups
Dried Fruits	
Apples	4 rings
Apricots	7 halves
Dates	2½ medium
Figs	1½
Prunes	3 medium
Raisins	2 tablespoons

Vegetables

Unlike fruit, vegetables are similar to one another in calorie content, so all servings are approximately the same size. One serving is one cup of raw vegetable, or ½ cup of cooked vegetable. Since each serving is a low 25 calories, and most people do not eat enough vegetables, I always encourage unlimited use. Following is a list from which to choose, with the cruciferous (cross-leafed) vegetables marked with an asterisk.

VEGETABLES
(4 OR MORE SERVINGS A DAY)

Artichoke	Leeks
Asparagus	Mushrooms
Beans—green, wax, or Italian	Okra
Bean sprouts	Onions
Beets	Pea pods
Broccoli*	Peppers
Brussels sprouts*	Rutabaga
Cabbage*	Sauerkraut
Carrots	Spinach
Cauliflower*	Summer squash (yellow)
Eggplant	Tomato
Greens	Turnips
(collard, mustard, turnip, kale)	Water chestnuts
Kohlrabi	Zucchini

Starchy Vegetables

Starchy vegetables are listed separately, and considered by dietitians to be starch rather than vegetable since they have 80 calories per serving (versus 25). An added 55 calories should not steer you away from starchy vegetables, which are complex carbohydrates and therefore a source of immediate energy. Many people cut down on potatoes to lose weight but nutritionally, as well as calorically, potatoes are a food bargain. One small baked potato provides a lot of food for only 80 calories, the same amount of calories as in *one ounce* (which practically cannot be seen) of most meats. Visualize switching from the typical American high-animal-protein diet to a high-carbohydrate diet. Picture an 8-inch dinner plate with one half of its surface covered with some animal food (chicken, beef, etc.), a quarter of its surface covered with vegetable, and the other quarter containing the starch (one small potato). By reducing the animal portion by one-half, you could add another three potatoes, for a total of four, keeping the calories equal and your heart healthy! And that's a lot of food!

STARCHY VEGETABLES
(4 OR MORE SERVINGS A DAY)

Corn	Potato, mashed
Lima beans	Squash (winter, acorn,
Peas	butternut)
Plantain	Yam, sweet potato
Potato, baked, 1 small	

Breads and Grains (7 servings a day)

Grains are the chief source of fiber in our diet, therefore I recommend whole-grain breads, whole-wheat pastas, and brown rice. You cannot always tell if a product is made of whole grains by its title or color. Some breads that claim to be whole are actually made with a flour blend, and the brown color of many breads is achieved with molasses. The ingredient list of a food tells the true story, with the word "whole" being the key word to describe a full-fiber grain. Each serving is approximately 80 calories, and while serving sizes vary, one ounce of cereal, bread, or crackers is a good practical measure. Seven servings of starch a day may mean that in one day you would have one cup of cooked cereal, four slices of bread, and a baked potato.

BREADS AND GRAINS (7 SERVINGS A DAY)

Cereals

Bran cereals, concentrated	⅓ cup
Bran cereals, flaked	½ cup
Bulgur, cooked	½ cup
Cooked cereals	½ cup
Grape-Nuts	3 tablespoons
Grits, cooked	½ cup
Puffed cereal	1½ cups
Wheat germ	3 tablespoons

Pasta and Rice

Pastas, cooked	½ cup
Rice, white or brown, cooked	⅓ cup

Breads

Bagel	½
Bread sticks 4 x ½"	2
Crackers, whole-wheat (Wasa, Ak-mak)	2–4 pieces
Croutons	1 cup
English muffin	½
Graham crackers	3 squares
Matzo	½ square
Pita, 6" across	½
Plain roll, small	1
Popcorn (popped without fat)	3 cups
Raisin bread	1 slice
Rye, white, and whole-wheat bread	1 slice

Low-Fat Dairy Products (2 to 3 servings a day)

Dairy products are the best source of calcium and the chief source of riboflavin in the diet. Although there are nondairy calcium sources, it would take enormous portions of these foods to meet our calcium needs. For instance, you would need to eat one large serving of salmon, half a cup of nuts, and three cups of dark green leafy vegetables every day to meet the minimum requirement. Some alternative health programs prohibit dairy because of its mucus-producing qualities. Doctors and nurses observe that some patients in acute phases of lung disease have a problem with milk, yet it is no problem to most healthy people. As a dietitian, I have seen children admitted to the hospital with rickets, the bone disease that is caused by inadequate calcium intake. Also, considering the debilitating effects of osteoporosis, why worry about a little mucus? Many new low-fat dairy products are coming onto the market, providing a wide choice of milk, yogurt, and cheeses. Calories are 80 to 100 per serving.

LOW-FAT DAIRY PRODUCTS
(2 TO 3 SERVINGS A DAY)

Skim milk	1 cup
Low-fat milk (1 percent fat)	1 cup
Low-fat buttermilk (1.5 percent fat)	1 cup
Evaporated skim milk	½ cup
Dry nonfat milk	⅓ cup
Plain nonfat yogurt	1 cup
Low-fat cheese (5 or less grams fat per ounce)	1 ounce

Protein Foods (5 ounces a day)

Many foods contain protein—meat, poultry, fish, dairy, beans, nuts, starches, and a small amount in vegetables. Animal sources provide complete proteins, which our bodies can use as they are. Protein in grains, beans, and nuts need to be combined with one another to become complete. I have listed only low-fat meats. Each serving has 50 to 75 calories. Five servings a day could be ½ cup tuna at lunch and 3 ounces of cooked chicken at dinner. These portions may appear small, since the average American eats twice as much protein (and with it, fat) as needed, but if there is any place in the diet I suggest getting picky, it is here. I recommend weighing meats to establish the right portion size.

PROTEIN FOODS (5 OUNCES A DAY)

Beef, lean cuts such as round, flank, tenderloin	1 ounce
Pork, lean cuts such as lean hams, Canadian bacon, trimmed center cut	1 ounce
Veal (all cuts are lean)	1 ounce
Poultry, chicken, turkey, hen, without the skin	1 ounce
Fish, fresh or frozen	1 ounce
Shellfish, crab, lobster, scallops, shrimp, clams	2 ounces
Oysters	6 medium
Tuna, water-packed	¼ cup
Herring	1 ounce
Sardines, canned in water	2 medium
Cottage cheese (preferably low-fat)	¼ cup
Egg	1

Vegetable Proteins

Tofu 2½" x 2¾" x 1"*	4 ounces
Beans: kidney, garbanzo, pinto, lentil, navy, lima, soybeans (cooked)	½ cup
Peanut butter	1 tablespoon

* Tofu is a complete protein by itself. Beans or peanut butter eaten in combination with grains such as brown rice or whole-grain bread provide complete protein.
Source: ADA Exchange Lists for Meal Planning

Fat (4 teaspoons a day)

Although a low-fat diet is important for a healthy heart, fat is still a necessary nutrient. Several fats, called essential fatty acids, are important to the hair and skin. Our bodies can produce most of the essential fatty acids except for one, linoleic acid, which is in polyunsaturated fats, such as safflower and sunflower oil. To make sure you get the daily minimum requirement of polyunsaturated fats, which is 10 percent of total fat calories recommended, 4 teaspoons is a desirable amount for someone eating 1,500 calories a day. You can meet your requirement with any of the liquid vegetable fats such as canola, corn, and soy oils, which are polyunsaturated, or olive and peanut oils, which are high in monounsaturated fats and also heart-healthy.

Other areas of nutritional concern for women over forty are sodium, calcium, and vitamin supplements.

SODIUM

Sodium, which, in our diet, is found mainly in salt, has been associated with high blood pressure, although family history and obesity are the greater contributors to this condition. Current theory maintains that, of the general population who do not currently have high blood pressure, 10 percent are sodium-sensitive—that is, having salt for these individuals may eventually contribute to high blood pressure. This theory suggests that for 90 percent of the population salt intake may pose no problem. In addition, many women anecdotally report sensitivity to salt as they get older, in the form of fluid retention and swelling.

Since there is no way to identify diagnostically those who may develop high blood pressure because of sensitivity to sodium, the National Research Council recommends keeping daily sodium intake under 2,400 milligrams. Most Americans consume much more than this amount each day, with 75 percent of this excess sodium coming from prepared foods.

My menus are geared for convenience, and you may be surprised to find prepared foods included, but it is possible to stay within the NRC recommendation for sodium and still use some canned and frozen foods with moderate amounts of sodium. Many food companies have lowered the amounts of sodium in their products, or have created special low-salt lines. Although it is not required by law, sodium amounts are often listed on the label. The menus in Chapter Ten stay within current recommendations.

Eating a diet rich in calcium and potassium and maintaining your weight in an ideal range will do the most for controlling your blood pressure.

CALCIUM

The Recommended Dietary Allowance for calcium is 800 milligrams a day. The newest RDA in 1989 was expected to include an increase in the recommendation of calcium for menopausal women, but the National Research Council did not find enough evidence that bone health would be altered by increased intake. Other researchers report that, considering individual differences in calcium absorption, 800 milligrams may be insufficient for many women, and they are recommending 1,000 milligrams a day for premenopausal women and 1,500 after menopause. If you are on estrogen-replacement therapy, the premenopausal recommendation of 1,000 milligrams can continue.

Caffeine, alcohol, and smoking hinder absorption of calcium, while vitamin D and estrogen enhance absorption. High-protein diets adversely effect bone health by increasing calcium loss in the urine. In order for the bones to make use of calcium available, there must be stress placed on bones.

A calcium supplement may be necessary, since most women now consume only half of their daily requirement through meals. Food is the best source for balanced consumption, however, since bone health also involves many other nutrients, including vitamin D, copper, zinc, manganese, fluorine, silicon, and boron. Recently some calcium supplements were discovered to be useless because they did not dissolve fast enough to be absorbed in the intestines. Chain-store and generic brands were the chief offenders. One way to test your supplement is to place it in some vinegar. If it does not dissolve within fifteen minutes, it will not dissolve quickly enough in your stomach to be absorbed and, therefore, cannot work for you. Using a supplement beyond the recommended intake can be hazardous, with one study suggesting that too much calcium supplementation can enhance gallstone formation in older women. As with all supplements, choose wisely and do not use a supplement as a substitute for food.

DIETARY CALCIUM, IN MILLIGRAMS
(TARGET: 1,000–1,500)

Milk

Low-fat, 1 cup	291
Nonfat, skim, 1 cup	297
Buttermilk, low-fat, 1 cup	285

Cheese

American, 1 ounce	163
Cheddar, 1 ounce	205
Swiss, 1 ounce	273
Cottage, lowfat, ½ cup	77
Feta, 1 ounce	140
Mozzarella, part-skim, 1 ounce	183

Yogurt

Low-fat, plain, 1 cup	415
Nonfat, plain, 1 cup	452
Flavored, low-fat, 1 cup	389

Frozen Dairy

Ice cream, 1 cup	176
Ice milk, 1 cup	176
Frozen yogurt, 1 cup	249

Seafood

Sardines, water-packed with bones, 4 ounces	496
Salmon, pink, canned, 6 ounces	333
Oysters, fresh, raw, 8 ounces	213
Shrimp, 3 ounces	98
Lobster, 3 ounces	55

Nuts

Almonds, ½ cup	152

Peanuts, 1 cup	104
Brazil nuts, shelled, ½ cup	130
Soybean nuts, ½ cup	75
Tofu, 4 ounces	145

Dairy products are the best sources of calcium, providing 55 percent of the average intake. Low-fat dairy products, while low in calories, not only have high amounts of readily absorbable calcium, they are also a good source of protein, riboflavin, and potassium. An added benefit is that calcium and potassium are also protective against high blood pressure and may do more for controlling blood pressure than eliminating salt. Potassium, widespread in all foods, is most plentiful in fruits and vegetables such as bananas, oranges, grapefruits, potatoes, winter squash, broccoli, and spinach. To maximize bone health with your diet:

1. Eat at least one serving of dairy foods daily, plus two other calcium-rich foods.
2. Add a daily supplement to your diet containing 600 milligrams of calcium in the form of calcium carbonate.
3. Avoid smoking and excessive intake of caffeine and alcohol.
4. Keep your protein intake moderate by following the high-carbohydrate meal plan.
5. Exercise daily, preferably a weight-bearing exercise such as walking, although any form of exercise works in your favor.

Vegetables

Dark green leafy vegetables are good calcium sources, although the calcium in certain leafy vegetables (spinach, Swiss chard, and beet greens) is not as readily absorbed by the body when eaten. Calcium is bound to a high amount of oxalic acid in these foods, which prevents its release. Spinach, Swiss chard, and beet greens are not to be neglected, however, since a certain amount of calcium is released when they are eaten and they are also an excellent source of many other necessary vitamins and minerals. In general, green leafy vegetables are the lowest-calorie, highest-nutrient food in the world.

PREFERRED GREENS AS CALCIUM SOURCES, IN MILLIGRAMS

Mustard greens, 1 cup	193
Broccoli, 1 cup	136
Okra, 1 cup	147
Bok choy, ½ cup	126
Collards, raw, ½ cup	149
Turnip greens, raw, ½ cup	126

Adapted from *Menopause Management* 3 (no. 1) (June 1990), p. 15.

SUPPLEMENTS

Folklore has it that if you eat a balanced diet you don't need any vitamin pills. This may have been true in 1900, when people commonly ate 3,000 calories a day and walked all over the place. Today the average woman eats 1,500 calories a day, which may make it difficult for her to meet her vitamin and mineral needs. In addition, nutrient absorption, storage, and usage may decrease with age. Other special situations may enhance the need for certain nutrients. Intense exercise increases the need for riboflavin, smoking can deplete vitamin C levels, and coffee in large amounts will flush out water-soluble vitamins.

For these reasons I recommend a one-a-day multivitamin-and-mineral supplement that contains 100 percent (and no more) of the Recommended Dietary Allowances.

High doses (more than ten times the RDA) of any vitamin or mineral are not recommended. Not only do they upset the balance of the body, but many supplements are toxic, including those that are water-soluble and eliminated in the urine.

I am often amazed at where people find nutrition information. I remember a client telling me she took vitamin B_{12} religiously. Why? Because someone on an airplane told her it was good for her. One of the biggest problems of any dietary advice is that it tends to focus us on one detail. Vitamins and minerals work in close coordination with one another. For instance, high intakes of zinc depress copper and iron; excess vitamin E inhibits vitamin A production; too much iron reduces zinc absorption. The list goes on. Who can keep track of all that as we fuss with one particular nutrient over another?

Since multivitamin pills usually contain only small amounts of calcium, calcium supplements are a separate product. Some calcium supplements also contain vitamin D, which you will be getting in your multivitamin. Vitamin D is a fat-soluble vitamin that is stored in the body and is toxic in high amounts. Therefore, use a calcium supplement that does not contain vitamin D to avoid this duplication.

While I recommend a multivitamin to fill in the gaps in your diet, it is important to remember that, as I have already noted, nutrients in pill form are not as well absorbed as food. Also, supplements do not provide energy, carbohydrates, protein, or fat, which are all basic body requirements. We have evolved over millions of years by eating a wide variety of foods. In terms of overall health there is no substitute for well-balanced meals.

DAILY SUPPLEMENT RECOMMENDATION:
- 1 multivitamin with minerals, which has 100 percent of the RDAs (but no more)
- 1 calcium supplement, with 600 milligrams of calcium and without vitamin D

WATER

Hydrating the skin is not the only important use of water. It is the largest component of the body, acting as a transporter of nutrients to cells and as a remover of wastes. Daily water needs depend on the amount of calories consumed, with approximately a quart of water for every 1,000 calories, although needs vary greatly, depending on climate and daily exercise. Water can be obtained in the form of juices, soups, milk, and other fluids. Coffee, tea, and other caffeine-containing drinks should not be counted as water, since they dehydrate, causing more fluid to be lost than gained. For cosmetic reasons, limit any fluids after nine o'clock in the evening, as they tend to accumulate overnight around the eyes, stretching that tissue.

Many people assume that they do not need fluids if they are not thirsty, but thirst, ironically, is not a good indicator of hydration. Dehydration will occur before thirst sets in. A more reliable way to know if you are getting enough fluid is to check the color and amount of your urine. If it is dark and cloudy rather than light and clear and the volume of urine is low, more fluid is needed.

"You are what you eat" is more than a catchy expression. Whenever I eat poorly, I feel it within a few days. I can also see the benefits of eating well on my skin, hair, eyes, nails, and teeth.

The effects of poor eating habits cause disease over a period of many years. Eating well, on the other hand, produces a feeling of well-being that is available immediately.

CHAPTER 10

One Month of Menus

Can you inform me of any other pleasure which can be enjoyed three times a day, and equally in old age as in youth?

—CHARLES MAURICE DE
TALLEYRAND PÉRIGORD

Eating styles have changed drastically since I was a young mother. My father owned a butcher shop. Every afternoon I would visit him with my two little girls and he would give me fresh meat for our evening meal. I started preparing dinner at three o'clock in the afternoon, and dinner was at six. I still love preparing a meal this way, filling the house with smells of freshly cooked food, but for me, as for many women now, spending that time in the kitchen is a luxury.

At my first job as a nutrition counselor I was horrified to find that many of my clients got home from work and ate things like cheese sandwiches for supper. A number of my colleagues, I soon realized, who should have and did know better, did the same thing. I lectured ceaselessly on the importance of finding time to prepare fresh meals as a way to take proper care of ourselves. But as the demands of work grew, cheese sandwiches often replaced a home-cooked meal in my own house, too.

PREPARED FOODS: NOT NECESSARILY BAD

I remember pitying anyone who would stoop so low as to feed themselves with a TV dinner. Yet, between constraints on my own time and in considering the needs of my clients, I have slowly been forced to explore the market of prepared foods myself and have found many products out there that are healthy and worthwhile. At present, most prepared foods are high in sodium, which can be a problem if you are one of the 10 percent of the population that is sodium-sensitive. Certain products *are* available with less salt, and there are several lines of low-sodium canned foods, which might need spicing up for taste.

The best way to find wholesome prepared foods is to shop around in a supermarket and a health food store and see the many new products that are always coming onto the market. I recommend many items later in this chapter. Identify a healthful prepared food by reading its ingredient list. Ingredients are listed according to weight, with the heaviest ingredient listed first. Some labels will tell you the amount of fat, which is useful. Fat is usually listed in grams, with each gram of fat containing 9 calories. Therefore, by multiplying grams of fat by 9, you will know the fat calories of the item. These should be under 30 percent, or about one-third, of the total calories.

Be aware of what is printed on labels. At this time, no legal definition exists for many of the claims made on food packaging, such as "natural" or "lite." I remember trying to understand why one of my extremely conscientious diabetic patients was showing very high blood sugars. Finally, we discovered she had been drinking a popular lemonade drink every night because it had been advertised as "natural." The drink was very high in sugar—which, technically speaking, of course, is natural.

In an ideal world, fresh, locally grown foods are best, and processing has its cost in nutrients and fiber. I found, however, that with less time available to prepare fresh foods, my diet was suffering, since I had not found an alternative and tended to eat sporadically or on the run. I started working with prepared foods because as a nutritionist I consider eating well a must. Since I gave in to the prepared foods market, I eat well more regularly and my diet has improved. This compromise allows me to work both sides of the fresh-versus-prepared street. For instance, I can put together a fast meal by heating a canned soup and adding fresh vegetables from the refrigerator, cut up several days before, into the pot.

By doing some batch cooking in a couple of hours on a free day, and filling in with quality canned and frozen foods, anyone can eat well all week, even with a busy schedule. The following month of menus is my answer to the "cheese sandwich syndrome."

THE MENUS

The first two weeks of menus require two hours of food preparation each week, which can be done all at once. Week Three consists of all prepared foods with no cooking involved, for those times when everything has gotten the best of you (but you need a meal anyway). Week Four is a nutritionist's dream—all fresh foods. These menus:

- Average 1,500 calories a day which, along with exercise, will result in weight loss,
- Are high in carbohydrates, with less than 30 percent of the calories as fat, for heart health,
- Are high in fiber which, in addition to its health benefits, provides satisfaction in meals,
- Include many foods that are thought to be "forbidden" but do fit into well-planned meals, providing pleasure and avoiding deprivation,
- Provide spacing of meals so that energy is always available and fat does not accumulate,
- Incorporate foods that reduce cancer risk, and
- Are designed to be fast, easy, and convenient, to fit into a busy schedule.

* * *

The actual calorie count for each day has been omitted intentionally. Fussing around with minute calorie differences is for, well, old ladies. Eat heartily, enjoy the food, and you will never be overweight if you stick to these amounts. Remember, less food than this will encourage fat accumulation rather than produce weight loss. Less is not better.

Week One

(Recipes are provided for dishes that have an asterisk after them. Also, snacks are listed at the end of the day but can be eaten at any time. In fact, the earlier in the day the better, for weight control, energy levels, and digestion.)

Monday

BREAKFAST:	1 slice Banana Pudding* topped with 1 cup plain nonfat yogurt
LUNCH:	Smoked turkey sandwich (2 slices dark rye bread, 2 ounces turkey, 1 teaspoon low-cal mayonnaise), lettuce and tomato, if desired
DINNER:	1 serving Fish Stew* heated with Steamed Vegetables* and Greens*
SNACK:	6 ounces pineapple juice
	3 fat-free cookies

Tuesday

BREAKFAST:	2 slices whole-wheat toast topped with 1/4 cup low-fat cottage cheese and 1 tablespoon toasted sesame seeds
LUNCH:	1 serving Apple-Granola Crisp*
	1 cup plain low-fat yogurt
DINNER:	1 serving Hain pea soup heated with Steamed Vegetables*
	1 slice whole-wheat bread spread with goat cheese
	15 grapes
SNACK:	4 graham crackers, 1/2 grapefruit

Wednesday

BREAKFAST:
1 serving Apple-Granola Crisp*
1 cup plain low-fat yogurt

LUNCH:
1 serving Steamed Vegetables,* mixed with 2 ounces low-fat cheese (hot or cold)
1 tablespoon salad dressing (toss with above)
2 Wasa crackers (can top with a purchased bean spread)
1 oatmeal cookie

DINNER:
1 Le Menu Light roasted chicken
Green salad with 1 tablespoon dressing
1 serving Birds Eye Dijon vegetables
1 cup canned diet fruit salad

SNACK:
6 ounces cranberry juice
2 large whole-wheat pretzels

Thursday

BREAKFAST:
1 serving Banana Pudding*
2 Ak-mak crackers topped with 1 tablespoon almond butter (or other nut butter)

LUNCH:
Tuna sandwich (2 slices whole-grain bread, 2 ounces water-packed tuna, 1 tablespoon low-calorie mayonnaise, lettuce)
1 cup low-fat milk
1 piece of fruit in season

DINNER:
1 Legume Mexican enchilada with tofu sauce (frozen entrée)
1 toasted tortilla
Steamed Vegetables*
Fruit juice bar (sold in freezer case)
3 cups popcorn

SNACK:
1 piece fresh fruit

Friday

BREAKFAST: 1 bagel, toasted, with 1 ounce low-fat cheese

1 orange

LUNCH: 1 slice Banana Pudding*

6 saltine crackers with 1 tablespoon peanut butter

DINNER: 1 serving Fish Stew* heated with 1 cup Greens* and 2/3 cup frozen corn

1 serving Apple-Granola Crisp* topped with 1/4 cup lemon sherbet

SNACK: 6 ounces apple juice

3 plain cookies

Saturday

BRUNCH: English muffin pizza (3 whole-wheat muffin halves spread with 1 ounce low-fat cheese, 1 slice tomato, pinch oregano, and toasted until cheese bubbles)

1 banana

DINNER: Roast beef sandwich (2 slices rye bread, 3 ounces deli roast beef with fat trimmed), spread with mustard and/or mayonnaise to taste, sprinkled with sprouts)

3 cups popcorn

1 apple

1 cup 1-percent milk

3 plain cookies or 1 piece angel food cake

SNACK: 12 nuts of choice

Sunday

BRUNCH: 3 bagel halves, toasted, with 3 ounces smoked turkey (sliced tomato, if desired)

1 cup pineapple chunks

1/2 cup low-fat cottage cheese

Sunday (continued)

DINNER: 1 Weight Watchers chicken nuggets
1 Lean Cuisine zucchini lasagna
Green salad with 1 tablespoon salad dressing
1 cup 1-percent milk
3 whole-grain cookies
1 apple

SNACK: 1 slice rye bread with 1 tablespoon peanut butter

Recipes for Week One

APPLE-GRANOLA CRISP

SERVES 4

This is a low-fat version of an old favorite, and a good way to include fruit during the winter months, when you may not feel like having fresh fruit. With a dollop of yogurt on top, it makes a quick meal. It's also good with pears and/or cranberries mixed with the apples. In the summer using blueberries makes a nice imitation blueberry pie.

TOPPING:
1 cup granola
1 tablespoon safflower oil
¼ cup whole-wheat flour
¼ cup warm water, approximately

FILLING:
4 large apples
½ teaspoon cinnamon
¼ teaspoon nutmeg
¼ teaspoon allspice
¼ teaspoon cloves
4 tablespoons raisins
½ cup orange juice

1. To make the topping, mix granola, oil, and flour. Add water until consistency is mushy. Set aside.
2. To make the filling, wash apples and cut, unpeeled, into chunks, removing core.
3. Mix together apples and spices in an 8 x 8″ baking dish, using hands to mix and coat apples with spices. Sprinkle raisins over top of apples. Cover with the topping. Pour the orange juice evenly over the topping.
4. Bake 40 minutes at 350°F.

Calories per serving: 250 (73 percent from carbohydrate, 1 percent from protein, 26 percent from fat)

BANANA PUDDING

SERVES 4

Again, an updated version of an old favorite provides a healthful, low-fat, low-sugar dessert. It tastes deceptively sweet, is filling, and can serve as a complete meal, since it contains a complete balance of foods. This is also a good way for people who don't like to drink milk to include calcium in the diet.

  2 slices whole-wheat bread, crust removed
  2 medium bananas, ripe
  2 cups 1-percent milk
  2 eggs (or use Fleischmann's Egg Beaters to avoid cholesterol)
½ teaspoon cinnamon
¼ teaspoon nutmeg or allspice
  1 tablespoon maple syrup

1. Place the bread in an 8 x 8″ baking dish.
2. Mash the bananas and spread over the bread.
3. Beat the milk with the eggs, add the seasonings and syrup, and mix thoroughly. Pour the mixture over the bananas. Let stand for 15 minutes.

4. Bake 1 hour at 350°F.

Calories per serving: 190 (67 percent from carbohydrate, 19 percent from protein, 14 percent from fat)

FISH STEW

(Specifically Good For Skin)

SERVES 4

This complete meal in one pot provides a generous amount of protein. While heating, a variety of frozen or fresh vegetables can be added to the pot. I suggest keeping a bowl of fresh washed greens in the refrigerator for just such an occasion.

1   large onion, diced
1   tablespoon olive oil
1   large tomato, diced
¼   cup dry white wine
3   medium potatoes, washed and diced
⅔   cup water
1   bay leaf
¼   teaspoon pepper
1   tablespoon parsley
½   teaspoon salt (optional)
1½   pounds fish, fresh or frozen, assorted varieties such as cod, halibut, and scallops, cut in pieces.

In a large pot, sauté the onion in the oil for 5 minutes. Add the tomato, stir, and sauté another 5 minutes. Add the wine and boil off the alcohol. Add the potatoes, water, and seasonings. Cover and cook over medium heat for 15 minutes. Add the fish and cook another 5 minutes, or until fish is done.

Calories per serving: 329 (18 percent from carbohydrate, 47 percent from protein, 35 percent from fat)

GREENS

Greens are a good calcium source, but some greens have bound calcium, making the nutrient less available. The following greens are good calcium sources.

Mustard greens
Turnip greens
Dandelion greens
Collards
Kale
Romaine lettuce

Wash and dry the greens. Trim them and break into pieces. Store in a covered bowl in the refrigerator.

STEAMED VEGETABLES

SERVES 4

Steaming is an excellent way to cook vegetables because it is fast and it keeps vegetables from being soaked in water. Steaming also assures minimal loss of vitamins and minerals in cooking. Any variety of vegetables and beans can be used for this dish. Vegetables have the greatest amount of nutrition for the least calories and they provide the satisfaction of chewing. Include beans in your steamed mixture, then mix with a whole grain like pasta or rice for a complete meal. Add a handful to any soup or stew.

1 10-ounce package frozen black-eyed peas
3 carrots, peeled and sliced
3 large stalks broccoli, stems and leaves removed
½ pound mushrooms, sliced
   Juice of 1 lemon

Steam black-eyed peas for approximately 5 minutes. Add carrots and cook 5 minutes. Add broccoli and cook another 5 minutes. Place in a bowl with the raw mushrooms. Add the lemon juice. Store, covered, in refrigerator.

Calories per serving: 130 (72 percent from carbohydrate, 28 percent from protein, 0 percent from fat)

Week Two

Monday

BREAKFAST: 1 slice Pumpkin Pudding*
              ½ cup applesauce
LUNCH: Spinach* salad with 4 ounces canned crab, 1 tablespoon dressing
              1 ounce crackers of your choice
DINNER: 1 serving Lamb Stew*
              1 serving Protein-Rich Corn Pudding*
              8 ounces flavored nonfat yogurt
SNACK: 1 orange
              3 large whole-wheat pretzels

Tuesday

BREAKFAST: 1 cup plain nonfat yogurt
              1½ cups berries in season
              1 slice whole-wheat toast with 1 tablespoon almond butter
LUNCH: Weight Watchers pizza
DINNER: Spinach* salad (1 sliced Hard-Boiled Egg,* 1 tablespoon salad dressing)
              2 servings Fruit Compote*
              2 whole-grain crackers spread with baba ghanoush (can be purchased in supermarkets)
SNACK: 4 graham crackers
              4 ounces juice

Wednesday

BREAKFAST: 1 bagel with 2 tablespoons cream cheese

Wednesday (continued)

LUNCH: 1 slice Pumpkin Pudding* with 1 cup
          plain nonfat yogurt
DINNER: 1 serving Lamb Stew*
          1 slice dark bread
          Spinach* salad with 1 tablespoon salad
          dressing
          1 cup pineapple chunks sprinkled with
          ½ cup granola
SNACK: 1 can low-sodium V-8 juice
          6 small crackers

Thursday

BREAKFAST: 1 slice Pumpkin Pudding*
           ½ cup orange juice
LUNCH: Egg sandwich (2 slices whole-grain
           bread, 1 boiled egg, sliced, 2 table-
           spoons baba ghanoush, and a sprin-
           kling of sprouts)
           10 peanuts
DINNER: 1 Mrs. Paul's fish Dijon
           1½ cups Campbell's low-sodium tomato
           soup
           1 ounce crackers
           1 serving Fruit Compote* with ½ cup
           plain nonfat yogurt
SNACK: 1 apple
           3 whole-wheat bread sticks

Friday

BREAKFAST: 1½ cups cold cereal
           1 cup 1-percent milk
           1 banana (if you want hot cereal, put this
           mixture in the microwave for 2 min-
           utes)
LUNCH: Smoked turkey sandwich (2 ounces
           turkey, sliced tomato, lettuce, 1 table

Friday (continued)

spoon diet mayonnaise, on whole-wheat Syrian bread)

10 whole almonds

DINNER: 1 serving Lamb Stew*

1 serving Protein-Rich Corn Pudding*

1 cup frozen brussels sprouts

SNACK: 1 can low-sodium V-8 juice

Saturday

BRUNCH: Canadian bacon and cheese sandwich (2 ounces Canadian bacon and 1 ounce low-fat cheese toasted on 2 slices rye bread)

1 cup fruit cocktail (without sugar)

DINNER: Armour Lite sweet-and-sour chicken (place on plate with 1 cup frozen broccoli for microwave cooking)

½ cup vanilla frozen yogurt (low-fat) with 12 toasted almonds

SNACK: 3 cups popcorn

Sunday

BRUNCH: 3 bagel halves with 2 tablespoons cream cheese, 3 tomato slices, and 4 ounces drained canned kipper

4 pear halves, canned, packed in juice, or fresh

DINNER: Chef salad (dark greens, 2 ounces diced turkey, 1 ounce part-skim mozzarella cheese, 1 sliced tomato, 1 coarsely grated carrot, 3 coarsely grated radishes, ½ cup croutons, 2 tablespoons salad dressing)

1 large bunch grapes

SNACK: 4 Ak-mak crackers with ¼ cup cottage cheese and jelly

Recipes for Week Two

LAMB STEW

SERVES 5

This meal-in-one-pot gives the impression that you have slaved over it all day. Serve with a green salad with a light vinegar or lemon dressing and top with a dollop of yogurt, if desired. Be sure to trim the fat from the meat carefully.

1 large onion, diced
1 tablespoon safflower oil
3 tablespoons flour
1/2 teaspoon salt
1/2 teaspoon pepper
1/4 teaspoon garlic powder
1 1/2 teaspoons paprika
1 1/4 pounds lamb, cut into chunks
1 cup water
2 medium potatoes, scrubbed and quartered
2 large carrots, thickly sliced
2 cups frozen peas

1. In a large Dutch oven, sauté onion in oil for 3 minutes. Push onions to one side of the pot. Mix together flour, salt, pepper, garlic powder, and paprika. Coat the meat in the flour mixture; sauté the meat in the Dutch oven, turning to brown on all sides.
2. Add the water. Stir the mixture with a wooden spoon, scraping the bottom of the pot. Cover and simmer over low heat about 1/2 hour.
3. Add the potatoes and carrots. Continue cooking another 1/2 hour.
4. Add peas. Cook another 5 minutes.

Calories per serving: 375 (25 percent from carbohydrate, 29 percent from protein, 46 percent from fat)

PROTEIN-RICH CORN PUDDING

SERVES 7

Whole-grain corn, milk, and cheese make this pudding a snack or lunchtime meal. Not only is it delicious, but it is convenient for wrapping up and taking along to work.

 ¾ cup yellow cornmeal
 1 teaspoon baking powder
 ½ teaspoon salt
 1 egg
 ½ cup whole milk
 3 tablespoons safflower oil
 1 8-ounce can cream-style corn
 3 ounces reduced-fat cheddar cheese, diced

1. Combine the cornm   aking powder, and salt in a mixing bowl.
2. Beat together the egg, milk, oil, and corn.
3. Combine wet and dry ingredients, blending lightly.
4. Mix cheese into batter.
5. Pour into a greased 8½ x 4½ " loaf pan. Bake at 350°F. approximately 40 minutes.

Calories per serving: 200 (33 percent from carbohydrate, 12 percent from protein, 55 percent from fat)

FRUIT COMPOTE

SERVES 5

Cooking fruit is a good way to enjoy fruit during the winter months, when many varieties are not available. Add this compote to the Fruited Frosting for a sweet dessert, use as a topping on hot or cold cereal, or top with yogurt and granola for a "sundae." Keep the skins for added nutrients and fiber. By using a glass pot you can cook and store this in the same container.

FRUIT COMPOTE *(continued)*

2 apples
2 peaches
1 pear
1 fresh apricot
2 tablespoons raisins
1/2 cup water

Thoroughly wash and dry apples, peaches, pear, and apricot. Cut into bite-sized chunks, leaving the skins on, and place in a small pot. Add raisins. Add the water to the fruit, cover, and simmer approximately 15 minutes. Store in a covered container in the refrigerator.
Calories per 1/2 cup serving: 88 (100 percent from carbohydrate)

HARD-BOILED EGGS

Eggs have nutritional pros and cons. Although the yolk is high in cholesterol, eggs provide one of the most usable, nutrient-rich sources of protein. They are also highly digestible for anyone needing extra protein and having digestive problems. The American Heart Association recommends limiting egg yolks to three per week.

2 eggs
Water
1 teaspoon vinegar

Place eggs in water to cover. Add the vinegar. Bring water to boil. Boil eggs 10 minutes. Cool. Refrigerate.
Calories per egg: 75 (0 percent from carbohydrate, 38 percent from protein, 62 percent from fat)

PUMPKIN PUDDING

SERVES 3

*This pudding is a pungent pick-me-up. Pumpkins are
very high in vitamin A, and the molasses adds iron
while sweetening. Spoon the pudding into a container
and take it to work as a one-dish lunch.*

1 16-ounce can pumpkin
1 teaspoon vanilla extract
1 cup skim milk
1 egg
1 egg white
1/2 teaspoon nutmeg
1/2 teaspoon cinnamon
1/2 teaspoon allspice
1/4 cup molasses
   Nonstick spray or vegetable oil

Combine all ingredients except oil and mix thoroughly.
Coat an 8 x 8″ baking dish with nonstick spray or rub
on a thin layer of oil. Pour in the pumpkin mixture. Bake
at 350°F. for 40 minutes.
Calories per serving: 182 (70 percent from carbohydrate,
20 percent from protein, 10 percent from fat)

SPINACH

*For convenience, pre-prepare a pound of spinach for a
variety of uses all week. Although spinach is one of the
dark green leafy vegetables that does not release much of
its calcium, it is a good source of many other nutrients,
including iron and fiber. Unlike many of the greens, spinach can also be enjoyed raw as a salad as well as cooked.
Top with hummus salad dressing and chopped egg.*

1 pound spinach

Clean, wash, and dry the spinach. Remove stems and
large veins. Place in a bowl, cover, and refrigerate.

Week Three

No recipes, no cooking; all prepared foods

Monday

BREAKFAST: 1 bagel spread with ¼ cup low-fat cottage cheese, topped with 1 tablespoon toasted sesame seeds
              ½ cup orange juice

LUNCH: Salad (from salad bar with greens and plain vegetables, 3 ounces water-packed tuna, 1 tablespoon prepared dressing) Many supermarkets now have salad bars. Otherwise, use lettuce, sliced carrots, and sliced mushrooms or any other vegetables you may have on hand.
              ½ medium round whole-wheat Syrian bread
              1 cup 1-percent milk

DINNER: 1 Weight Watchers chicken nuggets (cook two packages; use one for lunch tomorrow)
              1 cup frozen mixed vegetables
              1½ cups pasta salad (can be purchased at supermarket salad bars or deli counters)

SNACK: ½ cup low-fat frozen yogurt

Tuesday

BREAKFAST: 1½ cups nonsugared dry cereal
              1 cup 1-percent milk
              1 banana

LUNCH: Leftover chicken nuggets
              1 oatmeal cookie

DINNER: 1 cup Walnut Acres cream of pea soup heated with 2 ounces lean ham and ½ cup frozen carrots

Tuesday (continued)

6 whole-wheat crackers

SNACK: 1 medium bunch grapes

Wednesday

BREAKFAST: 2 slices toast with 2 tablespoons peanut butter

½ cup grapefruit juice

LUNCH: 1½ cups pasta salad (from salad bar)

2 ounces low-fat cheese (sometimes found cut up at salad bars)

1 banana

DINNER: 1 Legume manicotti florentine

1 cup fruit cocktail (packed in juice)

SNACK: 1 cup 1-percent milk

2 oatmeal cookies

Thursday

BREAKFAST: 1⅓ cups shredded-wheat cereal

1 cup 1-percent milk

2 tablespoons raisins

LUNCH: Turkey sandwich (2 slices whole-grain bread, 3 ounces sliced turkey, lettuce, tomato slices)

1 apple

DINNER: 2 cups Hain vegetarian vegetable soup with ⅓ cup chickpeas and 2 tablespoons grated Parmesan cheese

½ cup croutons

SNACK: 2 Wasa crackers with 1 ounce low-fat cheese

Friday

BREAKFAST: 1 cup 1-percent milk

½ cup granola

½ cup fruit cocktail

LUNCH: Vegetarian sandwich (pita bread with tofu spread, shredded cabbage,

Friday (cont.)

sprouts,1 slice mozzarella cheese, 1 tablespoon salad dressing)

1 medium bunch grapes

DINNER: 1 package Gorton's shrimp scampi heated with 1 cup frozen cauliflower

SNACK: 1 toasted whole-wheat English muffin spread with 1 teaspoon margarine

Saturday

BRUNCH: 3 bagel halves topped with 2 tablespoons almond butter, ½ cup low-fat cottage cheese

1 cup pineapple chunks

DINNER: 1 Tuna salad (4 ounces water-packed tuna, lettuce, 1 tomato, cucumber, green pepper, grated radish, 1 tablespoon salad dressing, ½ cup croutons)

1 slice rye bread

1 banana

½ cup ice cream (it's the weekend!)

SNACK: ¾ cup cold cereal and ½ cup 1-percent milk

Sunday

BRUNCH: 1½ cups raisin bran with 1 cup strawberries (fresh in season, or frozen)

1 cup 1-percent milk

1 slice toast with 1 tablespoon almond butter

½ cup fruit juice

DINNER: Amy's or Fantastic Foods macaroni and cheese (available in health food stores)

Green salad with ½ cup canned beets, ⅓ cup chickpeas, 1 tablespoon salad dressing

SNACK: 1 piece fresh fruit

Week Four (All Fresh Foods)

Naturally, home-cooked meals will take more time to prepare. To cut down on preparation time, soups and main dishes can be cooked in a batch and used later in the week. Recipes for soups can be doubled and frozen.

Monday

BREAKFAST: 1½ cups nonsugared dry cereal
              ½ banana
              1 cup 1 percent milk
LUNCH: 1 serving Indian Pudding*
              1 orange
              12 nuts of choice
DINNER: 1 serving Minestrone Soup,* heated with
              1 ounce feta cheese and topped with 2
              tablespoons Parmesan cheese
              6 Ak-mak crackers or other whole-wheat
              cracker
SNACK: Grapes, approximately 16

Tuesday

BREAKFAST: 1 cup oatmeal*
              1 cup 1-percent milk
LUNCH: Hummus sandwich, 1 serving (approx-
              imately ¼ cup) Hummus,* shredded
              lettuce, sliced cucumber, and sprouts
              on whole-wheat pita bread
              1 pear
DINNER: Baked Fish Paprika*
              Italian-Style Broccoli*
              Milk and Wheat Sesame Bread* (large
              piece, approximately 2 ounces)
SNACK: 3 large whole-wheat pretzels
              1 cup fresh fruit salad

Wednesday

BREAKFAST: 2 slices toast with 2 tablespoons peanut
butter
1/2 grapefruit

LUNCH: Minestrone Soup*
2 whole-wheat crackers with 1 ounce
low-fat cheese
1 small banana

DINNER: Steak (low-fat cut, such as tenderloin
or flank; 3 ounces, broiled)
Fake French Fries*
Chinese Greens*

SNACK: 4 ounces 1-percent milk
2 graham crackers

Thursday

BREAKFAST: 1 cup oatmeal*
1 cup low-fat milk
1/2 cup fresh fruit salad (leftover)

LUNCH: Sardine sandwich (3 ounces sardines
packed in water, sliced tomato, lettuce, 1
teaspoon Miracle Whip, on rye bread)

DINNER: Greens with Bean Soup*
Pasta with Oriental Peanut Sauce*
Indian Pudding,* topped with plain
low-fat yogurt, if desired

SNACK: 1 pear

Friday

BREAKFAST: Toasted whole-wheat bagel, spread with
low-fat cottage cheese and sprinkled with
toasted sesame seeds
1 pear

LUNCH: Green salad with sprouts (use romaine,
red leaf, or green leaf lettuce; do not
use iceberg, because it has minimal fiber and nutrients)

Friday (*continued*)

2 ounces feta cheese
Hummus Dressing*
½ medium round whole-wheat bread

DINNER: Chicken Curry*
½ cup brown rice
Indian Cauliflower*
Broiled Grapefruit*

SNACK: 1 small banana
1 cup nonfat flavored or plain yogurt

Saturday

BRUNCH: 2 ounces Quick Maple-Raisin Loaf*
1 cup plain low-fat yogurt, topped with fruit, raisins, and ¼ cup Grape-Nuts

DINNER: Pasta with Oriental Peanut Sauce*
Chinese Greens*
1 large bunch grapes

SNACK: Sandwich of homemade bread and leftover Fish Paprika

Sunday

BRUNCH: 3 slices whole-wheat toast with 2 scrambled eggs (Scramble the eggs in 1 teaspoon margarine or butter. If you prefer butter, use it. The most important thing with fat is the portion size, so carefully measure 1 teaspoon. It is doubtful that cholesterol will be a problem using this style of menu, and satisfaction is important.)
1 fresh orange

DINNER: Greens with Bean Soup*
Milk and Wheat Sesame Bread,* spread with Hummus or 2 ounces low-fat cheese
Quick Maple-Raisin Loaf* topped with Fruited Frosting*

SNACK: 1 apple

Recipes for Week Four

INDIAN PUDDING

SERVES 8

Sweet-tasting foods are naturally satisfying. This low-sugar and low-fat pudding can be a complete meal that is rich in protein and fiber. It provided the basics for the American Indians and can do the same for us.

1 quart 1-percent milk
1/3 cup cornmeal
2 tablespoons butter or margarine
1/2 cup molasses
1/2 teaspoon salt
1/2 teaspoon cinnamon
1/4 teaspoon cloves
1/4 teaspoon ginger
1/8 teaspoon allspice
1/8 teaspoon nutmeg
1 egg
1 egg white

1. Heat milk to boiling. Reduce heat and add cornmeal. Cook, stirring, until thick, about 15 minutes.
2. Remove from heat and add butter, molasses, and seasonings. Stir to mix completely and until butter melts.
3. Beat egg and egg white together, add to mixture, and stir thoroughly. Pour into 9 x 12″ greased baking dish.
4. Bake at 300°F. for 1½ hours.

Calories per serving: 155 (53 percent from carbohydrate, 18 percent from protein, 29 percent from fat)

MINESTRONE SOUP

SERVES 4 GENEROUSLY

The beans and pasta in this soup make it a complete protein. Serve with bread and low-fat cheese and top with grated Parmesan, if desired. Alone, it can be a very filling and low-calorie, nutrient-rich meal.

1 onion, sliced
1 tablespoon plus 1 teaspoon olive oil
1 8-ounce can Italian tomatoes
6 to 8 cups water
1 tablespoon chopped fresh parsley or 1 teaspoon dried
2 teaspoons oregano
2 teaspoons basil
1/2 teaspoon freshly ground pepper
1/2 teaspoon salt (optional)
2 cups (1 19-ounce can) kidney beans, drained
4 cups assorted vegetables (celery, carrots, green pepper, broccoli, cabbage)
4 ounces whole-wheat pasta

Sauté the onion in the oil. Add tomatoes, water, and seasonings. Stir and bring to a simmer. Add beans, celery, carrots, and green pepper and cook for 15 minutes, uncovered. Add broccoli and pasta and cook another 10 minutes. Add cabbage, cover, and cook an additional 15 minutes.
Calories per serving: 300 (68 percent from carbohydrate, 17 percent from protein, 15 percent from fat)

OATMEAL

SERVES 2

Oatmeal is a high-fiber dish that can be cooked in advance and reheated for a quick meal or snack. It can be served with milk, juice, or yogurt. A hot cereal is a good source of fast energy.

Prepare 2 cups of oatmeal according to package directions. Add 2 tablespoons raisins and ½ banana, sliced, while cooking. Refrigerate and reheat portions as needed in the microwave or on stove top. Add a little water when reheating. Calories per serving: 200 (89 percent from carbohydrate, 11 percent from protein, 0 percent from fat)

HUMMUS

SERVES 8

Hummus is basically a bean spread. Similar spreads can be made with kidney beans, split peas, or lentils, usually leaving out the tahini. Spread on crackers or bread or use as a dip for a tasty low-fat source of protein.
Beans are the backbone of vegetarian diets.

 1 cup raw chickpeas or 1 20-ounce can chickpeas
    Juice of 1 lemon
 1 clove garlic, crushed (optional)
½ teaspoon cumin
¼ teaspoon paprika
¼ teaspoon dry mustard
½ cup water
 2 tablespoons sesame tahini
    Salt and freshly ground pepper to taste

1. If using raw chickpeas, soak overnight. Boil until soft, approximately 2 hours (yields 3½ to 4 cups). Or use the canned chickpeas, which is a lot easier (you can rinse them to remove sodium).
2. Blend the chickpeas, lemon juice, garlic, seasonings, and half the water in a blender or food processor. Mix in the tahini by hand. Gradually add the remaining water for an easy spreading consistency. Add salt and pepper to taste.

Calories per serving: 100 (57 percent from carbohydrate, 18 percent from protein, 25 percent from fat)

BAKED FISH PAPRIKA

(Specifically Good For Skin)

SERVES 4

This is a low-fat adaptation of an old family favorite that we used to make with sour cream in the good old days. Serve with rice or boiled potatoes and a green salad.

    2   large onions, thinly sliced
    2   carrots, coarsely grated
 1 1/2   pounds white fish fillets
         Salt and white pepper to taste
    1   teaspoon dried dill
    2   teaspoons paprika
    1   cup plain low-fat yogurt

Arrange onion slices over the bottom of a 9 x 12 " baking dish. Sprinkle the carrots over the onions. Lay the fish over the onions. Sprinkle the fish with the salt, pepper, and dill. Spread the yogurt over the fish. Sprinkle the top with paprika. Bake at 350°F. for 30 minutes.
Calories per serving: 295 (9 percent from carbohydrate, 57 percent from protein, 34 percent from fat)

ITALIAN BROCCOLI

SERVES 4

Broccoli is one of the cruciferous vegetables recommended to reduce cancer risk. It is also one of the nondairy foods that are rich in calcium, and all in all one of the most nutritious foods.
Broccoli is versatile, and this Italian version blends well with meats, fish, or Italian food. The finished dish is crisp—and if you prefer it softer, add another tablespoon of water and cook it an additional 5 minutes.

1 medium head broccoli
1 tablespoon olive oil
2 cloves garlic, finely minced
  Freshly ground pepper to taste
2 tablespoons red wine vinegar
2 tablespoons water

1. Wash, dry, and trim the broccoli, and cut into small florets, leaving stems 1 to 2" long.
2. Heat the oil in a large skillet and sauté the garlic until it starts to soften and renders its odor, approximately 1 minute.
3. Add the broccoli and sauté for 5 minutes, stirring frequently.
4. Add the remaining ingredients, lower the heat, cover, and cook until broccoli is soft, stirring once or twice, approximately 10 minutes.

Calories per serving: 90 (45 percent from carbohydrate, 18 percent from protein, 37 percent from fat)

MILK AND WHEAT SESAME BREAD

SERVES 40

This delicious bread will make your house smell like a bakery. The flour mixture can vary to include more whole-wheat flour, if desired. I use this mixture for a lighter texture for parties and holidays. Spread with hummus or cheese and call it lunch.

1½ cups milk
¼ cup (½ stick) butter
4¼ cups all-purpose unbleached flour
2 cups whole-wheat flour
¼ cup sugar
2 teaspoons salt
1 package yeast
2 eggs
1 egg white, slightly beaten
1 tablespoon water
  Sesame seeds

1. Over medium heat, heat the milk and let the butter melt in it. Milk should be warm but not hot.
2. Combine 1 cup of the white flour with the sugar, salt, and yeast.
3. Combine the flour mixture, the 2 eggs, and the milk-butter mixture.
4. Start stirring in the remaining flour, holding out the last ¼ cup until the dough no longer sticks to the sides of the bowl.
5. Turn the dough out onto a lightly floured board and knead briefly.
6. Place the dough in a covered bowl in a large pan containing about 2″ of hot tap water. Let stand for 1 hour, or until approximately double in bulk.
7. Punch down the dough and knead for 10 minutes, using more flour if the dough sticks to the board. Form the dough into 2 large loaves or 4 small ones, and place on a greased baking pan. At this point, some of the loaves can be frozen for future use.
8. Let the dough rise again as before, for 1 hour.
9. Brush the egg white mixed with water over the tops of the loaves and sprinkle generously with sesame seeds.
10. Bake at 375°F. for 35 to 40 minutes. Bread is done when it sounds hollow when tapped on the bottom. Turn out onto a rack to cool.

Calories per serving: 100 (66 percent from carbohydrates, 13 percent from protein, 21 percent from fat)

FAKE FRENCH FRIES

SERVES 4

Once you eat these, you will wonder why anyone ever ate the greasy ones—"fakes" are crispy and tasty without the grease. Serve with meals to your family and don't say a word about "fake." Potatoes are also one of the best sources of vitamin C, and a good satisfying low-calorie snack.

1 pound white potatoes, scrubbed and dried
2 teaspoons safflower oil
  Salt (optional)

Preheat oven to 425°F. Cut potatoes into french fries and pat them dry with paper towels. Rub the potatoes thoroughly with oil, using your hands to coat all surfaces. Bake in a shallow baking dish or on a cookie sheet for 30 minutes. Salt lightly, if desired.
Calories per serving: 100 (66 percent from carbohydrate, 8 percent from protein, 26 percent from fat)

CHINESE GREENS

SERVES 4 GENEROUSLY

Greens are virtually calorie-free, providing many of the same nutrients we get from meats. They are rich in B vitamins, iron, and zinc, and are one of the most neglected foods in the American diet. My Asian clients often eat greens at every meal.

2 large bunches greens (select from the list on page 183)
1 tablespoon plus 1 teaspoon safflower or canola oil
2 cloves garlic, finely chopped
1" cube fresh ginger, peeled and finely chopped
2 tablespoons light soy sauce
2 tablespoons balsamic vinegar
2 tablespoons water
1 tablespoon sesame seeds (optional)

1. Wash, dry, trim, and chop the greens.
2. Heat the oil in a large skillet or wok. Sauté the garlic and ginger together, approximately 2 minutes, until the garlic just begins to turn golden. Add the greens, stirring intermittently as they sauté, until they start to wilt, approximately 5 minutes. Add the soy sauce,

vinegar, and water and cover. Cook until greens appear cooked, approximately 5 minutes.
3. Add sesame seeds.
Calories per serving: 50 (100 percent from fat—all from sautéing oil and soy sauce)

HUMMUS SALAD DRESSING

This low-fat dressing hugs the vegetables, giving the salad flavor and added nourishment.

Cautiously add 2 parts water and 1 part white vinegar to your chosen amount of hummus until it reaches the consistency of a creamy salad dressing. Add toasted sesame seeds, if desired. (One-quarter cup of hummus will yield approximately ½ cup of salad dressing.)

GREENS WITH BEAN SOUP

SERVES 4 GENEROUSLY

This soup has a pleasingly thick consistency—it is almost a stew. Make a double portion of it so you can keep some in the freezer. Reheat with any available vegetables and serve as a side dish, or serve it with crackers and/or bread as a main course. Add feta cheese or grated Parmesan for added protein and flavor.

2 tablespoons olive oil
2 leeks, washed, trimmed, and chopped (Use only half of the green part and be sure to separate leaves well and wash individually to ensure thorough cleaning)
2 stalks celery, diced
8 cups water
3 tablespoons regular or low-sodium vegetable or chicken bouillon
1 bay leaf
1 teaspoon dried basil

  1½ cups cooked beans
   1 cup brown rice, washed and drained
   4 cups greens, or 1 large bunch, washed and chopped

1. Heat the oil in a wok or large frying pan and sauté the leeks and celery for 10 minutes, stirring frequently.
2. Add the water, bouillon, bay leaf, basil, beans, and rice and simmer, covered, for 30 minutes.
3. Add the greens and continue to simmer for 15 more minutes.

Calories per serving: 290 (62 percent from carbohydrate, 15 percent from protein, 23 percent from fat)

CHICKEN CURRY

(Specifically Good For Skin)

SERVES 4

Chicken (white meat and no skin) has less saturated fat than most meats. Serve this delicious curry with brown rice and top it with yogurt. The curry flavoring is strong and you may want to adjust the amount, starting with 1 tablespoon and adding more as desired.

    1 tablespoon olive oil
    1 medium onion, diced
    1 medium clove garlic, finely chopped
    1 pound boned chicken breast, cut into 1 x ½" cubes
   ½ cup chicken broth (use salt-free, if desired)
1 to 2 tablespoons curry powder
   ½ banana, sliced
    1 medium apple, peeled, diced, and cored
    1 fresh tomato, diced

Heat the oil in a large skillet and sauté the onion for 3 minutes. Add the garlic and continue sautéing until garlic renders its odor, approximately 1 minute. Add the chicken and cook, stirring, until all the surfaces start to brown, approximately 3

minutes. Add the broth, curry, banana, apple, and tomato.
Mix, lower heat, cover, and cook 15 minutes.
Calories per serving: 230 (14 percent from carbohydrate, 44
percent from protein, 42 percent from fat)

INDIAN CAULIFLOWER

SERVES 4

*This cruciferous vegetable takes on an exotic taste with
these Indian seasonings.*

 1 large head cauliflower
 2 tablespoons safflower or canola oil
 2 teaspoons whole fennel seeds
 1 tablespoon whole mustard seeds
 1 tablespoon whole cumin seeds
 1 tablespoon finely minced garlic
¼ teaspoon turmeric
½ teaspoon salt
½ cup water

1. Wash and dry the cauliflower. Cut into small florets.
2. Heat the oil in a large skillet. Add the fennel seeds,
   mustard seeds, and cumin seeds and sauté until the
   mustard seeds start to pop, about 1 minute.
3. Quickly add the garlic and continue cooking, stirring
   until the garlic starts to brown, about another minute.
   Add the turmeric and mix through.
4. Add the cauliflower, salt, and water, and stir. Cover and
   cook for 10 minutes, stirring occasionally. The cauliflower should be crisp, but if it is still hard, turn off the
   heat and cover the pan for another 5 to 7 minutes.
5. Stir once more to coat the cauliflower with the seasonings.
Calories per serving: 100 (24 percent from carbohydrate, 10
percent from protein, 66 percent from fat—the high percentage from fat is because the oil is so high in calories in relationship to the cauliflower. The actual amount of fat is 7 grams.
You can try this with less oil.)

BROILED GRAPEFRUIT

SERVES 4

If you're not happy without a sweet at the end of a meal, this recipe can satisfy you with no fat and minimal sugar.

4 teaspoons maple syrup
2 grapefruits, halved and sectioned

Spread 1 teaspoon maple syrup on each grapefruit half. Place 5 inches under a preheated broiler and broil for 5 minutes. Serve immediately.
Calories per serving: 55 (all from carbohydrate)

PASTA WITH ORIENTAL PEANUT SAUCE

SERVES 6

This dish can replace meat to provide a satisfying, protein-rich vegetarian meal. Including several vegetarian meals each week cuts down on the intake of fats, particularly saturated fats. This dish also has a lot of fiber and is rich in many nutrients. Since the fat rises to the top of natural peanut butter, you can reduce the fat content by pouring this oil off and turning the jar upside down over paper towels for several hours so more oil will drain out.

SAUCE
 2 tablespoons chopped and peeled fresh ginger
 1 teaspoon coriander
 1 tablespoon peanut oil
 ½ cup natural peanut butter (no added fats or sweeteners)
 ¼ cup soy sauce (you can use light soy sauce for less sodium)
 1 teaspoon sugar
 3 tablespoons rice vinegar
 ½ cup hot water

NOODLES

½ pound flat thin somen noodles
1 tablespoon oriental sesame oil
3 fresh scallions, chopped, with greens (excluding tips)

To make the sauce, place all the ingredients in a food processor. If you are using a blender, omit the peanut butter and work it in by hand afterward. If you prefer the sauce thinner, add more hot water. The sauce should be a thick pouring consistency.

To make the noodles, bring a large pot of water to a boil and add the noodles. Cook until tender, about 10 minutes. Drain. Toss the noodles with the sesame oil and the peanut butter sauce, and top with the scallions.

Calories per serving: 460 (33 percent from carbohydrate, 13 percent from protein, 54 percent from fat)

QUICK MAPLE-RAISIN LOAF

SERVES 8

If you love dessert, this one provides good food that's a piece of cake, literally.

2 eggs or Fleischmann's Egg Beaters
1 cup whole milk
1 tablespoon safflower or canola oil
¼ cup maple syrup
3 cups whole-wheat pastry flour
2 teaspoons baking powder
1 teaspoon salt
¼ cup raisins
¼ cup chopped walnuts

Beat eggs, milk, oil, and syrup together. Mix in flour, baking powder, and salt. Fold in raisins and nuts. Pour into a greased loaf pan and bake at 350°F. for 1 hour, or until the loaf just starts to separate from the sides of the pan.

Calories per serving: 275 (63 percent from carbohydrate, 14 percent from protein, 23 percent from fat)

FRUITED FROSTING

SERVES 4

This mixture adds glamour when poured over fruit, cake, or cereal.

1 cup plain low-fat yogurt
1 cup diced fruit (for summer use strawberries and raspberries; for winter use frozen berries)

Blend ingredients in a blender or food processor.
Calories per serving: 46 (70 percent from carbohydrates, 20 percent from protein, 10 percent from fat)

Even if you follow these menus as best as you can for a month, there will still be the week when you have not shopped and have not batch-cooked a thing. By keeping a full house of nonperishable foods, you can put together fairly healthful and tasty meals in minutes.

FOR THE PANTRY

*Walnut Acres canned products**

Chicken stew	Beef stew	Ground beef
Beans & hot dogs	Braised beef hash	Chicken rice soup
Chili con carne	Mild turkey chili	Cream of water
Vegetable beef soup	Chicken corn soup	cress and potato
Lentil soup	Black bean soup	soup
French onion soup	Noodles in ground beef	Tomato rice soup

(*Quality Foods: Catalog available 800-433-3998)

Other foods
Raisins   Health Valley vege- Almonds
                           tarian

FOR THE PANTRY (CONT.)

Trail mix
Smoked oysters
Baked beans
Kidney beans
Light canned fruit
Health Valley lentil
  chili

Peanuts
Nonfat dry milk
Salmon, canned
Bottled spaghetti
  sauce
Miso soup mix

Water-packed sar
  dines
Vegetarian chili
Chickpeas
Light canned fruit
  in six-pack

FOR THE REFRIGERATOR

Natural peanut butter
Whole-wheat crackers
(refrigerator keeps them
  fresh)
Grated Parmesan cheese
Toasted sesame seeds
Eggs
Pepper salad
Nonfat plain yogurt
Low-fat milk (prefer
  1 percent)

Feta cheese
Natural almond butter
Low-fat cheese—e.g., cottage

(available part-skim or all-skim)
Corn or wheat tortilla
Herring (in the jar)
Mexican salsa
Maple syrup or light maple
  syrup

FREEZER

A huge selection of frozen dinners that go from freezer
to microwave produces a meal in five minutes. Many of
these brands are low in fat and approximately 300 calories per meal. Most are high in sodium. Healthy Choice
is a brand that contains only moderate amounts of sodium. Also, check your local health food store for other
product lines with moderate sodium.

Some concern has been expressed recently regarding
the safety of the packaging of microwavable foods. Some

of the packaging chemicals may be absorbed by the food when heated. While this is under investigation, I recommend glass or Corning materials for heating in the microwave. I find it easy to remove foods from their containers onto a dinner plate to be heated uncovered, although heating directions suggest keeping foods covered. If you find covering dries out the meal, place the food in a glass bowl so the top can be covered without direct contact with the food.

Following are some items to try. Stock up and rest assured—you will now always be able to produce a meal on those "just too busy" days.

FROZEN DINNERS

This is a sampling. Check the frozen food section of your supermarket or health food store.

Healthy Choice: Chicken Parmigiana Dinner, Salisbury Steak Dinner, Turkey Dinner

Stouffer's Lean Cuisine: Zucchini Lasagna, Chicken Tenderloin in Barbecue Sauce, Oriental Beef, Filet of Fish Divan

Weight Watchers: Pizza, Lasagna, Veal Parmesan, Imperial Chicken

Budget Gourmet Slim Selects: Sirloin Beef in Herb Sauce, Chicken au Gratin

HEALTH FOOD STORE PRODUCTS

Jaclyn: Grilled Tofu in Peanut Sauce

Legume: Tofu Manicotti, Lasagna, Shells

Freezer Stock Items

VEGETABLES: Bagged vegetables are easy to portion. Keep a large variety of vegetables in the freezer and drop them into soup, or add to a microwave dinner. Frozen vegetables are of good quality and are sometimes fresher than fresh, when produce is shipped long distances.

Try collards, black-eyed peas, okra, mustard greens, mashed turnip, cauliflower, mixed vegetables, butternut squash, broccoli florets, peas, Italian green beans, carrots, corn, stew vegetables, lima beans, asparagus, pea pods, french-cut green beans, whole onions, corn on the cob. There are also vegetables prepared in sauces, but watch for extra fat here.

BREADS: Keep a variety of whole grains on hand: pumpernickel, rye, and an assortment of whole-wheat choices, bread, pita bread, bagels, and English muffins. They defrost quickly and can go from the freezer directly into the toaster.

OTHER ITEMS: Cheese blintzes, blueberry blintzes, cooked rice, baked potato.

PUTTING TOGETHER SOME MEALS

You've just come into the house at 7:30 P.M. and nothing is prepared for dinner. From your full cupboard you can combine a meal that is high in carbohydrate, low in fat, and moderate in calories. And you can do it *fast*. A microwave oven produces a meal in minutes, a fact much appreciated by the American public. Three quarters of American homes are now equipped with microwaves, and one-stop microwavable foods are a $2 billion industry. If you are one of the 25 percent still holding out on this type of cooking, adjust the recipes as follows: Instead of using the microwave, assemble the recipe, place in a baking dish, and heat in the oven at 350°F. for approximately 30 minutes.

CHILI CON CARNE

½ cup canned chili con carne
 1 tortilla
    Frozen mustard greens
    Salsa

Spread chili on tortilla. Roll and place on dinner plate. Add mustard greens. Microwave on high for 3 minutes. Serve with salsa.

TURKEY CHILI

½ cup canned turkey chili
1 tortilla
1 ounce part-skim mozzarella cheese
½ cup frozen peas

Spread chili on tortilla. Top with cheese and peas. Heat in microwave on high for 3 minutes.

ITALIAN NOODLES AND BEEF

1 cup Walnut Acres noodles in ground beef
1 tablespoon Parmesan cheese
1 cup Italian green beans

Arrange on plate and microwave on high for 4 minutes.

QUICK RAVIOLI

4 frozen ravioli
1 small jar spaghetti sauce
1 cup frozen broccoli
¼ cup skim-milk ricotta

Boil ravioli until tender. Meanwhile, remove the top from the jar of spaghetti sauce and place in microwave. Place frozen broccoli in a bowl with 1 tablespoon water. Microwave on high for 5 minutes. Serve ravioli with sauce, broccoli on the side, and ricotta on top.

TOMATO-RICE SOUP WITH BROCCOLI AND CHEESE

1 can tomato-rice soup
½ cup frozen broccoli
2 ounces feta cheese

Heat soup on stove top with broccoli and cheese for approximately 10 minutes.

HERRING AND VEGETABLES

½ package Birds Eye Dijon vegetables
2 ounces herring
1 slice dark bread

Heat vegetables in microwave for 4 minutes. Serve with herring and bread.

SALMON-MISO DINNER

1 package miso soup mix
1 package frozen kale
½ cup salmon mixed with 1 tablespoon low-calorie mayonnaise
2 slices rye bread

Prepare soup on stove top with kale, approximately 15 minutes. Serve with salmon and bread prepared as a sandwich.

YOGURT SUNDAE

1 cup plain nonfat yogurt
½ cup trail mix
1 cup canned fruit

Put yogurt in a bowl, arrange the fruit around the edges, and sprinkle the trail mix on top.

SANDWICHES FOR LUNCH

Quick-to-prepare sandwiches are high in bulk, taste, and nourishment, and can be made simply by having the right sandwich fillings on hand. Sandwiches can be made on a variety of whole-grain breads that have been kept in the freezer. The frozen bread will defrost by lunch. Perishable sandwiches need to be refrigerated until lunch, since these foods can grow bacteria at room temperature after two hours. One way to do this is to bag your lunch along with a freezer ice pack (purchased in hardware stores).

SANDWICH FILLINGS

Vegetables	Low-fat Protein	Flavorings
Chopped spinach	Water-packed sardines	Toasted sesame seeds
Sprouts		Chopped walnuts
Sliced mushrooms	Water-packed tuna fish	Toasted sunflower seeds
Diced tomato		Marinated peppers
Chopped cucumber	Low-fat cheese	Pepper salad
Zucchini	Hummus	Onion relish
Grated carrots	Bean spreads	
Shredded cabbage	Chili	
Cooked asparagus	Tofu	

Choose one item from each list. Mix and match for a lunch that has variety and is healthy and satisfying. Add a glass of milk or yogurt for a fully rounded meal. A new product on the market that could be added here nicely is Frulait, an 8-ounce drink made of fruit juice and yogurt.

SWEET TREATS

Liking sweets is natural. Newborn infants are drawn to this taste, which they find in mother's milk, whereas other tastes, such as salt, are acquired. After avoiding salt for a time, when you do eat something salty you no longer care for the taste. This is not the case with sweets. You could avoid them for years and then still love your favorite pastry at first bite, as though you had never been away.

Calories in dessert come chiefly from the fat rather than the sugar. For instance, a piece of apple pie is approximately 450 calories, with more than 300 of those calories in the crust. The filling is actually a bargain, calorically speaking.

Many products now coming onto the market are low-fat sweets. Nutritionally, there is nothing particularly good about them, but there is nothing particularly bad, either, and they may be a good way to satisfy a sweet tooth without having a lot of fat. Weight Watchers carries a line of frozen desserts and Entenmann's offers low-fat cookies and cakes, while a wide variety of low-fat frozen yogurts and ice milks, for a low-fat ice-cream-like snack, have the nutritional value of milk, although they do have added sugar.

WHERE'S THE FAT?

Any recipe that appeals to you can usually be redesigned with much less fat than the original. This not only cuts calories but, more important, cuts fat calories. The following are two examples of adapted recipes that suit updated healthful tastes:

HOT CREAMED PASTA WITH MUSHROOMS

SERVES 4

This recipe is off to a good start, healthwise. To decrease the fat content even more, you can use low-fat (2-percent) cottage cheese and nonfat yogurt.

- ½ pound fettuccine noodles
- ½ pound mushrooms, sliced
- 2 teaspoons butter
- 1 teaspoon olive oil
- 1 large onion, chopped
- 1 large clove garlic, finely chopped
- ½ teaspoon salt
- ½ teaspoon pepper
- 1½ cups cottage cheese
- 1½ cups yogurt

1. In a large pot, bring 3 quarts water to a boil and boil noodles 10 to 15 minutes, until done to desired firmness.
2. Sauté mushrooms in butter and olive oil, approximately 5 minutes, stirring intermittently.
3. Add onion and continue to sauté another 3 minutes, or until onion is translucent.
4. Add garlic and sauté another 3 minutes, or until garlic renders its odor. Remove from heat and season with salt and pepper.
5. Drain noodles and place them in a serving bowl.
6. In a food processor, blend the cottage cheese and the yogurt.
7. Stir cheese mixture into sautéed ingredients and toss with fettuccine.

Original: 400 calories per serving (53 percent from carbohydrate, 22 percent from protein, 25 percent from fat)
Lower-fat version: 320 calories per serving (64 percent from carbohydrate, 21 percent from protein, 15 percent from fat)

ITALIAN CHEESE PIE

SERVES 8

    4 eggs
    1 cup sugar
1 1/2 teaspoons vanilla
1 1/2 pounds ricotta cheese
    3 tablespoons toasted pine nuts

TOPPING
 1/2 cup graham cracker crumbs
    1 tablespoon butter, melted
    1 tablespoon sugar
 1/2 teaspoon cinnamon

Beat together the eggs, sugar, and vanilla. Blend the ricotta into the mixture. Add the pine nuts and mix well. Pour into a 9″ pie plate and bake for 20 minutes at 350°F. Combine graham crackers, butter, sugar, and cinnamon. Sprinkle crumb mixture over top of pie and continue baking another 20 minutes. To revise this standard recipe: Use 2 eggs plus 2 egg whites; change sugar from 1 cup to ½ cup; use all-skim ricotta cheese. If you prefer a creamier and sweeter taste, take a middle ground on this pie. Use part-skim ricotta cheese and reduce sugar to ¾ cup rather than ½ cup.

Standard recipe: 245 calories per serving (53 percent from carbohydrate, 11 percent from protein, 36 percent from fat)

Revised version: 140 calories per serving (60 percent from carbohydrate, 19 percent from protein, 21 percent from fat)

The following chapter takes the same thorough, effective, and convenient approach to daily exercise as I have taken here with food. Combining a balanced diet with daily exercise is an excellent lifelong formula for ensuring both great looks and great health.

CHAPTER 11

Exercise: A Science with Magic

I just bought a music video called "Sweatin' to the Oldies." Most music videos have Jane Fonda. I don't even like to look at them because it reminds me of how fat I am. So this one is Richard Simmons, wearing this old-fashioned swimsuit with his knobby knees sticking out. And all these fat men and women behind him and music from the forties and fifties.

—SANDRA LITTLETON
Fifty-six

When the urge to exercise comes over me, I just lie flat on my back until it passes.

—W. C. FIELDS

Exercise is magic. Physiologically, it is the answer to weight control. It lowers blood pressure, lowers the heart rate, stabilizes blood sugar, elevates mood, improves sleep, and builds bone mass. The list is very long, but the real reason I exercise is for its inexplicable magic.

It's been twenty-five years since I took my first yoga class. I have been in and out of shape a hundred times since then, and I remain amazed at how renewable our bodies are. The yogis say we get a totally new body every six years, with every cell regenerated. That's enough to cause an identity crisis.

During the five years I studied to be a dietitian, I didn't exercise at all. I thought I was hopelessly out of shape. I have since found out that it is never too late to start working out. Studies on monkeys in the past ten years have shown that "lifestyle changes"—which can mean revised diet, revised sleep patterns, and/or revised exercising—can reverse the course of diseases. Arterial plaque, once considered permanent, has been shown to decrease in size following diet and exercise changes. Exercise programs done in nursing homes, along with calcium supplements, have increased bone mass in the elderly. In recent unconfirmed studies, exercise was shown to increase the body's own TPA (tissue plasminogen activator), a potent blood-clot buster. Any amount of exercise has impact. A minimum amount, below which no benefits accrued, was once thought to be required to produce cardiovascular benefits, but recent research shows that even small amounts of exercise help. In fact, the most valuable part of exercise is the first twelve minutes of the workout.

EXECISE AND WEIGHT

How *much* we eat does not have that much to do with how much we weigh. We all know someone who weighs 250 pounds and has been dieting all her life. She says she hardly eats anything and she is telling the truth. Conversely, if you know someone who eats like a horse but never gains weight, chances are they do, or *once did*, exercise.

Keeping an ideal body weight may be the most important health measure you take in life. When weight goes down, along with it goes blood pressure, cholesterol levels, triglycerides, and blood sugars. Obesity is the major risk factor in uterine cancers and a risk for all cancers. I have worked with many people who eliminated the taking of otherwise necessary medicines by bringing their weight into an ideal range.

Each body has a basic way of handling food. As mentioned in Chapter Nine, part of this handling of food has to do with the body's percentage of muscle mass versus fat. Dieting encourages the body to *decrease* muscle mass and *increase* fat, *even though weight may go down*.

The only way to build muscle while burning fat is through a combination of aerobic exercise, which burns fat, and weight training, which builds muscle. Weight training can be achieved with actual weights, Nautilus equipment, or a muscle-building system, such as yoga. The fat burned during aerobic exercise is relatively small, but the effect on the overall mechanism (the body) is continuous. The most fat is burned during moderate to slow exercise. Exercising very hard burns sugar and calories but not much fat. The way to speed up the fat-burning adaptation is to spend more time exercising slowly and gently. As you will see, the slow route also provides the greatest mental benefits.

As we exercise, our body fat decreases automatically and our new muscles hold everything in place. Women are designed so that lower body fat will not be reduced until the upper body fat is low enough, so give your body the time it may need to reach any special areas of concern.

EXERCISE AND MOOD

Exercise affects emotions by altering brain chemistry. Researchers have found that moderate-intensity exercise—as opposed to short, high-intensity workouts—lasting at least twenty to thirty minutes produces the greatest increase of blood endorphins, a form of morphine. Norepinephrine, another brain chemical associated with fighting depression, is also increased during exercise.

A friend of mine once said, "I never saw a runner smile." Maybe not during the run but definitely afterward. Covert Bailey, the exercise physiologist, does not recommend running or jogging to people over fifty, although an eighty-year-old woman did run the Boston Marathon in 1989. Nevertheless, walking will produce the same changes in mood.

EXERCISE AND OSTEOPOROSIS

Hip fracture is the second leading cause of accidental death for women aged forty-five to seventy-four. After seventy-five, it is the leading cause. Exercise stimulates the activity of the osteoblasts, the cells that make bone, while slowing down the osteoclasts, the cells that break down bone. Exercise will not make our bones grow larger, but it may make them more dense. Additionally, exercise increases muscle mass, and a heavier layer of muscle protects bones better when falls occur. People who have regularly exercised throughout their lives have fewer bone fractures than those who have not. We used to think that exercise had to be weight-bearing to have benefit on the bone. The skeleton's ability to absorb calcium *is* increased through weight-bearing exercise, but studies have shown that any exercise that tugs and pulls on bones, such as swimming, stimulates calcium deposition. In a study done with the elderly, the bone mineral of the wrist was increased by 3.4 percent as a result of squeezing a tennis ball as hard as possible for 30 seconds a day over 16 weeks. Of course, women with osteoporosis should consult their doctors before beginning any exercise regime.

DO WE OR DON'T WE?

In November 1989 *The Boston Globe* reported on a survey of 160 male and female swimmers, ages forty into their sixties. Those who continued regular exercise had sex lives similar to people in their twenties and thirties.

With exercise as with sex, there often seems to be a lot more talk about it than action. While exercise is big business, with $6 billion spent on running shoes last year, and the virtues of exercise extolled everywhere, only 20 percent of the population has a consistent exercise program in place. The women with whom I spoke were doing a little better than average, at 26 percent. The other

74 percent would like to, plan to, are going to, want to, used to, and will be getting back to it soon.

Evelyn Glenn, the fifty-eight-year-old woman who was amazed that she was still attractive to men when she surfaced after her divorce, was one of the 26 percent who did exercise, with a routine of active aerobics three times a week. Evelyn emphatically stated that the physical and psychological benefits of exercise increased for her as she got older. Even though she claimed not to enjoy exercise that much, skipping a few days left her "achy and cross. The less I feel like doing it now, the more I feel I have to." In response to friends who wonder how she keeps it up, she said, "I don't know how they could *not* exercise!"

Neither do I, considering the benefits. It is just crazy not to. Along with its other regenerative powers, exercise is the one true source of permanent weight maintenance. And it is great for looking good. All that circulation is the best beauty treatment I have found to date. So why not?

WHY NOT?

Many women just "didn't feel like it." "When I get home from work I'm tired and I'm hungry and I just need time to unwind," said Diana Ramsay, the Citicorp VP. "That leaves just the weekend for exercise, and since it can't do me that much good once a week, I'll make it never." She grinned at her conclusion, recognizing that logic such as that had not gotten her where she was professionally.

The comments of others continued with "I haven't felt like it"; "Time is a problem"; "Household responsibilities get in the way."

A favorite recommendation of mine to clients concerned with losing weight was to join a health club. After all, once the money is spent, they would naturally use the place. Linda Meyerhold, a sixty-two-year-old social worker, put that idea to rest when she reported that she has a membership at a spa but never shows up. "My doctor tells me I'm the people those places make their money on."

And yet everyone was planning an exercise program. "There will come a day," Janine Hayes, fifty-one, assured both me and herself. "One day when I will wake up and just get going."

Tess Berkley told a familiar tale of how easily a hard-won exercise regimen can fall by the wayside. The forty-six-year-old nurse said, "I have a system of exercise, and it keeps falling apart. I was running all summer, and I think I stopped after having bad bronchitis. I also got into a new relationship."

I can relate to that one. Once you've got a guy, why bother? Mary Zazzera, known as T, who runs the Today's Woman division of Ford Models, undoubtedly found the best way to avoid exercise. She sent her coach, who is also one of her models, away on a shoot in Europe.

Finally, there was Betty Rogers, a forty-nine-year-old office assistant. "Exercise for the moment is out. I'm not doing anything with exercise." That's telling it like it is!

Is *not* exercising a problem for you? A solution is at hand. Here is what to do:

THE COMBINATION PROGRAM

I recommend combining a variety of aerobic exercise with a yoga routine. After forty, it is important to change exercises to avoid injury from overuse of certain muscle groups. Also, combining activities uses all of the body's muscles for a well-rounded program. And variety means more fun. Try alternating walking, running, bicycling, and rowing.

The system of hatha yoga is a wonderful time-efficient method that emphasizes stretching, breathing, and relaxation. The postures also intensely contract the muscles, bringing the full muscle into active metabolism and use. A paradox of the system is that it is at once gentle and kind to the body while its intensity firms and strengthens very quickly. It is the perfect workout for a busy life, since it can be done anywhere, needs no equipment, and produces a lot of results in a short amount of time.

For all its grace-giving, balancing, and toning qualities, yoga is not aerobic. Combining aerobic exercise with a yoga routine provides the invaluable benefits of both and covers all your exercise needs.

Starting is the hard part, because you immediately feel what poor shape your body is in. You will easily notice if you haven't worked out in a while. You might have imagined you could do more than you can. Don't be discouraged—you will see results soon. Yoga is so gentle, it may seem as though nothing is happening, but the body follows the patterns being set quickly. Many adult education centers and YMCAs offer yoga classes. A class offers the benefit of working with a group and also provides a pure environment away from distractions at home. Since the training of yoga teachers has not been formalized, and the choice of a teacher is often personal, I suggest trying a class to make your own assessment.

In the beginning the effort is greatest and the benefits least. As practice continues, effort becomes less and benefits increase dramatically.

YOGA

The following poses provide a complete yoga session. For a balanced routine, be sure to bend your body in all directions: forward, backward, sideways, twist, and upside down. You can select from these poses according to your needs or use the 5-, 15-, and 30-minute routines provided. I recommend a padded exercise mat for comfort and for protection of the spine. It is best to work with bare feet.

Take a deep breath and relax after each pose. This

deprograms the body before starting the next pose. Listen to your body to know whether it is deprogrammed from the previous pose.

You begin making progress at this point: During the holding part of the poses, your attention should be in two places: on the breath going in and out, and on where your body feels most resistance. You will notice the point of resistance changing, which means the muscles are stretching. Progress is made by your body letting go, not by any force you apply. As you come out of *each position*, take a deep breath, allowing your body to relax before going on. Photographs are included of most of these exercises, especially those that might be difficult to visualize.

Forward Bends

FORWARD STRETCH

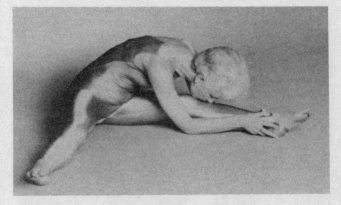

1. Sit straight, with your legs apart.
2. Inhale; stretch your arms up.
3. Exhale; lower your body over your left leg.
4. Natural breath; grasp your leg. Hold for a count of 20.
5. Inhale, sitting straight, stretching your arms up, and bringing them back to your sides.
6. Deep breath; relax. Repeat on the other side.

While holding, stretch from the base of the spine, up each vertebra to your nose, lengthening your torso over your leg.

FORWARD BEND

1. Sit straight, with your legs extended in front; legs are together, hands resting on thighs.
2. Inhale, raising your arms over your head.
3. Exhaling, lower your upper body over your legs, holding your legs wherever you can reach. Hold for a count

of 20. Breathing is natural. As you hold, continue to draw your nose toward your knees.

4. Inhale as you raise to sitting position, stretching your arms over your head.
5. Exhale, returning your hands to your thighs. Take a deep breath.

CHEST EXPANDER

1. Stand straight; extend your arms forward.
2. Inhale; bring your arms behind you. Clasp your hands behind you as high as possible.
3. Exhale; bend forward.

4. Normal breath, draw your clasped arms over your head. Hold for a count of 20.
5. Return to standing; bend back, sliding your clasped hands down the backs of your legs.
6. Return to standing straight.
7. Take a deep breath and relax.

Backward Bends
(Avoid if you have back problems.)

COBRA

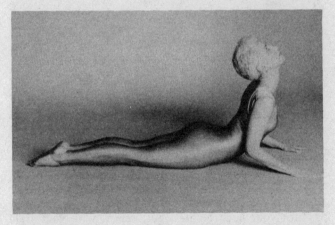

1. Lie on your front, your legs together. Place your hands with palms down on the floor, a thumb's distance from your shoulders. Elbows should be down.
2. Imagining a chainlike structure of spine, slowly raise head, neck, shoulders, chest. Your hips should remain on the floor. Your hands and arms will support you.
3. Hold for a count of 10, advancing eventually to 20. Breathing is natural throughout.
4. Return to prone position, one vertebra at a time.

HALF LOCUST

1. Lie on your front with your legs together. Place your hands palm up under your thighs. Your head should face left.
2. Inhale, lifting your left leg while exhaling.
3. Hold your leg at maximum height, with natural breath, for 15 counts, eventually advancing to 20.
4. Lower your leg; know where your leg is at all times.
5. Turn your head to the right; repeat with your right leg.

LOCUST

1. Lie on your front with your legs together. Place your hands palm up under your thighs.
2. With your chin on the floor, inhale.

3. Exhaling, lift both legs. Hold for a count of 5, eventually advancing to 10 and then 15.
4. Concentrate on breathing in and out, slowly lowering your legs.
5. Take a deep breath.

KNEE STRETCH

1. Lie on your front with your knees a little apart.
2. Bring your left foot up, reaching back to catch it with your left hand.
3. Draw your heel down toward your buttock. Breath is natural.
4. Come to a point of resistance. Hold for a count of 20.
5. Release your foot. Return your leg to the floor.
6. Repeat on the other side.

Be gentle with the joints, because they progress slowly and injure easily.

KNEE LIFT

1. Lie on your front, your knees a little apart.
2. Bring your left foot up, reaching back with both hands to catch the ankle.
3. Lift the knee.

4. Hold for a count of 10. Breathing is natural throughout.
5. Slowly return your knee to the floor.
6. Release your ankle. Return your leg to the floor.

The trick here is to try not to force the knee up, but rather to release the large thigh muscle. It is an exercise in letting go. Allow it to happen. Repeat on the other side.

CAT ROUTINE

This exercise is of *benefit* to bad backs. It flexes the spine in all of its directions without contraction or lifting.

1. Start on hands and knees, with your fingers facing each other.
2. Slowly lower your chin to the floor, followed by slowly lowering your chest to the floor.
3. Lift and arch your back, tucking your chin into your chest (like a cat).
4. Return to straight back.
5. Raise your left leg, bringing your head up and back.
6. Bring your left knee toward you and draw your head down so your forehead meets your knee.
7. Return to hands and knees.
8. Repeat with your right leg.
9. Complete by sitting back on your heels, stretching your hands forward by walking them away on the floor (stretching like a cat).

Side Stretches

TRIANGLE

1. Stand straight, your legs comfortably apart, your arms at your sides.
2. Inhale, bringing your right arm straight up parallel to your ear.
3. Exhale, sliding your left hand down your leg, bending at the side.

4. Resume normal breathing; hold for a count of 10.
5. Slowly return to a standing position, returning your arms to your sides. Repeat on other side.

SIDE STRETCH

1. Stand straight, your legs comfortably apart.
2. Inhale, bringing your left hand over your head and placing it on your right back.
3. Grasp your bent elbow with your right hand.
4. Exhaling, bend to the right, pulling your elbow.
5. Resume normal breathing; hold for a count of 10.
6. Return to a standing position; return your arms to your sides. Repeat on the other side.

Twists

SHARK TWIST

1. Sit with your right leg straight, placing your left foot on the floor, outside of your right knee.
2. Place your left hand firmly on the floor behind you, close to your body.
3. Bring your right elbow against the outside of your left knee, keeping your hand straight up.
4. Use your elbow for leverage, twisting to the left. Look over your left shoulder. Hold for a count of 10. Breathing is shallow and normal throughout. Repeat on the other side.

Put weight on the hand behind your body to decompress spine, which will allow more twist.

Inverted (Upside Down) Poses

SHOULDER STAND

1. Lie on your back, hands by your sides, palm down.
2. Inhale; stretch and then raise your legs up to a 90-degree angle with your torso, exhaling.
3. While breathing normally, continue to roll your body up until your legs are over your head, behind you, and parallel to the floor.
4. Support your hips with your hands.

5. Walk your hands up your back as you raise your legs toward the ceiling, until your entire weight rests on your shoulders. The body is a straight line in the air from the neck to the feet. Hold for a count of 20. Build up to 2 minutes over time.
6. Roll spine, one vertebra at a time, back to a prone position. Lower your legs to a count of 10.
7. Take a deep breath and relax.

Yogis say if you can do only one thing, do the shoulder stand, otherwise known as the Whole Body Pose.

PLOUGH

1. Starting in the shoulder stand, bring your left leg over your head toward the floor behind you. Let gravity do any work to be done and control the action with your abdomen. Hold for a count of 5.
2. Return your leg to shoulder stand, again using abdominal muscles.
3. Repeat with the other leg.
4. Continue lowering one leg at a time until they reach the floor.

5. Then lower both legs at once. Concentrate on abdominal muscles. Place the legs rather than dropping them. Breathing is normal throughout.

HEAD STAND

It is important to do the head stand in steps, without moving to the next step until you have mastered the one before. This may take some time, so it is best to forget the goal and just do the steps. Work in front of the couch to avoid fear.

1. Kneeling, intertwine your fingers, making an equilat-

eral triangle with your hands and elbows on the floor in front of you. The distance between your elbows should be the same as the length of your forearm.

2. Place the back of your head inside your palms and find a comfortable spot for your head on the floor. Straighten your knees and rest on the elbow base, head, and feet. Your rear end is in the air here, and your knees are straight.

3. Walk knees in toward chest, allowing them to bend while the back remains straight. If they do not reach, continue with forward stretches until they do.

4. When knees come comfortably to chest, lift your feet off the floor and come into an upside-down-egg position. Hold here until your balance is secure.

5. The work here is in the abdomen. Raise body up until your knees face the ceiling. Hold here until strength is gained and balance is secure.

6. Continue to raise your feet until you are straight.

That's it. You are standing on your head. Now that you know the pose, the real work begins! Congratulate yourself for getting to this point. (See Exercise Resources, page 319, for books on advanced positions.)

Joint Flexibility

HALF LOTUS

Be very gentle with this, because joints are delicate.

1. Sitting, bring your left foot to rest on your right leg, as far toward the groin as comfortable.

2. Inhale, and with both hands, embrace your knee and draw it toward your body.

3. Exhale, gently easing your knee down toward the floor.

4. Hold at the point of resistance; breathe easily in and out for a count of 10. Repeat on the other side.

Timed Routines

FIVE-MINUTE YOGA ROUTINE

1. Forward Stretch. Roll back to prone position when complete.
2. Shoulder Stand. Relax the shoulders while holding.
3. Forward Bend.
4. Cobra. Complete by sitting back on your heels.

Relax in a prone position for 30 seconds while breathing deeply.

FIFTEEN-MINUTE YOGA ROUTINE

1. Triangle.
2. Forward Stretch.
3. Cat Stretch.
4. Cobra.
4. Half Locust. Complete by sitting back on your heels. Lie flat and relax 30 seconds.
5. Shoulder Stand, advance to
6. Half Plough. (One leg at a time.) Roll down to prone position.
7. Forward Bend.
8. Shark Twist.

Relax flat on your back for one minute. Complete by massaging the temples.

THIRTY MINUTE YOGA ROUTINE

1. Triangle. Keep your arms parallel to your ear.
2. Chest Expander. When done, lie on your front and relax 20 seconds.
3. Cobra.
4. Half Locust.
5. Full Locust.
6. Knee Stretch.

Relax on your back 30 seconds. Draw your knees into your chest to relieve tension.

8. Forward Stretch.
9. Shoulder Stand.
10. Plough on each side, advancing to full plough (both legs at the same time).

Relax 30 seconds.

11. Forward Bend.
12. Half Lotus, twice on each side.
13. Twist.

Relax one minute. Massage your temples and your head.

The benefits of each pose will become clear to you as you do it. The yogis say a flexible spine is the key to a youthful body. You will see strengthening and firming in all muscle groups, and you will experience a grace and flexibility throughout your body. Yoga is also wonderful for stress, and each session should leave you energized and relaxed, a rare combination. There are also claims, though unproven scientifically, that many of the poses have disease-preventing properties.

AEROBICS

The way to tell if an exercise is aerobic is how you feel. If you are warm, breathing heavily, and using most of your muscles for 12 minutes without interruption, the exercise is aerobic. Exercise using fewer muscles, such as walking, requires more time to be aerobic (at least 20 minutes).

Beginners should have a medical checkup before starting an exercise program. Women with osteoporosis will need to have a doctor approve the specific exercise they undertake. Wearing shoes that provide strong support for the feet and cushioning to protect the back and knees is very important. Be sure to replace your shoes according to the manufacturer's recommendation.

I first tried aerobic exercise as a way to get back into shape after I had finished my nutrition degree. I started with walking. Impatiently, I advanced to running, which turned out to be torture, broke my discipline, and sent me back to a warm house to start the process over again. I went through this cycle many, many times. Finally, I settled into a walking program, and after several years, when my walk had evolved to the speed of a slow run, I started to jog. I now jog at the speed of a fast walk.

Many outdoor aerobic exercises are available for beginners: bicycling, cross-country skiing, swimming are only a few. For winter months, beginners can try a stationary bicycle, rowing machine, treadmill, cross-country-ski machine, video aerobics classes, or trampoline. All of these can be done at home, or at a health club along with aerobics classes.

MINIMUM TIME TO PRODUCE AEROBIC EFFECT

12-Minute Minimum	15-Minute Minimum	20-Minute Minimum
Jumping rope	Jogging	Walking
Running in place	Running	Outdoor bicycling
Jumping jacks	Cross-country skiing	Stationary bicycling
Chair stepping	Rowing	Ice skating
	Dancing	Roller skating
	Mini-trampoline	Swimming

From Covert Bailey, *Fit or Fat*

Choose one or, preferably, more inside and outside activities. Variety will be your best protection against injury. I find I get different benefits from different exercises. For instance, walking gives me the best physical feelings of strength and balance, while jogging seems to leave me clear-minded and in a wonderful mood. From aerobics classes, I notice strong cosmetic benefits such as higher color, smoother skin, and the disappearance of lines under my eyes, which may be from the excessive sweating.

Purchasing the equipment needed to include weekly indoor and outdoor workouts can cost between $50 and $6,000. For instance, you may choose walking and a video aerobics workout for a minimum cost. Or you may set up your home with a rowing machine, trampoline, and several videos, and buy a bicycle for outdoors, for an approximate cost of $1,700.

Setting up the environment is important. When you return from work in the evening, your home will either invite you to exercise or invite you to fall into an easy chair. At the moment when you need all the help you can get, the right environment sets you up to win.

Don't wait until you have bought equipment to start your program, however. A clutter-free room with flowers in a vase and an exercise mat is an inexpensive and very inviting environment. What is important is to start *now*!

SAMPLE PROGRAM

Monday	Wednesday	Thursday	Saturday
Before work: 15-minute fast walk and 15-minute yoga	After work: 25-minute indoor bicycle plus 5-minute yoga	Before work: 5-minute yoga and 30-minute indoor bicycle	30-minute outdoor exercise and 30-minute indoor bicycle yoga

Remember: If you exercise *twice* a week, you will be less fit than if you exercise *three* times a week. If you exercise three times a week, you will maintain your fitness. If you exercise *four* times a week, you will gain in fitness.

Plan in advance exactly what exercise combinations you are going to do and *write them down* in your weekly calendar. You will be setting aside 2½ hours a week. Once your exercise plan is written on your schedule, you can avoid the day-long "Should I? Shouldn't I? Will I? Won't I?" syndrome.

THE RIGHT FIT FOR YOU

Exercising takes a certain amount of effort, but it is well worth it, to which women who make it a priority attest. "More energy," "less hunger," "calm," "less body pain," "essential" are all words used to describe the benefits.

Success in putting a long-term exercise program in place, so that it becomes a beneficial habit, can take time. You may find that you will go through months of experimentation, trying different types of exercise, seeing which ones work well together and at what times of the day. Allow yourself repeated failures, but do not give up. You will find the right fit.

A "right fit" program will meet your particular psychology. For instance, Rachel Diver, fifty-one, a sales and marketing manager in San Francisco, said she hated to plan, so she developed a large variety of exercises she enjoyed, including walking the hills of the city, and did what worked with her schedule. "I don't do well with strict regimens, so the way I get exercise is different each week."

Finding the right activity means putting up with failed attempts. Cynthia Richards, the community organizer who has lived through so many hot flashes, first tried jumping rope, because she thought it would be a fast way to work out. Except she found that her knees buckled and "when you're older your bladder doesn't hold up, and the rope would always ravel." After two or three years of trying on and taking off different possibilities, she discovered that bicycling was perfect for her.

After she found the perfect activity, she then fit it into her schedule by bicycling to work. "I really can't exercise unless it's built into my day-to-day life and I get something else out of it. Bicycling is a great workout and it also gets me to work without costing me anything. No more parking problems!'' Of all the women with whom I spoke, Cynthia impressed me as the only woman who claimed to be unconcerned about her own beauty. Yet she looked great as she parked her bicycle outside the restaurant where we met for our interview. ''I think that may be the basis of my entire happiness, the benefits of that bicycle thing.''

Exercise does take time, and a certain amount of effort. But the return on health is unbeatable, and immensely satisfying when you find what works for you. Cynthia described her commute to work: ''It's eight in the morning. It's cool. I go right down Mass. Avenue. I go through Harvard Square and get on that gorgeous bikeway by Memorial Drive. I feel like I have been on vacation by the tme I get to work. It's heaven.''

CHAPTER 12

Already Beautiful

> *They aren't making mirrors the way they used to.*
> —TALLULAH BANKHEAD
> *But am I really really really beautiful?*
> —SASHA
> from *memoirs of an ex-prom queen*
> by Alix Kates Shulman

If you're *still* not sure if you're really beautiful, test yourself with the following quiz:

1. You've just returned from your high school reunion. You look _____ the girls you went to school with.
   A. younger than
   B. older than
   C. the same as
   D. you wore sunglasses and couldn't see very well
2. A free copy of *Vogue* came in the morning mail. Compared with the cover girl you _____.
   A. are older
   B. are not as smooth-skinned
   C. earn less money
   D. are infinitely more intelligent
3. You are _____ your mother.
   A. more beautiful than
   B. less beautiful than
   C. a completely different type from
   D. not at all competitive with
4. What do you say when a man says, "You look beautiful"?

A. "Why, thank you."

B. "Are you crazy?"

C. Nothing, while you look around to see who he's talking to.

D. Nothing. You have a hot flash.

Did you pass the beauty test? Are you more or less beautiful than you have ever been? Do you care?

Even the woman who claims not to be concerned about her looks hardly ever passes up answering a beauty questionnaire, even if she takes it on the sly in the doctor's office or hairdresser's from a magazine she would not be caught dead reading at home. And it is the rare woman who resists judging herself by the standards of beauty, just or unjust, that we have internalized since we were girls. These standards circulate through a network of influences, which include hard-to-ignore film, television, and advertising media. But we also receive messages from our husbands, boyfriends, fathers, mothers, sisters, and friends. Our identities, in large part, have been shaped according to our physical appeal.

GETTING THE MESSAGE EARLY

Standards of beauty vary from culture to culture and change over time, but a widely accepted equation links beauty to youth. I remember a party I attended with my husband and some friends when I was first married. The music played, the crowd milled about, and my friend's husband turned to me and my friend. In case we should get any funny ideas he informed us, "There are a lot of young, beautiful girls here tonight. I mean, these girls are nineteen years old. You can't compete. You just can't compete." I remember feeling I had lost a step, somehow. And I was twenty-two.

Margaret Gullette is the author of *Safe at Last in the Middle Years*, a book that explores themes of four middle-aged writers—Margaret Drabble, Anne Tyler, John Updike, and Saul Bellow. I interviewed Gullette because I was drawn to the thesis in her book that midlife could be lived and perceived as a time of growth. During our interview in her office, we ranged over topics from the personal to the cultural. For Gullette, one is intricately related to the other. She remembers being shocked when she first realized, in her thirties, that growing older meant she was expected to be concerned about losing her looks. And she saw that for women in general, losing looks could have broader, more terrifying implications. "In our thirties, we begin to get cultural signals that we are supposed to be looking for our first gray hairs and worrying about other signs of aging. And of course, men were leaving women and you might be one of the ones who was left. I was in a stable marriage. I was not personally worried that I would be left, but I could see that every woman was supposed to be worried that she was going to be."

WHAT WE ALREADY KNOW

Does this mean that women in their middle years are desperate over every new line on their face, over every gray hair or every added pound? On the contrary. Women in midlife have too many other things going on in their lives to become obsessed with age-related bodily change. In fact, most of the women I interviewed felt they had gained a quality over time that made them more attractive than ever before. While their lives defied many myths associated with middle age, they were the embodiment of a type of woman Europeans have appreciated for a long time: the woman in her choice years who is already beautiful.

Janet Lowe, the forty-six-year-old Digital Equipment Corporation executive who raised her daughters alone after her husband was killed in Vietnam, agrees. On a gray Friday afternoon in her Concord, Massachusetts, condominium, Janet's energy did not seem diminished at the end of a workweek. She spoke about feeling more attractive than ever. Didn't she have a sense, however, that she wasn't getting any younger?

"I guess I thought that I would have trouble with getting older, and I can see that my skin sags in ways that it didn't twenty years ago. But I don't think being more attractive necessarily has to do with how I look," she said, as she pondered over what this quality she knew she had was. "Sometimes I look at myself in the mirror and think, I'm just not holding anything back. What youth might have provided in glow or something, whatever youth provides, I now provide something else. I'm more attractive to men than I used to be. I hold a promise to men that I didn't hold before. I'm not sure I totally understand that, but I think they find me more attractive than they did."

What Janet didn't understand but undeniably sensed psychotherapist Adrienne Garrity, forty-six, called "Presence. Being there, available to people." Would she prefer to look twenty-six instead of forty-six, I wanted to know. "Actually, despite some wrinkles, I think I might look better now. I work out more consistently and my body's better trained," she said. As if thinking and speaking at the same time, she added, "Yeah, I like the way I look. Above and beyond wrinkles, what I lost in elasticity I've made up for in something that's not that easy to define."

"It's confidence," said Louisa Curran, fifty-four, a housekeeper and a grandmother of six. "I think I'm getting more attractive, although I don't think anyone would call me a beauty. I was prettier when I was younger, but I have more confidence now. If I had had the confidence and the attractiveness together, now that would have been something."

Confidence. Every one of the women with whom I spoke said she had some special essence—confidence, presence, experience—that gave her a new dimension of attractiveness. Despite the culture's equation of beauty with youth, women at midlife know inside themselves that they are beautiful and powerful. While women know this individually and might even be telling it to one another, this well-kept, underground secret is only now beginning to go public. Part of the secrecy is connected to a dilemma a woman at midlife experiences. While she has no trouble considering *who* she is in terms of a psychological and spiritual identity, it is another thing altogether for a woman to consider how she should look.

IS THERE A STANDARD LOOK?

The media do not seem to know how a middle-aged woman should look either. The majority of advertisers continue to use younger-looking models, since they assume that "most mature consumers perceive themselves to be ten to fifteen years younger than they are." This is a costly mistake. Middle-aged consumers are a $265 billion market. While women might have questions about how to approach beauty, they do feel great about themselves and are not buying the message that they would rather be young.

The approach advertising takes angers many women, who are frustrated by cultural pressures telling us how we should or should not look. Julia Phillips resented that advertising imposes its standards on us. "There should be a respect for maturation. We should appreciate the lines on our faces. They have been earned. It is an insult that we are expected to look like fifteen-year-olds or twenty-five-year-olds."

Francine Lewin agreed. "I have some wrinkles and some sags and a few lines that I didn't have before. According to advertising, such effects that come along with age are not meant to be." While she told me she looked and felt beautiful, she acknowledged that pressure existed to make women feel over the hill—and desperate to do something about that. Friends of hers, for example, believe that since there are so many things available to prevent aging, why should the process be allowed to happen? She uses her gray hair as an example. "It is not popular to have gray hair. How do I know? My friends look at me and say, 'Oh, that looks very nice on you!' In other words, they certainly wouldn't want to have it, but on me it looks okay. Don't you think it's miraculous how so many women at the age of sixty suddenly turn blonde?''

I would not go so far as to say we are not allowed to look our age, for we certainly have the option to look any way we want. The question is, *do* we want to look our age? What does fifty look like, anyhow? Or sixty? Our mothers looked older then than we do now. Is there a standard? And how far do we want to go to achieve a standard if there is one? After all, we have all seen someone who has been overly facelifted and made up, trying to look like a kid and ending up just looking sad. But we do have a long span of years ahead of us, and those years call for us to pay some attention to our looks. We have the freedom to choose how our physical appearance will express our inner strength and beauty.

TIME TO APPRECIATE OURSELVES

Margaret Gullette noted that middle age is a time when many women actually start to appreciate themselves. They stop being so self-critical and are more able to see their own attractiveness. Yet, aging may be difficult for traditionally beautiful women. Gullette recalled a very beautiful friend who is now in her sixties. She was a knockout at one point, and aging was very hard on her. Gullette went on to note the women ''for whom beauty was just a burden, distorting all their relationships with men. They came to this period when the culture said they were declining. Maybe that was a hardship initially, but they came out the other side, and now they are saying the whole thing was a burden, both initially being beautiful in their youth, then the alleged decline thing.

''I don't know the way out,'' Gullette concluded. ''Nobody yet knows the whole way out. But we are not going to find it by reproducing an old question about getting 'older'. We're going to get the answer by saying, 'Look what the culture is making us think.' "

Julie Hatfield, forty-nine, the fashion editor of *The Boston Globe*, is one of those women suspected of having more difficulty with time passing because she has always been a "knockout." She was dressed for our interview in a close-fitting above-the-knee skirt and she looked great. She turned her philosophical eye on the question, Are you beautiful?

"I look at Jane Fonda, and I look at Jackie. I think they are great role models, physically. I don't know about mentally. I think physically those two women are wonderful role models for what our bodies can look like at this age. As far as my looks go, I notice that men on the street don't turn around as much as they used to. No, it probably has nothing to do with menopause, nothing at all. Because on certain days if I am dressed up or if I am dressed provocatively for evening, I still get those comments. It is partly our attitude. Am I beautiful? I have been told that. People tell me, but I don't always believe it, although I have always been attractive to men."

"Has that changed with time?" I asked, not without some anxiety.

Hatfield felt it had, but not for the worse. "Even though there is something in our culture that says a girl is better, every woman our age seems to have a 'je ne sais quoi,' something that shows in our eyes, the sense of humor we have. Maybe from raising children and making it through."

Despite this quality, she is a woman whose business is beauty, and she often pondered the question of how far we should go to make ourselves over. Should we try to look like the young models on the fashion-show ramps, wearing bikini pants? Should we flatten our stomachs through liposuction? When can we eat a cream puff and not feel guilty? "When will the wrinkles be all right and the gray hair? In this society and in this day and age, maybe never.''

Out loud I wondered, ''What is there to do?''

Hatfield suspected most women were concerned that they might give in to the aging process fully. Yet many women she knew were not sure how to maintain themselves, without the drastic measures of surgery. ''A bit of advice I would give to older women is posture. Stand in front of a mirror in your normal posture and then really stand up straight, shoulders back. That makes an incredible difference. Poor posture gets more dramatic as you age, and if you stoop over, you look like an old lady. So posture is critical to fashion. Every woman can do something about her posture. We cannot help reaching sixty-five years old, but we *can* help how we hold our bodies.''

Despite Hatfield's affirmative suggestions about how attitudes and actions can influence how we present ourselves, the conversation returned to attracting men. ''Some businessman about two weeks ago was quoted in the paper as saying he is sick and tired of old, fat stewardesses, aging stewardesses on airplanes. When he gets on a plane he wants to see a stewardess who is eighteen years old and under 115 pounds. That is a very cruel statement to make. What I want to know is, do most men feel that way?''

WHO CARES?

Why all this ambivalence about their own beauty and glamour from women who are already beautiful? I suspect it *is* a pressure we feel about men. After all, isn't it the men whom we are trying to please?

Doreen Amato sees it differently. She is the chief dietitian at an urban hospital. She is also thirty-six, younger than most of the women with whom I spoke. When I asked her if she was more or less attractive to men now than ten years ago, she answered, ''Who cares? I'd like women to join together with one another and say that what we look like when we get older is okay." Wouldn't such a shift in attitude require men to change their opinions about older women?

"Look," she told me, leaning across her desk and fielding interruptions as we talked, "I think the way a man sees a woman is what his mother and the other women in his life project. Men just go along with the tide, like shells in water. And the woman is the water. So if women tell men, 'Look, an older woman is beautiful,' eventually a man is going to say, 'Yes, you're right.' "

Doreen has tried this theory out in her own life and found that it has worked. "I decided I was beautiful at some point," she said, shrugging as though that explained everything. "Even though I knew I wasn't really. I made it up and talked myself into it. I feel it's up to women to change the ideas about themselves and men will come along."

Doreen's ideas about beauty being "made up" reminded me of the last time I had been to the doctor, a specialist I had never met before. He sat across his desk from me, behaving in a very businesslike fashion, listening to my history with the slightest air of being distracted. When I told him I was a model, he perked up and leaned forward a bit in his chair. Suddenly he seemed much more interested in who I was—attracted to me, perhaps.

That doctor didn't even know I was alive until I told him, through my profession, that I was beautiful. And that is, I have concluded, before any makeup is applied, the older woman's job—to inform the world that she is beautiful. As Doreen Amato said, everyone will then just come along.

As middle-aged women we need to take a strong stand about ourselves, about who we are and what we want to project, and to hold firm to that stand. It is up to us to be less secretive about our inner selves, our sense of beauty, and to stop hiding the wealth of resources each of us harbors. Deep down inside, we women who are forty, fifty, and sixty know we have something. If the way we act in our lives mimics that inner state, then our beauty will be unmistakable and unfaltering. We will express that ageless beauty, inside and out, for which there is no competition.

Although role models may not have been apparent for a number of years, recently it has been impossible to ignore the powerful middle-aged women in public life. The list is endless and you can fill in the blanks yourself.

All we need to do is look around us. We are everywhere.

TO PUT IN THE EFFORT, OR NOT

Just when we are starting to figure life out, when we are feeling great about ourselves, more gratified and very beautiful on the inside, the job of maintaining our outer looks looms larger. We love it, we hate it, we resent it. We should grow old gracefully, fight it every step of the way, fix it, ignore it, make the best of it, accept it, give it up, analyze it, understand it, write about it, and somehow find an answer.

Most of the women I interviewed had made minor changes in their skin and hair-care routines and in their use of makeup since entering the menopausal phase of their lives. Most were using some old tried-and-true moisturizer, and many had no particular skin-care program in place at all. Makeup was kept to a minimum, with the notion that it would not make any difference in their appearance and that their appearance was just fine as it was. I have never met a woman who felt that way about her living room, a place where change is always welcome.

Maybe we are all sensitive to the hint of contempt attached to a woman pursuing beauty, particularly an aging woman. But we are trapped in that dilemma again, caught between not wanting to give in to pressures about aging yet wanting to look good. The dilemma feels like a no-win proposition—we are subject to cultural contempt if we do and an accusation of sloth if we don't.

As a model I may be more sensitive to appearance changes than most women. For example, skin changes are gradual, and unless forced to keep track of them many women may not notice the degree to which their skin has altered. Once they have noticed, most women are not sure what they should do. In general, how far should someone go? What is the line that separates enhancing your looks and radically altering them? Is there any agreement on how to grow older gracefully? Should every woman dye her hair or have a facelift?

TAKING A GOOD, HARD LOOK

The decisions are personal, yet they start with an ice-cold self-assessment of how we want to look and how we actually do look. From there, it is a matter of design. The technology exists for us to look almost any way we would like, and therefore choices need to be made. Some women panic over every new wrinkle. If wrinkles are causing low self-esteem, perhaps a surgical procedure is in order. I don't mind wrinkles. In fact, I think a wrinkle-free face is boring. Recently, a fashion magazine ran a feature story on models and their mothers. My eyes were continuously drawn to the mothers, whose faces showed intelligence, character, and yes, some wrinkles. Yet it does bother me to see the shape of my face change, which I feel detracts from my looks. To counter such changes, I have investigated a number of techniques that lift and strengthen my facial muscles, all described in the next chapter.

Perhaps the easiest and most immediate way to enhance your looks is through skin care. To the women whose beauty program consists of some moisturizer plus soap and water, I would say that a reevaluation of how to care for your skin will result in a big improvement. Cared-for skin shows. Even wrinkled and full of sags, it has a glow and tells people that here is a woman who is vital and interested in herself.

Betty Rogers has found midlife the perfect time for reassessing beauty habits and changing her style. ''There are lots of things I find that I do now for myself that didn't interest me before, like my nails. My daughter came home and said to me, 'You know, Mama, your nails are so nice,' and I said, 'Honey, who had time to think about nails all those years when my hands were in dishwater or the washing machine?' Ten years ago my body was different from what it is now. But the things I do now make me look attractive. I recently got into colors. I was a person of basic colors, and my daughters would say, 'Come on, Mama, you've got to wear colors. They look nice on you.' I'd wear gray, browns. Now I wear red.''

Like Betty Rogers, I changed my habits in midstream. Although I had a healthy lifestyle for many years I dragged my feet when it came to using cosmetics to enhance my looks. Since I started modeling, at forty-seven, I have lifted those feet. Now I try everything, as though my new career offered a certain permission to pay this kind of attention to myself. I love doing it and I am glad to be able to affect my appearance.

I've always had a fantasy of being a happy old lady, all wrinkled, who could care less about her looks, working in the yard all day, and showing everyone her flower garden. When will I be that old lady? The answer is, not yet!

I expect I will continue with various beauty treatments, probably some cosmetic surgery, maybe change the color of my hair as time goes on. I do hope I do this in good taste, and I assume my daughters will let me know if I go over the line. (Daughters are the ideal fashion police.) When I am that old lady in the garden showing off my flowers, I suspect I will have on a new shade of lipstick, a large brimmed hat to keep out the sun, and pretty polish on my nails. Just in case some nice gentleman comes to call.

BEAUTY AND MEDICAL HEALTH

The desire for beauty is inherent in almost everyone, and even the medical world is beginning to notice. James Leyden, a dermatologist at the Center for Human Appearance at the University of Pennsylvania, notes the psychological and social importance of looking good. Michael Pertschuk, the center's psychiatrist, thinks it is possible that our desire to be beautiful stems from an innate survival urge rather than from narcissism. The need is so basic it dates back way before Madison Avenue. Madison Avenue does not exist in Siberia or in the outback of Australia, yet standards of appearance are very much alive in those cultures. The Center for Human Appearance is the first institute of its kind, bringing together world-renowned surgeons and physicians to medically treat human appearance. Linton Whitaker, the center's plastic surgeon, feels that combining the concepts of inner and outer beauty provides a potential that has not been explored up to now.

Perhaps physical appearance is as important to health and well-being as is medicine. Hard-core evidence for this by scientific standards is scarce. One such study done in a gerentological research center showed that men evaluated to "look younger" actually did live longer. Barbara Bush noticed the effects of caring for her looks during an illness, as she reported in *The Washington Post*. "Everyone knows I've had a year with pop eyes and all sorts of weird things," she said, referring to her bout with Graves' disease. "Without my hairdresser, and my precious Mr. Scaasi, and other friends who made me feel like I looked good anyway, it would have been a different year."

An exciting program called *Look Good . . . Feel Better* provides beauty advice for women who are undergoing treatment for cancer. It is a coordinated effort of the Cosmetic, Toiletry and Fragrance Association, the American Cancer Society, and the National Cosmetology Association, and treatment centers are being established in major cancer hospitals around the country. In addition to makeovers, there is a national phone number (800-558-5005), through which women can reach experts in their area for advice on hair and makeup.

The first such center is at the Memorial Sloan-Kettering Cancer Center in New York City. Attending physician William Cahan notes, in the literature available from the *Look Good . . . Feel Better* program, "A woman's concern about her appearance is not all fluff and feathers. It is a fundamental part of her psyche and must be heeded when her sense of vanity is traumatized, which is often the case with chemotherapy and radiotherapy treatments for cancer. Makeup has to do with self-respect, vanity, and ego. A touch of lipstick, rouge, or shadow can make all the difference in the world— not only to her physical appearance, but also to a woman's sense of worth and well-being."

And as many of us know, for better or for worse, beauty is power. University of Maryland psychologist Harold Sigall reports that in every field of endeavor, an attractive person will have much more impact than an unattractive person. In other words, good-looking fund-raisers will raise more funds, attractive teachers will gain more attentiveness, a well-groomed salesperson will sell more. And anyone can do it.

Our looks are one of our resources. By the time we reach menopause, we are experienced and seasoned enough not to be controlled by the fashion standards of the day. But we should not disregard ourselves by ignoring our looks. It may be uncomfortable and unfamiliar for women who are used to taking care of others first to pay a lot of attention to themselves. But self-care does make a difference, and it is important, particularly during the menopausal years, when reduced levels of estrogen produce changes to which we are not accustomed. If we feel vital, energetic, productive, and gorgeous inside, why not look that way on the outside?

CHAPTER 13

Time for a Change

In the sixties, I never wore makeup or styled my hair. Now I think it's much more interesting to play with my appearance. Thank heavens, I recovered from the sixties.
—CARRIE BROUWER
Forty-eight

In modeling, last year's pictures are no longer worth anything, because they don't represent how a model currently looks. Without the feedback of pictures, however, I never would have noticed the real changes in my appearance that have taken place over time. While it was apparent from the mirror that my ''look'' changed from year to year, photographs made it impossible to deny that age had something to do with such change. Age-related changes were difficult to accept, particularly since my new career is based on my looks. But the photographs have forced me to be candid with myself. As one fashion expert told me, ''My eyes, and probably my eyesight, have adjusted to the changes of age. When I look in the mirror, I see the face that used to be there.''

In my late forties, I could see that a complete makeover was in order. First, I went through my closets, which were filled with things I had not worn in years, and asked, ''Does this color still work for me?'' Getting rid of all those clothes broke my heart, even though they rarely saw the light of day. After clearing out my closets and making room for new styles, I went to work on my skin. I developed a skin-care routine through experimentation, and I started to work with makeup. I had had acne when I was young, but now my skin looks better than it ever did.

Every woman should periodically have a makeover. After all, everything else we do goes through changes season to season. We eat differently, work differently, play differently this year than we did last year, and certainly than we did ten years ago. Our looks could benefit from the same evolution. I recommend having your colors evaluated, having your hair redone, and having a professional skin-care evaluation every five years. And let professionals do it for you, no matter how frivolous and indulgent that seems. I have observed that none of us sees our own style and beauty potential, and it is a treat to let someone else guide you and give you tips. For instance, if you are the type who feels the stores hide the good clothes when you go shopping, ask for a professional shopper. Some stores provide this service, or you can find an individual consultant who will redesign your wardrobe for a fee. We do not hesitate to renovate everything else in our lives that requires maintenance, such as our cars or our homes—why not ourselves?

SELF-CARE ROUTINES

Before I became a model and was shocked into a makeover, my method of skin care was haphazard. Having always been a "natural" type, I was proud of the minimal care I put into my own beauty. But little hints started to fall my way. For one birthday almost everyone I knew gave me moisturizer and makeup. On a modeling job in New York, high from the excitement of working with a famous fashion photographer and makeup artist, I heard the photographer say, "Don't worry, I won't light her neck." A house didn't have to fall on me. I took a cold look in the mirror and decided some attention was in order.

I started to research the subject, asking every makeup

artist I worked with, "What tips do you have for the older face?" I read books, consulted aestheticians, and interviewed representatives from cosmetics companies. Some of the programs I explored offered free introductory sessions, and I was so impressed with the results that I signed up for the programs. I invested some money and I gave my face up to experimentation, not in the name of vanity, of course, but for the sake of science! What I found is that three methods made a difference in my appearance: skin care, makeup, and facial toning, all of which I discuss in this chapter.

A note about cost: Launching a beauty program is possible without incurring a huge expense. This program, available to a range of pocketbooks, includes products of many different prices, and tricks and tips for stretching the more expensive items. Although the quality of products does differ with price, you will get results by establishing a consistent regimen using the products you already have and replacing them as you please.

Because of the care I have taken in the past years, my skin has improved. Before this, it was definitely going in the opposite direction.

SKIN CHANGES

The top layer of skin, the epidermis, continually produces new cells and at its surface sloughs off old dead cells. The second layer, the dermis, contains elastin, collagen, sweat glands, hair follicles, and sebaceous glands. Below the dermis lies a supply of blood vessels and nerves.

As we age, various changes occur as the result of chronology, lifestyle, and, at menopause, reduced levels of circulating estrogen. Separating the contribution of each of these factors is difficult, but studies of young women who have had surgical menopause show that many age-related skin changes occur as the result of decreased estrogen.

New cells are produced at a significantly slower rate as we age. The renewal cycle for epidermal cells is 50 percent longer, so that skin cells are really older by the time they push their way to the surface. Cells give up their moisture more readily, so that the whole look of the skin is drier and thinner, while oil glands are less active. And as collagen and elastin break down in the dermis, that layer shrinks, leaving the epidermis larger in relation to it, so that sagging starts. Circulation in the skin is slower, so that it becomes blotchy with broken capillaries. Skin shading lightens and the texture roughens because of enlarged pores.

Estrogen therapy helps keep the skin plumped up and smooth and is associated with a decrease in collagen and elastin breakdown.

The challenge of caring for mature skin is to find ways to retain moisture, remove dead cells, and keep the dermis thick and vital. The dermis can be taken care of from the inside through exercise and good nutrition. The epidermis is available to treatment from the outside through good skin care.

SKIN CARE

Catherine Hinds has been in the beauty business for over twenty years. She is the founder of the Catherine Hinds Institute for Estheticians in Medford, Massachusetts, and the former president of the Massachusetts Chapter of the National Association of Estheticians. In her fifties, with bright blue eyes and a shock of gray hair, she does, I must say, have beautiful skin. In speaking about skin care, she revealed, in addition to her years of experience, a gift for straight talk.

"Look," she told me, "there are only four things you can do to skin: cleanse it, protect it, moisturize it, and exfoliate it." Although she has her own line of skin care products, she candidly admits that the product isn't as important as consistency, similar to caring for your teeth.

"European women know this. Facials are important, but any good aesthetician should share the information needed to do your own at home. We know there's a cost involved."

Shopping Strategies

Shopping for skin-care products can be overwhelming, and I think most women are turned off by the constant advertising and packaging hype. Perhaps this is why so many of the women with whom I spoke were sticking to some old favorite skin-care routine that was doing an adequate job. First, newer products do not necessarily mean better products. Second, you need a Ph.D. in creams and lotions to wade through the available products, and there are always more to try. I recently bought a leg-tanning lotion only to find out from the package insert that this skin-care line had twelve (yes, twelve) other sun-care lotions available. A good way to begin differentiating between products is to check the consumer columns of magazines geared to women our age.

Trying new beauty items, of course, can be a lot of fun and sometimes fruitful. Cosmetics companies are fully aware that once you, the consumer, have success with a product, you will stick with it. As a result, many companies have redesigned their sales techniques so that customers are educated about products and understand how they should be used.

A cosmetics section of a major department store, with its endless array of items and smells, and a salesperson who does not look like someone you would describe as "supportive," can be intimidating. Developing a shopping strategy helps the situation. First, decide what products you are going to buy and your price range. Although it is the job of the salesperson to sell, she is a well-trained specialist. Use her. Her job is to make sure that you find the right product and know how to use it. She will analyze your skin and make suggestions for the type and combination of products you may need. And if the product does not work for you, take it back. Tony Michaels, senior vice president for Lancôme, says, "If you're not happy with a product you've bought, exchange it, as you would a blouse. We don't want anybody wasting money on products."

Each counter is set up with "testers," which are samples to experiment with before buying. Ask for a sampler of a product that interests you. If no samples are available, bring your own plastic container and ask if you can take a small amount home to try. I have found that many salespeople are helpful and fully enjoy answering questions and talking about their products. While knowing what you are shopping for is important, try everything while you are there. Asking a question and having someone work with you does not mean you are required to buy. I have left cosmetics and skin-care counters with my arms looking like a Picasso from cosmetic samples, having made a minimal purchase or none at all.

PRICE RANGES FOR SKIN-CARE PRODUCTS

Materials	Price Range
Cleanser	$ 4–$32
Toner	6–20
Exfoliator	5–40
Moisturizer	5–70
Sunblock	4–15
TOTAL	$24–$177

FOUR STEPS TO A GOOD SKIN-CARE SYSTEM

- Cleansing
- Exfoliating
- Moisturizing
- Protection

Cleansing

I still like soap for makeup removal and once-a-week deep cleansing. While most women assume soap should be avoided because it is drying to the skin, a moisturized soap and warm water worked into a good lather and gently massaged onto the face with your hands cleans the face with the least amount of irritation. Cleansers used to remove makeup require too much tugging and rubbing, leaving the face irritated. Be sure to use a soap containing moisturizer, which can be determined by the ingredient list. The most prominent ingredient, in all cosmetic products, is listed first, with the others following in descending order of amount.

Cleanse the face twice a day, in the morning and evening. In the morning use warm water only, as the face is still clean from the night before and warm water will rehydrate without removing any natural skin oils produced overnight. Splash the water over the face and neck, allowing the water to rinse the eyes as well.

In the evening, if you are wearing makeup, first remove your eye makeup with eye-makeup remover, and your lipstick with a light moisturizing lotion such as Kiss My Face (see Moisturizing, page 269) or Neutrogena. Wash your face with soap and warm water once lightly or until the makeup is removed fully, making sure to rinse the face thoroughly to remove all the soap. If you are not wearing makeup, use a cleanser.

Cleansers contain varying amounts of creams. Often the more lotion-rich products do not leave the face feeling clean. Since almost all over-forty skin is dry, I have listed mild products. If you are the exception, with still-oily skin, consult a product specialist at a major department store, as your skin may require different treatment for different areas of the face. Spread the cleanser over your face using your hands as you do with soap and water. After all, only your hands know all the ins and outs of your face. Rinse it off with warm water rather than tissue, which can pull and irritate the skin. Pat the face dry with a towel.

Toning is an additional step of the cleansing process. A toner will deep-cleanse and tighten the pores, remove any residual makeup or dirt, and start to exfoliate gently. While some experts feel toning is essential, I find it dries my skin after a soap-and-water cleansing. I use toner on special occasions to give my pores a tighter appearance. Using a cotton ball, apply the toner over the more oily areas of the face where pores appear large. This may be on either side of the nose, and on the chin. Toners are made with and without alcohol. I recommend an alcohol-free toner, such as Ultima, or Aubrey Organics Herbal Facial Toner.

Soap	Cleansers
Dove	Aubrey Organics Sea Soap
Caress	Annemarie Borlund Cleans-
The Cleansing Bar by Ultima	ing Milk
Purpose Gentle Cleansing Soap	Cetaphil

Exfoliating

Exfoliating is really a continuation of cleansing since it removes dead cells that constitute the top layer of skin and allows new cells to regenerate more rapidly. Since skin cells make their way to the surface for removal, the part of the skin that we see is the oldest. Without exfoliating the skin regularly, everything else you do is being added to layers of dead skin. You can exfoliate with various products such as Retin-A and scrubs, or more simply with an abrasive sponge.

Retin-A is an exfoliator that reverses photoaging (skin damage caused by the sun). Highly publicized as a magic formula, it has also been the subject of controversy. All the publicity is reminiscent of many health food fads that promise miracle results. While Retin-A has been clinically shown to reduce wrinkles, fade blemishes, and thicken the skin, which it does over time, it is not magic. The results are subtle, leading many to argue that it does not work.

Photoaging starts to appear ten to twenty years after exposure, which means that a lot of the obvious skin changes I see now started twenty years ago when I was outdoors with a young family, before anyone ever heard of sunblock. I decided to give Retin-A a try. To purchase it I needed a prescription (and in general I advise anyone interested to consult a dermatologist, since improper use of the product can be harmful). I initially found the results disappointing, until I was instructed properly in its use.

Ruth Tedaldi, dermatologist at Newton-Wellesley Hospital in Massachusetts, feels that many people could benefit from Retin-A use. After following her directions carefully, I have found it not only effective but the simplest nighttime skin-care program.

Retin-A is applied every night before bed. Put a pea-sized amount in your hand and dab it over the face, keeping it one inch from the eyes and a half inch from the lips. Also dab it on the upper chest and the backs of the hands. Then spread gently. The product can be irritating and cause peeling, but this diminishes with time. Fair-skinned people, who tend to wrinkle more, get better results. If you find Retin-A drying, which it can be, apply moisturizer over it. It also makes the skin more sensitive to future sun damage, so it becomes extra important to protect the skin always (see Protection, page 272). The price of Retin-A has skyrocketed since I began using it, from $17 to $28 a tube, which lasts approximately three months. But I love the results. My skin feels thicker and smoother and holds more moisture. While I still have certain creases, such as two lines between my brows, the lines are not as deep. If it cost less, I'd put it all over my body!

For a simpler approach to exfoliating, I recommend

Buf-Puf twice a week. Buf-Puf is a rough-surfaced spongelike product that sloughs off dead skin cells. The Buf-Puf can be very harsh, so it is important to lather it richly with its accompanying cleanser and to rotate the puff in rapid circles so that speed rather than pressure works against the skin cells. You want to remove dead cells without damaging blood vessels. Delicate skins may find Buf-Puf too harsh. In such cases, a scrub cleanser might be better. Since using Retin-A (for over a year now), I only use the Buf-Puf once a week.

With either treatment, light complexions should proceed more cautiously, starting with terry cloth and mild scrub, and advancing only as the skin can tolerate. Darker complexions can start with Buf-Puf and Retin-A, although there may be some initial peeling. All of the following methods will work to some degree, but the most important thing is to start some consistent exfoliating.

Mechanical Exfoliation	Chemical Exfoliation	Cleansing Scrubs
Buf-Puf Terry face cloths	Retin-A	Clarins Gentle Facial Peeling Ultima Refining Scrub Mask The Body Shop Azuki Bean Exfoliating Scrub

Moisturizing

All skin needs moisturizing, even a baby's. As skin matures, it loses its ability to hold moisture. This is due to a combination of chronological aging, sun damage, and, for women in menopause, estrogen depletions. The skin is most oily in the teen years, when many adolescents have acne. After this period, a continued loss of natural oil occurs. Fair skin tends to be drier, and moisturizer becomes necessary sooner. At menopause, everyone needs some moisturizer, even women who were desperately trying to keep their skin dry in years past.

Women with drier skin don't necessarily require a different type of moisturizer, but they need to apply it more frequently, as their own natural production of oil is less.

Moisturizing does not add moisture but seals it in. Moisture is added by water only. Maisie Tam, a Lahey Clinic dermatologist, reports, "How skin looks depends on the integrity of the stratum corneum (the uppermost layer of skin). The only way to make it look and feel good is to hydrate it with water and then seal the water in with a moisturizer. Applying moisturizer without first hydrating the skin is pointless." The skin takes up moisture in the first ten minutes of a bath or shower. After twenty minutes of bathing, moisture starts to be drawn out of the skin. When you see your fingers begin to wrinkle, you will know you have been in too long. Ten to fifteen minutes should be enough time to hydrate your skin without drawing any moisture back out.

Here is a wonderful way to feel smooth all over and seal in moisture right after bathing: Immediately after a shower or bath, while you are still wet, shake excess water off your body. If you are showering in the morning, place approximately two tablespoons of body lotion in one hand, pour half into the other hand, and quickly rub it all over your body. Because you are wet, it will spread well. Start with the legs, move up to the torso, and finish with the chest, arms, and shoulders. You can include the face, although you will just be adding protection and additional moisturizer to your morning face routine. Then pat dry with your towel. The ingredient list is your best guide to the amount of cream contained in any moisturizer and generally a product tryout will tell if it works for you. I love olive oil on the skin, but since it does leave me smelling a little bit like a pizza, it's best saved for an evening bath or shower. I find it wonderfully soothing and protective, and it's inexpensive.

Adding moisturizer to the hands and face several times during the day is important, especially if your skin is dry. Remember, the moisturizer only seals in moisture, and as it wears off, the skin continues to evaporate water continuously. (You are losing moisture even as you read this!) Before bed, apply moisturizer to the hands and face. If you are using Retin-A, it may double as your moisturizer, but dry skin may need an added coat, which can be applied over the Retin-A cream.

The first thing a makeup artist does on a modeling job is rub moisturizer all over the face. If it doesn't apply evenly and leave the skin surface smooth, we're in trouble for the rest of the day. Finding the right moisturizer, therefore, was crucial for me. Many experts claim that the least expensive and the most expensive products have the same ingredients. My perusal of ingredient lists does not bear this out, and I have found the proof of the pudding on my face. I used to use Lubriderm, and it was effective in my twenties and thirties. I've used several products regularly since, and each time they seemed effective until something better came along. I'm currently using Annemarie Borlund Regeneration Night cream. (I use it during the day.) It is quite a bit more expensive than the Lubriderm I started with, but I love how soft it leaves my skin. One way to cut down on the cost of an expensive moisturizer is to apply it once in the morning and then use another product for touch-up through the day. For nighttime, olive oil or safflower oil is very effective.

One of the products I have tried along the way that worked well on my skin is vitamin-E cream. Interestingly, my experience with the effects of vitamin E went against the grain of my scientific training as a nutritionist. I tend to look for proof before acting. Scientific literature says that topical vitamin E can do nothing for the skin. It must be ingested for it to have any value at all. At some point I was given a jar of vitamin-E-rich cream, and boom, my skin was smoother than ever with much better color.

The following are some recommended products:

FACE

Annemarie Borlund Regeneration Night cream

Rachel Perry HiPotency "E" Cellular Treatment (thick and may be sticky)

Jason Natural Products Vitamin E Creme

Olive oil, which contains vitamin E

Safflower oil, which contains vitamin E

BODY

Kiss My Face Vitamin A & E Moisturizer

Status Nourishing Day Lotion

Olive oil

Safflower oil

Baby oil

Protection

Some dermatologists now believe that up to 70 percent of skin changes once thought to be due to aging are caused by exposure to the sun and other elements. The body protects itself naturally against the sun's rays by its pigment, so that the darker the skin, the more natural the protection. The ultraviolet rays of the sun pass right through the epidermis of light skin and penetrate the dermis, where they cause damage to the elastin and collagen contained in the dermis. The sunburn heals and fades quickly, but sun damage is permanent and will start to show ten to twenty years later. Injury to the collagen and elastin causes premature sagging and leathery, wrinkled skin. Also, pigment changes will cause uneven coloring. While cosmetics can improve the appearance of the skin temporarily, to date Retin-A is the only topically applied cream that can naturally reverse some of the past damage. While Retin-A will change the texture of sun-damaged skin, it does not affect deep wrinkles and sagging. These are the province of the plastic surgeon and will be discussed later. The more serious possible effect of sun damage is skin cancer. The American Cancer Society predicted that in the United States in 1990, more than 600,000 new cases of skin malignancies would be diagnosed, most of them caused by the sun. Figures are not yet available to check their prediction.

Whether the diminished ozone layer is causing more sun exposure is still under debate, but I do remember a time when to sit in the sun felt warm and healing. Now sun on my face feels like an abrasion. Something has changed, although I am not certain if it is the atmosphere or my attitude, created by all the horror stories I have heard about skin damage.

After menopause the skin is lighter and the epidermis thinner, making it still more vulnerable to sun exposure. To protect the skin, sunblock is essential *at all times, in all places*. Dermatologist Ruth Tedaldi advises using at least an SPF 15 on the face and hands. Also, wear a wide-brimmed hat and sunglasses when walking about or sitting on the beach or in the yard.

A variety of views exist regarding differences in sunblock. The number 15 after SPF refers to the length of time a product remains effective. For example, if it takes you approximately 10 minutes to turn red in the sun, SPF 15 will protect you up to fifteen times as long as that, or 150 minutes. The higher the number, the longer the protection time. Some dermatologists believe higher SPF offer more protection minute by minute as well, although high-SPF lotions can be sticky and irritating to the skin. A dispute exists about the safety of PABA, a sunblock ingredient. PABA contains sulfur, a common allergen that can cause rashes and irritation.

Dr. Tedaldi suggests using PABA-free products. The trick here is to find a product providing adequate protection with no irritation. For every day (work, home, etc.), use an SPF 15 and reapply if necessary. Sunblock is applied in the morning after cleansing and moisturizing and before applying makeup. Since some moisturizers and foundations have built-in sunblock, they may double as protection. Don't forget that waterproof sunblocks are available for days at the beach.

SUNBLOCKS
PURPOSE, SPF 12, can be used between October and April. A combination sunblock and moisturizer that I have found very easy on the skin.
SHADE SPF 15
PRE-SUN SPF 29
SUNDOWN SPF 30, waterproof
These are all PABA-free.

DAILY CARE SUMMARY
MORNING:
- Rinse face with warm water
- Apply toner (optional)
- Apply moisturizer
- Apply sunblock (may be included in moisturizer and/or makeup)
- Apply makeup as desired

DAYTIME:
- Apply moisturizer on the hands several times through the day

EVENING:
- Wash face with soap and water
- Exfoliate (how often depends on the method, e.g., twice a week with Buf-Puf or scrub, once a day for Retin-A)
- Shower or splash face with water
- Apply olive oil

RETIN-A USERS:
EVENING:
- Wash face with soap and water
- Apply Retin-A
- Add olive oil if extra moisturizer is needed

When reviewing new products, identify their use (cleanser, exfoliator, etc.), then fit them into your skin-care routine to help decide if they work well with your other products and if they are worth purchasing on a regular basis.

Weekly Care

Facials provide an in-depth version of cleansing, exfoliating, and moisturizing. Although salon facials are not essential, they are a wonderful treat, and an aesthetician will most probably take more care and time with your face than you will at home. Your State Board of Cosmetology can recommend a reputable salon. I recommend working with a licensed aesthetician. You can also give yourself a good facial at home with a weekly routine that is easy and fast.

First exfoliate with Buf-Puf, a rough sponge, or a scrub. Don't forget, the surface layer of skin that meets the public is made of dead skin cells, with effective exfoliation increasing dead-cell turnover. This allows the alive, glowing skin that is underneath to show through.

After exfoliating, apply a green clay mask to firm and tighten the skin. I recommend green clay because it is inexpensive and natural and does not irritate skin, although other masks are effective as well. A mask is actually a continuation of the cleansing process. By providing a deep pore cleansing, it allows pores to close, which gives the skin a smooth appearance, erases light surface lines, and actually tightens the entire surface of the skin, giving the face a firmer look.

Green clay can be purchased in health food stores in powder or paste. The powder needs to be mixed with water to form a paste the thickness of peanut butter. It does the job well, without any of the harsh chemicals found in many masks that leave the face burning and blotched. Spread the clay over your face and neck and let it dry for approximately 10 minutes. While the mask is drying, rub olive oil all over your body, legs, torso, arms, and chest. Shower, rinsing off the mask using water and your hands, and let the water of the shower run over your body, removing the excess oil. If your skin is particularly dry, rub an additional tablespoon of oil over your body just before towel-drying.

Some people object to the use of a mask, because it doesn't last. This is true. It doesn't. But what in life does? The effects of cared-for skin accumulate, so that the overall appearance of the skin is good and the skin stays looking good over time. Masks also clean out pores, and that effect lasts if masks are used regularly. Since the effect of the mask is greatest for several hours after it is done, you may want to apply a mask before going out to a special occasion.

The mask will leave your face feeling tight and maybe dry, so now is the time to apply moisturizer, although under no other circumstances should you bother to moisturize without hydrating. After washing the mask off in the shower, and before bed, apply 100-percent vitamin-E oil. Try this first on a small area since some women have allergic reactions to vitamin E. The oil is very thick and sticky, so be prepared. While the mask affects the small surface wrinkles, the vitamin E diminishes the deeper facial wrinkles like the furrows between the eyebrows and the lines that run from the nose to the mouth. You'll wake up with smooth and freshened skin from head to toe!

MAKEUP

Over the past four years I have been made up by many well-known and talented makeup artists, and "artist" is an accurate word to describe them. I have never met people who love what they do more than the makeup artists. Just to test my hypothesis I always ask, "How do you like your work?" The first time I heard the answer—"I could never imagine doing anything else"—I was amazed. Rarely do people say that about their jobs.

Makeup is fun. The brushes and the colors remind me of an artist's studio and palette. I've really come to see that beauty is created. With some practice you can achieve the illusion you want—glamorous, natural, professional—in very little time.

Tips for the Older Face

Before attempting makeup tricks, it is most important to establish your skin-care system. Skin that is cared for maintains its smooth surface and fresh glow, minimizing the amount of makeup needed for a natural and highlighted look. I remember Akira, whose makeup work graces the covers of many national magazines, doing my makeup for a *Lear's* story on yoga, and laughing as he said, "I follow you around all day, watching your face and working on your face, so you will look 'natural.' "

I am in full agreement with Truvy, the beautician in *Steel Magnolias,* who says she built a business on the premise that "there's no such thing as natural beauty." But I also understand what makes a lot of women timid about using makeup—the fear that they will end up looking like Bette Davis in *Whatever Happened to Baby Jane?* My observation is that most older women underdo their makeup. I want to be sure to look "natural," and I create that look by following all the steps outlined below, using subtle shades and a light hand in application.

SUPPLIES

4 BRUSHES: • For eyebrows, eye shadow, blush, and powder

MAKEUP: • Concealer
- Foundation (optional)
- Powder
- Blush
- Eyebrow powder
- Kohl eyeliner
- Powder eye shadow
- Mascara
- Kohl lipliner
- Lipstick

Work with counter personnel to create the right color palette for your skin. Keep in mind that:

1. Concealer should match your basic skin tone as closely as possible, leaning toward the lighter side.
2. Foundation and powder should blend with your skin tone.
3. Blush should highlight your natural color.
4. Keep eye shadows in shades of gray and brown.

A dramatic look can be created with darker mascara, eyeliner, and lipstick. Your makeup choices should be based on your skin tones rather than the season, although your lipstick can reflect the season if you desire. As you will see, most of the effect of makeup is based on shading and lightening.

MISCELLANEOUS:
- Cotton balls (be sure they are 100% cotton)
- Small triangular sponges
- Eye-makeup remover

The first step when you begin to make up is to make the color of your face as even as possible, using concealer, foundation, and powder as described below. In this way you create the blank canvas on which you can achieve your desired look. In modeling this is known as getting the face "flat."

Makeup Steps

1. *Clean and moisturize* your skin and apply sunblock, unless you are using a sunblock-containing makeup. Look at yourself in a well-lit mirror, making believe your face belongs to someone else in order to be objective. (Warning: This may take some practice!) You will see a variety of skin discolorations, and shadings caused by your particular facial contour. Decide how you want your makeup to sculpt your face. In general, concealer covers blemishes and brings shadowed areas forward, while blush creates

shading in places, such as under the cheekbones, where you want it.

2. *Concealer* will lighten shaded areas and cover skin markings, and should be one to two shades lighter than your natural skin color. Use a product with a consistency that is liquid enough to apply easily. One concealer I like is Dermablend, which comes in several skin tone shades. Dermablend is often recommended by surgeons to cover scars and is very effective in covering skin discolorations. Many stick concealers pull on the delicate eye area. Dot concealer onto darkened or discolored areas (usually under the eyes and on either side of the chin) with your fingertip. If this area is very dark, or is blue because of broken blood vessels, first apply a layer of light green (for yellow-toned skin) or light lavender (for pinker skin) concealer and then continue with your usual product. Blend in with a sponge applicator. When blending, do not pull the sponge across the area. Rather, press the sponge against the inside area under the eye, then lift and move the sponge by releasing and reapplying light pressure as you progress to the outside of the eye area. This feels like a light rapid tapping, which applies makeup with minimal pulling of the skin.

A word about application. The trick, especially in areas that move a lot with facial expression, like around the eyes, is to get adequate coverage with the least amount of makeup. Check yourself later in the day and see if the amount of makeup you applied in the morning has been counterproductive. That is, have your facial motions creased the makeup, drawing attention to what you wanted to cover? Now you have a sense of how to compromise tomorrow on perfect coverage, with less makeup. Feel free to play with this. Many people give up on makeup completely when a small adjustment can easily solve the problem. Keep in mind that there is a difference between a real

face and a face on a magazine page. Most advertisements for makeup appear on an eighteen-year-old face, in a photograph that has been airbrushed to perfection. So let your makeup optimize what you have, and forget about perfection.

3. *Foundation.* I don't use any foundation for everyday use, because it tends to cake and crack when my face moves and by midafternoon I start to look like Frankenstein. I use foundation for photography, or for very short time periods, such as a meeting or a television appearance. Some very light foundations, which give some color and cover without creasing, are on the market: Lancôme Bienfait du Matin multiprotective day creme, which also contains sunblock, Dr. Hauschka Day Cosmetic (can be purchased in health food stores), and Chanel Teint.

Here's a foundation tip: blend your foundation with

equal parts of moisturizer in your hand before applying it. The mixture provides a thinner coating that moves more easily with your face over the course of the day.

Foundations come in various tones from ivory to beige, some pink or peach tones, bronze, and mahogany. Each skin has its basic undertone, such as pink, yellow, or olive. Black skin has many more tone variations than white. Flori Roberts and Fashion Fair Cosmetics are among the product lines offering diverse choices for black skin. As skin ages, it becomes lighter and more pink. Work with counter personnel, using samples to find a match to your undertone, and choose a shade that most closely matches your own. You may want to heighten or darken your tone slightly. Visage is a makeup line that custom mixes foundation, powder, blush, eyeshadow, and lipstick to match personal skin tones from very pale to very dark.

I use two foundations that have a basic olive tone— a light beige and a dark tan—and mix them according to the shade I want. And I vary the mix according to my clothing and the season. Since I avoid suntanning, I sometimes create a darker tone to mimic a tan, and with gray-white hair it provides a nice contrast.

4. Now apply *powder*, again experimenting with shades at the cosmetics counters. Ultima has a new line of very light coating powders, and my current favorite is Ultima Rice Powder, which is almost invisible on the face. The powder is mixed with crystals, which reflect light and give an illusion of smaller pores. With a large face brush, apply a light coating of powder all over the face.

Now that your face is flat you can start adding effect.

Before doing your eyes and lips and adding blush, decide what you want to accent. I suggest that if you want to make up your eyes strongly, let your lips remain softer by using a medium to light shade. Conversely, if you want strong lips, go lightly on the eyes.

5. *Eyebrows*. Keeping these clean and tweezed is very important. Straggling brow hairs, particularly gray ones, look unkempt. A salon waxing will achieve a very clean brow line. A well-defined and thick brow defines the eyes. On very busy days when time is at a premium, I will brush in eyebrows and put on lipstick. These two things alone can really heighten your face. For color, use a powder about the same color or a little darker than your natural brow. Using a magnifying mirror makes a big difference in how clearly you see your face and how well you can work on it.

Comb the eyebrows straight down. Brush in eyebrow color. Comb the eyebrows back into place.

6. *Eye Shadow*. Powder eye shadow gives the most subtle effect. Before purchasing a shadow, rub it between your fingers to make sure it feels silky. Avoid bright or iridescent colors, which bring attention to any excess skin that may be in the eye area. The purpose of eye shadow is to give the eyes a deep-set look. Therefore, no matter what your skin tone or eye color, choose colors that mimic natural shading, such as grays and browns. I suggest having both on hand and coordinating the color with your clothing. For instance, on a day or evening when you may wear royal blue, opt for the grays, and when you're wearing brown or orange, use the brown tone.

Apply eye shadow by dotting the area you want to shade with the tip of the eye shadow brush. Once the area is dotted in, use short brush strokes to blend. Start on the lid a half inch from the inside edge of the eye and shade the remainder of the lid to the outside. Then dot a diagonal line from the mid-eyelid crease to the outer edge of the eyebrow. Move the brush half of its own width down, continuing to dot back into the edge of the upper eyelid. (See illustration, page 283.) For a more finished look, use a lighter shadow underneath, covering the entire area between the upper lashes and eyebrow.

7. *Eyeliner.* Reserve eyeliner for times when you want to be dramatic. Some fashion experts feel that eyeliner is too stark for an over-fifty face, but I think it looks fine on Sophia Loren and Tina Turner! Use a color that blends with your eyeshadow, avoiding stark black or blue. I like dark gray and brown.

   Start your line halfway between the inside corner and middle of your eye at the edge of the eyelid. Draw a thin line outward to the edge of the eye. Darken the lower lid just over the lashes, bringing the pencil to the outside edge and meeting the top line.

8. *Mascara.* For evening, use a color one shade darker than your own lashes. Some new products are better suited to daytime use, such as Max Factor's Some Color, a lightly colored mascara, which is my favorite. I was told that models always use Maybelline, since it thickens lashes quickly and lasts long, and a quick peek at other makeup bags has confirmed this. I find it a little heavy for all day. Brush on upper and lower lashes and then go over with an eyebrow brush to separate and even the lashes. Repeat with a second coat on the top lashes only for thicker, longer-looking lashes. For a cleaner, more natural look use mascara on the top lashes only. This also prevents the smudging that leaves dark circles under the eyes.

9. *Blush.* For summer blush on white skin, use a tan shade to mimic a suntan. In the winter, a blush with

more pink adds some needed color. Bronze or mahogany tones are recommended for black skin. Ask for advice at the cosmetics counter for your particular skin tone. I prefer the powder blushes, which are easy to apply with a brush.

To apply, use the top portion of the brush and tap-tap-tap lightly over the area to be covered. Start dotting outside the eye rim, level with the corner of your eye. Continue dotting down over the cheekbone, staying outside the eye rim to the eye midpoint. Now move the brush down three-quarters of its own width and continue to dot just below the cheekbone, back up to the outside of the cheekbone. (See illustration above.) This dotting technique controls the amount of blush that goes onto the face and keeps the color even. Fill in with short brush strokes. You have given your face shape as well as color. This method is particularly good with the suntan shades.

10. *Lips*. A lipliner pencil is your best friend when it comes to shaping and reclaiming your lip line and keeping lipstick from spreading. Well-finished lips are important—as a matter of fact, if I used only one item of makeup, this would be it. First, evaluate your lips before using the pencil. Do you want to make them thicker, or thinner? A makeup artist pointed out to me that my lip arches were far apart. Therefore, I draw my lip line by placing the pencil inside the natural arch. For best control, use a lip brush to fill in, although a lipstick will do.

If the corners of your mouth turn downward, apply lipstick only up to one-quarter inch from the end of the mouth, leaving the corners free of lipstick. In addition, draw the lower lip out *slightly* beyond the upper lip. For an optional but beautiful touch, powder over the lips by dipping one of your triangular sponges into powder, shaking off any excess, and dabbing it over the lips. Add a second layer of lipstick. Then clean the edges of the lips with a clean portion of the sponge and blot lightly. Lipstick will stay on much longer. Your application does not have to be perfect the first time. The beauty of those little triangular sponges is that they clean up mistakes.

To keep your lips full and moist-looking longer, try this: first, apply a wax-based Chap Stick to your lips. Then draw in your lip line with your pencil. Next, use the pencil to fill in color within the lines. The look will be muted. If you want more glow, add

a layer of lipstick. Your lips will look great. Less
lines show and they stay moist and colorful for hours.

Styles change, but full and colorful lips are now
in fashion, so you may want to outline the lips
slightly outside of the natural lip line, as in illustration on page 285. Be careful not to overdo this, however, and end up with what my daughter refers to as
"that Bozo look."

Pulling It Together

As I noted, before you even start, decide what you
want to accomplish when you put on your makeup. When
you want to knock them dead you will probably go for
the "works," and you should count on twenty minutes
at the mirror. I have devised both a five-minute and a
two-minute routine to fit most situations.

Five-Minute Makeup

This will give you a finished look for day or evening.
For a natural effect, use a powder close to your own skin
color, a suntan-shade blush, eyebrow shadow the same
shade or one shade darker than your own, eye shadow
slightly darker than your skin tone, and a lipstick that
blends with your clothing. (Avoid the "nude" shades,
which make you look washed out.)

Use the five-minute routine with some contrasting colors to achieve a glamorous effect for the evening. The
array of colors is endless, and every season brings out a
new variety, so pick and choose as though they were
upholstery fabric. Using my coloring as an example—
gray hair and blue eyes—I change from a "natural" look
by using lighter powder, a pinker blush, the same eyebrow shade, a darker eye shadow, brown/black mascara,
and a strong lipstick like dark pink or clear red.

This is the sequence to follow for the five-minute
makeup:

- Clean and moisturize your face.
- Apply concealer.
- Brush on blush.
- Brush on powder.
- Brush on eyebrows.
- Use one shadow in the eye crease.
- Apply mascara.
- Apply lipstick.

Two-Minute Makeup

This faster routine is good for everyday makeup. Doing your lips takes the most time, but they are worth it, because lipstick can take you from invisible to attractive in one short step.

This is the sequence to follow for the two-minute makeup:

- Clean and moisturize your face.
- Brush on blush.
- Brush on eyebrows.
- Outline lips and apply lipstick.

Now your face is at least outlined and defined and has some color.

We have a great deal of control over our own appearance. While time does march on, when our best efforts are in action no one need know precisely how that time affects our looks.

1. NATURAL—NO MAKEUP

2. DAYTIME MAKEUP—ALL APPLIED AS ONE LIGHT COAT:
   concealer
   foundation and moisturizer mixture
   blush
   eyebrow powder
   eye shadow
   eyeliner
   mascara
   lips: lip pencil over Chap Stick

3. **CHANGE TO EVENING LOOK**
   increased blush
   darker eyebrows
   darker and expanded eye shadow
   added eyeliner
   one more layer of mascara

FACIAL TONE

The Question of Plastic Surgery

Every woman I know around my age, whether she will undergo cosmetic surgery in her lifetime or not, has stood by the mirror and pulled back the skin around her eyes, cheekbones, or neck "just to see" what she would look like if . . . Once prohibitively expensive for the average Jo, surgical procedures for cosmetic reasons are no longer just the province of the stars. One surgeon I interviewed told me that the majority of his patients earn between $25,000 to $35,000 a year. More and more young women are having eye lifts in their thirties and facelifts in their forties. The American Academy of Plastic and Reconstructive Surgeons reports that academy members performed 63 percent more procedures in 1988 than they did in 1981. If you are interested in finding a board-certified surgeon, consult the American Society of Plastic and Reconstructive Surgeons (800-635-0635) or the American Academy of Facial Plastic and Reconstructive Surgery (800-332-FACE.)

Despite such encouraging statistics, many people in this country are still skeptical about plastic surgery, if not for moral reasons, then for reasons of cost or concern about undergoing a surgical procedure. Certainly those were the overriding sentiments of the sampling of women I interviewed for this book. Also, we tend to think of plastic surgery as an indulgence for the rich and famous. It is interesting to note that Moscow's Cosmetological Clinic is the busiest and largest skin clinic in the world. In the Soviet Union plastic surgery appears to be viewed as a medical necessity.

In certain respects I agree with the concerns of the women I interviewed. I dread the thought of surgery and I consider the cost enormous. And a certain forbidden quality seems attached to going to such great lengths for the sake of beauty. I suspect, however, that I will not get through this life without some cosmetic surgical procedure. In her book *Always a Woman*, model Kaylan Pickford writes about having her eye area repaired. Another "classic" model friend of mine told me quietly that she had a "little work done" around her eyes. I find myself relieved when someone such as Frances Lear speaks openly in *Time* magazine about her one "very expensive makeup." Helen Gurley Brown is frank about her facelift, and Angela Lansbury explains that she decided to do only her neck and chin to avoid a change of expression. Last summer, *Vanity Fair* announced that Jackie O. had checked into a Manhattan hospital to have her face lifted by a well-known Park Avenue surgeon. Announcements such as these seem like a green light to go ahead with something that otherwise feels off-limits.

I recently consulted a plastic surgeon who described the various procedures available and told me that my skin showed stretching in many areas, but because of my strong bone structure, so far I was "getting away with it." He removed some of the mystery of the procedure by explaining that facial plastic surgery removes excess skin. He elaborated that, as we age, the skin of the cheeks becomes detached from their underlying supporting structures and starts to fall forward. At the same time as the skin is stretching, the underlying structures—bone, muscle, and deep skin layer—are shrinking. The result is an excess of skin, which the surgery removes.

As I sat there visualizing my insides shrinking and my outsides stretching on the one hand, and the risk of surgery on the other, I decided to see how long I could "get away with it" without plastic surgery.

Beyond surgery a youthful, and a healthy, appearance can be maintained by conserving bone structure (see page 152), maintaining skin thickness (see pages 124, 152–53, and 263), and toning facial muscles (see the following section on face exercises and Electrical Muscular Stimulation, or EMS).

Nonsurgical Facelift

The aesthetician Catherine Hinds, who was earlier reported as outlining the four approaches to caring for skin, says that only two major breakthroughs in skin care have occurred in the past twenty years. They are Retin-A cream and Electrical Muscular Stimulation (EMS). EMS, a process that tones the muscles of the face, is done in a salon with two small hand-held machines that look like eggs with metal plates attached. The metal plates are placed on certain spots on the face and a mild, adjustable electric current contracts the facial muscles. The muscle contraction feels similar to the contractions of facial exercises, only stronger. Two types of currents are used. Galvanic is the milder of the two and is used on delicate areas, such as around the eyes. Faradic is stronger and contracts the larger muscle groups.

An electrical current on the face requires application of foreign stimuli and brings into question the safety of the procedure, although EMS has been widely used for body building with no known side effects. Catherine Hinds has been practicing EMS in her Newton, Massachusetts, salon for eleven years and to date has had no reported ill effects. Another question about the procedure is whether or not it is effective. Hinds allows the individual client to decide for herself, although it is Hinds's opinion that once the skin has sagged a lot, EMS does not help. By and large, her clients say it works. The FDA, however, does not agree.

I had EMS done before discovering it is not approved by the FDA. The last ruling on this issue, passed in 1980, says that no scientific data exists to support the use of EMS for cosmetic application. Although the procedure is not illegal, regulated approval can be obtained for medical use only. In a medical capacity it can be used for relaxation, retardation of tissue atrophy, muscle education, increasing muscle blood circulation, and maintaining or increasing range of motion. One EMS machine distributor informed me that the machines are advertised in national men's magazines for body building and he rarely receives regulation complaints regarding that usage. He gets the most legal resistance from the FDA regarding the cosmetic application of EMS. "I think," he said, "that this may have to do with most of the people at the FDA being men." Another distributor summed up what appears to me to be FDA bias against using the procedure for cosmetic needs in this country. "Look, we're not talking about the Mafia. We're talking about a treatment that has been used widely all over Europe for twenty years. The rulings in this country are unlike any other in the world. There are fifty-three hundred beauty salons in Canada, and forty-six hundred of them use it."

Lack of regulation makes it difficult to decide on the safety of EMS. Catherine Hinds advises:

- Look for a reputable salon. Your State Board of Cosmetology can advise you which salons are properly licensed. (Licensed to practice cosmetology, that is. No formal licensing is currently available for the practice of EMS.)
- Ask for a licensed aesthetician.
- Ask for a free demonstration.
- Ask whether the practitioner has received special training in the use of EMS equipment.

Because of the series of EMS treatments I had, I feel that my face is more defined and in general healthier. I now occasionally have touch-up treatments, using facial exercises in between.

The cost for the initial series of twelve treatments is $500–$800. Monthly follow-ups are $30–$50.

A battery-driven small machine for home use, called Minitone, is now out on the market for approximately $220.

Acupuncture

Acupuncture is an ancient Chinese medical practice used to cure illness or alleviate conditions by placing very fine needles just below a person's skin. The placement of acupuncture needles relieves built-up tension in the nerves, and since the face has over a thousand nerve endings the results of acupuncture in that area are better tone, coloring, and firmness, and smoother and more relaxed skin. A series of treatments runs two to three times a week for six to seven weeks at a cost of $300–$500, with suggested once-a-month touch-ups costing $25–$40. A bonus of such treatments is that no recuperation time and no risk of infection or swelling are involved. Results are reportedly not as good with extremely wrinkled skin.

As a nutrition consultant in a holistic health practice, I received body acupuncture as an employee "perk," finding the sessions enormously relaxing. The center had done some facial programs and reported that the skin of recipients took on a vital glow. Small surface wrinkles diminished, facial muscles firmed, and dark areas under the eyes were markedly reduced.

When selecting among practitioners, be sure they are licensed in the state in which they practice. Confirm this by consulting your state's Professional Acupuncture Association, which may also offer a referral service.

Facial Exercises

In my quest for beautiful and healthy skin, I responded to a newspaper ad for the Face Life program and signed up for a four-class series that taught me a complete facial-exercise routine. I saw immediate results in the first class. I was struck by the fact that while I had exercised most of my muscles for most of my life, at age fifty I had let my facial muscles go their own way. Actually, before this program I hadn't even known I *had* facial muscles. As a result of my new awareness, I included my face in the exercise system I had for my body and it felt great! I recommend face exercises for anyone of any age.

Face Life was developed by Laura Hart, Ph.D., of Newton, Massachusetts, and is best learned visually. If you would like to learn the full system, contact Dr. Hart (see Resources, page 320.) The ages of the participants in the class, all women, ran from twenty to sixty. Some of the younger women were being treated for face injuries due to illness or accident, while others were interested in reshaping the contours of their face. The rest of us were interested in reversing age-related change.

I noticed a marked difference in everyone after the first session, and the changes accumulated over the three-month period of the class. I see no reason to wait for accident, illness, or middle age in order to learn these exercises, and I recommend that young women acquaint themselves with their facial muscles early in life. Along with Dr. Hart's program, several books are available that teach facial exercise programs (see your local library).

Under the layers of skin and fat of the face is an intricate system of muscles, which the anatomy books refer to as "muscles of expression." As discussed in more detail in the nutrition chapter, the usual process of aging involves losing muscle while gaining fat. Just as exercise returns the contours of the body, it can strengthen the contours of the face. The job of the facial muscles is to move the facial skeleton, as in chewing. Again, with technology being a double-edged sword, modern human beings chew much less since the advent of farming and the stove. Another job performed by the facial muscles is to hold up the face. Facial exercises can prevent and reverse the sagging that results from reduced muscle mass. Before I began doing facial exercises, I hated watching my chin sag and cheeks shrink as though they had a life of their own that I could not influence short of going through surgery. The beauty of developing a personal facial exercise program is that once you have it, no cost is involved, plus the benefits accumulate and grow with time.

Facial exercises have a stigma attached to them. Accumulated movements of the face are thought to cause wrinkling. In reality, one cause of wrinkles is the shrinking of muscle under the skin. Another cause is the diminished dermis layer, due to a decrease in elastin and collagen. Not only do facial exercises increase blood circulation to the face, the exercises enhance collagen and elastin production. I have found a new firmness and turgor to my skin and would say that wrinkles have diminished. Ironically, many women have lived their lives frozen-faced in fear that overuse of face muscles causes wrinkles, when in fact the exact opposite is true.

Facial muscles do not contract as strongly as body muscles do, so you will not build muscle bulk as you would in body training. The exercises are meant to be done mildly and frequently, at least twice a day. *Once learned* they can be done in about ten minutes. I do them while waiting at red lights, and just hope nobody is watching.

The following are exercises I have found to be effective:

SCALP TIGHTENER

This exercise will prevent the face from falling in the brow area. It tightens the scalp muscles, holding the scalp firmly on the skull.

Raise your eyebrows without frowning. Your forehead muscle will raise, and there should be no change in your expression. Doing this helps you find the scalp muscles. As you raise your brows, you will feel the forehead and top of the scalp tighten. The tightened area under your hair is the scalp muscles, which you are exercising. Finding them takes some practice, but once you have found them, you can move those muscles independently by contracting and releasing repeatedly.

If you are doing this exercise correctly, the face still has the feeling of being startled, while your hair moves

up and down as if you were wearing an ill-fitting wig.
Release, and repeat twenty times.

UPPER CHEEK LIFT

This exercise tones the muscles of the upper cheek,
which draws attention to the eyes and gives that *Vogue*-
model, high-cheekbone appearance.

Using a mirror initially, make a crooked grin with the
right side of your mouth. Hold this position throughout
exercise. Place a finger on your cheek, below the outer
corner of your right eye. Your finger is now resting on
the muscle to be exercised. Identifying the muscle with
your finger, use this muscle to slowly push the lower lid
of your right eye closed. Hold. Slowly return to normal
position. Repeat eight times. Repeat on the left side.

LIP LIFT

This exercise lifts the corners of the mouth, which tend
to turn downward with time. Place your teeth and lips
together in a relaxed position with the lips closed. Lift
the corners of your mouth toward the temples. Smile pur-
posefully, putting the outer corners of the mouth up and
out. Your face should be in a big grin. The contraction
is felt from the corners of the mouth to the upper cheek
muscles, which tremble slightly. Slowly return the outer
corners of your mouth to their natural position. Do this
as slowly as possible, controlling the muscles as you release them. Do four times with both corners of the mouth
together, then four times on each side of the mouth separately. When you have finished on each side, the lips
can relax open and the outside of the eye closes slightly.
This has been extremely useful to me in modeling because I can control just how happy I want to appear, from
mildly pleased to ecstatic.

CHIN TIGHTENER

I love this exercise. It tightens the area under the chin
by contracting what the yogis call antigravity muscles.

Tilt your head back and push your lower lip over your top lip. Place your finger on the chin muscle to help identify and move it. Push your chin muscle up toward your lip for a count of 5. Repeat eight times.

CHIN TIGHTENER II

This works the same area as the first chin tightener while using a second method.

Open your mouth, stick out your tongue, and point the tip of your tongue as far toward the tip of your nose as possible. Release, withdrawing the tongue back to between the lips. Repeat twenty-five times.

FACE STRETCH

This exercise stretches the cheek muscles after you have gone through all the above contractions. By including stretching with contraction, the work is balanced and the face is left feeling relaxed.

Close your mouth and push it as far to the right as possible while using the facial muscles on the left to pull the flesh of your cheek as far to the right as you can. The left side of your face will feel stretched, while the right side will be distorted-looking, because of the displacement of the skin. Relax your left cheek but not entirely, and stretch again, repeating eight times. Repeat on the other side.

As a woman in midlife you are already beautiful, so use the tips in this chapter to enhance the qualities that are already there. Keep in mind that beauty is not frivolous nor is it an indulgence. A dangerous myth about the older woman is that she is uninteresting, invisible, someone to be patronized, or someone to be ignored. We do not have to take such assessments lying down! Putting effort into our looks goes miles toward destroying that myth.

SECTION FOUR

❧

The Future

CHAPTER 14

Taking Risks, Making Noise, Being Courageous

Time and trouble will tame an advanced young woman, but an advanced older woman is uncontrollable by any force.

— DOROTHY SAYERS

If we are neither young nor old, neither depressed nor sick, neither a grandmother nor a vamp, who are we? And where are we headed with no map to guide us?

We are charting a course into a future that promises to be as varied and surprising as our pasts have been. Some of us are forty; some of us are sixty. We have first children and grandchildren. We have worked for years and are ready to retire. We are starting our second or third careers and are determined never to retire. We cannot be categorized and yet we share an undeniable will to be known—for having lived fully and for having something to offer.

"This is the richest time of a woman's life," asserted Mickie Kramer. "Yet we don't have role models, we don't know what to call ourselves. There's a way for us to dress, there's a way for us to look, there's a way for us to be. But we need a word like 'teenager' to describe us. Not being identified means we can't be marketed to, we can't be referred to."

Call us anything: middle-aged, menopausal, post, past, almost, going to—it doesn't matter. What does matter is that never before has a group of people had as much to

offer the world at large—discipline from years of taking
care of others, passion born and cultivated in an age of
romance, perseverance from having raised children to
adulthood, fortitude from waiting to have children while
working on careers, resilience and humor from having
survived life's blows. We are smart. We are hard-
working. We have an appreciation for fun. Since Madison Avenue for the most part has ignored us, we are not
jaded by images of who we should be. We have the resources and the freedom to accomplish anything.

OUR ROMANTIC GENERATION

That we can do anything, that we can write the script
for our own lives, is not empty rhetoric swept up as
crumbs from the "Me Generation." What we have to
offer is particular to our sensibility. We were not raised
to choose our destinies; we learned to exercise choice,
years after being encouraged to follow only one or two
paths.

Columnist Georgie Ann Geyer addresses "our romantic generation of women, those of us in our fifties and
forties," who valued love and relationships above all
else, as "the swing group in feminism. We personify
within ourselves the laboratory of change and the passion
and the glory of a noble cause passed on to the young,
whatever they now chose to do with it."

Coming of age in the fifties and early sixties, with its
dreams of love, was not all foolishness. We bring a depth,
a richness, and a passion to relationships, whereas
younger women seem to evaluate their romantic options
from a few steps removed. There is something for us to
learn from their looking before they leap, yet something
special is available when you jump in as we did and live
with all your heart.

And we stand on the shoulders of the women who came
before us. As thirty-eight-year-old Mary Zazzera says of
her mother, in her sixties, who raised nine children,

"What she says to me continually is, 'I still feel I have something to say and something yet to give this world.' In that respect my mother is available and she is open. She hasn't stopped growing. She hasn't stopped questioning. She hasn't found any answer, but she is questioning, and that's the part I think is incredibly important."

In my family, my mother, who is seventy-five, has wondered about my two sisters and me. What is to become of her three independent daughters, she wants to know, as she watches us juggle family life, money, and career changes. I asked her what her expectations of her sixties and seventies were when she was in her forties and fifties. "To tell you the truth, I wasn't looking for any great desires in my life. I went along and I turned seventy-five—I didn't know where the years went to." She paused, thought, and finally, never having had a career, she said, "When I come back in my next life, I would like to come back as Elizabeth Arden, or Estée Lauder. They are beautiful, they are businesswomen, and they made an empire for themselves."

GRABBING THE REINS OF OUR DREAMS

We have the opportunity to realize our dreams in ways the generation before us did not. Yet, we can start realizing such dreams only by giving ourselves credit for having gotten where we already are. Too often, in the quest for achievement and success, we forget to acknowledge what we have already done. In such a light, our dreams and goals are never as important as they should be (not selfless enough, too small and close to home) and are simultaneously unrealizable. Stepping back and enjoying what we have accomplished offers great pleasures and provides a significant boost as we plunge forward into the future.

Smoki Bacon, sixty-one, is known in Boston society as a socialite, a title she laughed at when I mentioned it to her, since the organizing and hosting of cultural events requires tremendous work. In her fantasy life she would "never have to worry about paying bills. I would have a lot of money to invest. I know this town backward and forward and I would love to head up some huge foundation to be able to give money to groups to use." Yet, her dreaming does not discount the significant contribution she felt she had already made. "My making a difference in life has been with my two daughters, and I am a firm believer," she insisted, banging her fist on the table, "that you start with what is right there before you, before you go and change the world."

Julia Phillips, fifty-nine, is proud of her work, as a wife, as a mother, as a teacher, and as a school principal. She knows she has touched many lives. For a woman who is used to working hard within a system, the contemplation of retirement brings with it mixed emotions. Speaking with me, she found herself debating two alternatives—continuing to make some sort of contribution through work or enjoying the comforts anticipated by no longer working full-time. "In reality, I have been working all my life, so why should I feel guilty for not working? I think it's very important to enjoy leisure. Yet, I'm so concerned about ecology and the environment. I wish I could do something in that area. I don't know if I will. I kind of feel as if I have an open future."

An open future. Sounds both limitless and threatening, inviting and confusing. What can such a future bring?

"The future," said writer Merlin Stone during our interview over coffee, "I will play by ear." The author of numerous books on ancient goddesses, Stone came to writing in her forties after making and teaching sculpture for twenty years. She has always found herself in the middle of some creative project. "I have a strong feeling that I am being guided and will be told what to do. My clue to the guidance is what I get excited by and feel energized to do. I go from project to project—lecturing, workshops, articles. The floor doesn't get washed too often because I don't get excited by that very often! But I feel I have as much potential now as when I was ten, maybe more.''

''I still have at least two more careers in me,'' said forty-six-year-old Janet Lowe, the executive with Digital Equipment Corporation. ''One thing I would like to do before I die is manufacture something. I owned an apartment building at one time, and I had a beauty salon and a gift shop at one point, but I've never manufactured something. Another thing I've wanted to do is generate money. I've always had enough money, but what if I had a resource to draw on to do the next thing? It's just something I never thought about.'' How much did she have in mind? ''I've sat down and figured this out and I thought probably about twenty million dollars.''

I gasped. ''Twenty million?'' I got that old feeling about girls not being good at math.

''Yes. The way I look at it, a million is way outside of how I usually think about anything, so maybe twenty million isn't enough.''

Claudia Nelson, fifty-five, broke out of her usual way of conducting her life when after many years as a housewife, mother, and artist she became an entrepreneur in partnership with her husband, Harry. They now own and operate a bakery, and they also run a school for disabled children. She told me about her business plans. ''Both Harry and I expect to work for the rest of our lives. We're expanding the bakery and we want to get into direct mail and retail sales. We have the school, and we're building another one in Delaware and one in Pennsylvania. So we've got a lot of construction projects on the board for probably the next eight years.'' Claudia notes that her middle age does not look like the middle age she expected. ''I remember my mother saying when she turned fifty, 'Well, I'm an antique now, I'm fifty years old and you get to be an antique.' She died at eighty-six, which is thirty-six years of being old. That's a long time to be old!''

Sandra Littleton, fifty-six, has laid out explicit plans for a new future after making her way through loss and setback. Excess weight and a painful divorce left her emotionally stunned in her forties. Now in her fifties, she told me, "First of all I'm going to do everything I can for my health. I'm going to start in a weight-loss program at Emerson Hospital and I'm already exercising an hour a day. Then I'm going to get this house cleaned up and get rid of a lot of stuff and move to a smaller place." What led to these changes was her realization that she wanted to "make the most of each decade, because you don't even know if you'll get to the next one. Even if you do get to the next one, it will probably be diminished from what this one has been. I need to tell myself to stop shuffling around and make the most of what I've got." At last count Sandra had lost, and kept off, forty pounds.

FORGING THE FUTURE

What will it take to forge a new future? Often we are jolted into change because of a tragedy or a crisis. The face of our future is then permanently altered by a force from outside. But shaping the next thirty-odd years does not necessarily mean uprooting or overturning what we already have. In fact, the idea of being *required* to have a useful, difference-making rest of our lives will probably send a lot of women running for cover, screaming, "I've gone through too much already! Leave me alone!" Yet, we somehow want to use our energies and we want to be heard.

"As women," said Merlin Stone, "we internalize what we're supposed to be doing at certain ages. So now we may think, I'm too old. The best thing for a woman to do, when she realizes that she's been held down, is to get angry. Feel your anger that things have happened this way, furious. Use that as fuel. We're considered useless? That's ridiculous! In ancient cultures older women were considered exceptionally wise. Now, we're considered ignorant. 'Foolish old lady,' 'crazy old lady,' 'silly,' 'hysterical.' For ourselves, to respect who we are and to trust who we are is crucial. Also, to respect one another helps us understand who we are as individuals. When you get a group of women together, older women, you hear the brilliance and the perceptions from experience that have been unable to be said. Wisdom regarding the earth, life, sanity. These resources are resources the world should draw on.''

Creating a future, personally or globally, in which our resources are used to their fullest extent does not come easily. Stone carves her future with openness and continual observation, always aware of her own responses. Janet Lowe looks way beyond the usual and the expected for herself and comes up with a business goal of $20 million. Claudia Nelson initiates the big change from artist to entrepreneur in the shadow of her mother's thirty-six years of old age. Sandra Littleton looks at her life with honesty and draws on courage to make a comeback from pain and disruption.

What seems most ''natural'' is just to drift into old age. Not drifting takes effort. Effort initially may require a certain sacrifice of comfort, whether that comfort comes from a habitual way of viewing something, as evidenced with the women above, thinking about something, or doing something.

In a PBS special about the renowned ballet dancer Margot Fonteyn, Fonteyn talked about dancing with Rudolf Nureyev when he was twenty-three and she was forty-two. Knowing that everyone would want to see how they looked together, she made sure she was strong enough to keep up with him. She did this by continuing to practice her most difficult dances so that her stamina, courage, and discipline would never drop below her highest standards for herself.

Until I heard Fonteyn, I was quite proud of my aerobic workout four times a week. Listening to her, I asked myself if I had dropped whatever for me were the most difficult challenges of keeping fit. I could see that I had.

Angela Lansbury reports that she stays in shape in her sixties because she's a workaholic. After a long successful career in theater and films, she became a star in another medium—television. Although her series *Murder, She Wrote* has been a "relentless workload," she has found new creativity within it, bringing in stars and directors with whom she wants to work. And the series does not preclude a return to films.

In her fifties, Liv Ullmann has not let herself rest on the laurels of her talents and successful acting career. In her book *Choices* she speaks of taking advantage of her celebrity status in order to help those who don't have her privilege, particularly the tens of thousands of children around the world who die every day from malnutrition. For the past twelve years she has put her anger into action by traveling extensively, visiting refugee camps for the International Rescue Committee, and as a goodwill ambassador for UNICEF. In between her travels she found time to meet her husband on a speaking engagement in Boston in 1983. In 1989 she hosted a party for the Boston Salvation Army as a celebration for her fiftieth birthday. When asked about her ability to keep up with the demands of her schedule, however, she laughed, insisting that she was basically lazy, preferring to lie on the sofa and watch old movies to doing anything else. Like Angela Lansbury, she has taken on "relentless workloads" for the sake of fulfilling her visions.

When my goals and visions feel particularly futile and out of reach, I have found the lives of accomplished women inspirational and encouraging. Women in the public eye like Fonteyn, Lansbury, and Ullmann are role models for leading an ongoing, productive, and creative life. Yet, I am also inspired by accomplished women who do not lead public lives, whose successes are not documented by the media but who achieve success through the acts of day-to-day living. I have been inspired by the women I interviewed for this book and for them I had the following question:

If you had one day or night of fantasy and could be anyone you wanted, who would that person be? A number of women said they didn't have many fantasies, because they were so satisfied with their lives. Yet, encouraged to answer, everyone was able to invent a dream future, untethered by the normal barriers.

The most popular fantasy was about dancing. Doris Lambert would fulfill her childhood dream of being a ballerina; Shirley Grant wanted her husband to lose a hundred pounds and get into the shape he was in when they married, so they could go out dancing all night; Julia Phillips and her husband would be resurrected as Fred Astaire and Ginger Rogers.

"Do you know what the Lambada is?" asked Linda Avery, her eyes full of mischief. "It's a Brazilian dance where the women wear high heels and little skirts that twirl around and little skimpy tops and a flower in their hair and a feather and they do this dance that involves a lot of bending, twisting, and spinning. When my husband and I were down in Key West recently, we had this idea about this new dance and we actually taught ourselves how to do it. Since few people knew how to do it where we were, we were doing it on the dance floor alone. And I loved it. That's my fantasy. Being just completely free and uninhibited. And being a leader of sorts, being a true individual."

Francine Lewin sees herself dancing on stage. "If I had one night in a dream world I'd be a fabulous dancer. A fabulous professional dancer on Broadway— like *Chorus Line*." Is that possible? "In my next life but not in this one."

Does every woman harbor a fantasy about dancing?

Adrienne Garrity, forty-six, is currently single, although she has been married three times. What she longs for is "romance. I'd like to be Ingrid Bergman in *Casa-*

blanca, and rest my head on Humphrey Bogart's chest and have him tell me he'll think for the both of us.''

Grace Devereaux, age fifty-nine, never finished high school. Given the chance, she would choose to have more education. Such a fantasy is more than possible in today's world. While singer Pearl Bailey, who died in 1990, missed that opportunity as a young woman, at age fifty-eight she went to college for the first time. She claimed, in an interview the year before she died, not to be motivated or clever, but just able to pick up and do whatever it was she decided to do. "My religion is action," she said.

Some fantasies are in the arena of political power. If Pauline Worlen could be anyone in the entire world for a day, she would be the president of the United States. "I've got a couple of things I could fix. I'm not sure how much I could do in a day, actually, but it would be great to be up there and say, 'Quit this crap!' " Recently, in Mississippi, a woman running for mayor encouraged two friends to run for the city council on the same ticket. Two other friends joined the ranks. The five women won and are running the city.

Gloria Steinem, in an interview with Joan Rivers, said she envisions an army of silver-haired women taking over the world. As I read the daily newspaper, full of world problems, I too can envision this army tackling and solving major social problems. One such problem is women's health, an area in which progress is finally being made in response to strong and relentless voices of protest.

Change started after a public spotlight landed on the National Institutes of Health, revealing that in 1987 health concerns affecting women accounted for only 13 percent of the NIH budget. Many major health studies completely eliminate women. As a result, overall medical conclusions have been based on studies performed on men alone. Such conclusions have been passed on as medical practice and advice for women, whose physiology may demand different conclusions. For example, a study of 22,000 men showed a beneficial effect of aspirin for those at risk for heart disease. Women, however, were excluded from the study *because of cost considerations*. This is shocking, considering that heart disease is the number-one killer of women over fifty. Soon after this study was made public another was published that related specifically to aspirin's effect on women. The two studies would appear to be parallel although careful reading shows the women who took aspirin were not monitored as specifically as the men were in their study. The conclusions regarding women and aspirin remain speculative. Another area of neglect is breast cancer, with incidences having risen 50 percent since 1960. In 1989, the NIH halted a major study on breast cancer, again because of cost considerations.

The Women's Community Cancer Project, a group based in Cambridge, Massachusetts, was formed in the fall of 1989 to lobby for changes in the medical approach to cancer, particularly as it affects women. In Congress, the Congressional Caucus for Women's Issues, co-chaired by Colorado Congresswoman Patricia Schroeder, introduced legislation to ''achieve parity in medical research.'' And in the fall of 1990, an office at the National Institutes of Health was established to monitor, coordinate, and enhance research on women's health. The office was formed in recognition of the need to include women in clinical studies.

The three-year, $10 million Postmenopausal Estrogen-Progestin Intervention Trial, launched in 1990 by the National Institutes of Health, is designed to chart the effects of various hormone treatments on postmenopausal women. This first major government-funded study of menopause we hope will be one in a series of many that will take the issue of menopause seriously. We can only assume that ongoing research will clear up the confusion surrounding hormone-replacement therapy so that the facts can be presented reasonably and not as canon fodder for media scares about cancer and other fatalities.

Ongoing organizations, such as Liv Ullmann's International Relief Fund and UNICEF; new projects such as the Women's Community Cancer Project; caucuses for ensuring research on women's health topics—what other beneficial change does this army of midlife women have the potential to inspire?

We know our capabilities. Does the rest of the world? With the resources we embody and our power base of sheer numbers, we are making our presence known more than ever. The strength of our numbers has brought to the surface areas, such as health care, where, until now, we have been ignored. If we exercised our strength and influence, if we used the resources of our life experience, imagine what headway could be made in medicine, in government, in the arts, in the environment, in our communities, in our families, and in our experiences of ourselves.

At this point in our lives, the strongest force capable of defeating us is our own complacency. Carolyn Heilbrun is the Avalon Foundation professor in the humanities at Columbia University and the author, under the pen name Amanda Cross, of a popular detective series. In her nonfiction book *Writing a Woman's Life*, she discusses women's biographies and the need we have for stories of women's lives in order to help shape our own. In these words from an interview, she warns us against getting too comfortable as she inspires us to express ourselves fully:

It occurs to me now that as we age many of us who are privileged— those with some assured place and pattern in their lives, with some financial security—are in danger of choosing to stay right where we are, to undertake each day's routine and to listen to our arteries hardening. . . . Instead, we should make use of our

security, our seniority, to take risks, to make noise, to
be courageous, to become unpopular.

We are the vehicles for change. As we carry the ball
into the next century, look out.

≋

Appendix:

Kegel Exercises

Kegel exercises are designed to firm the muscles of the pelvis. Strengthening those muscles can eliminate the problem of stress incontinence while strengthening and supporting the bladder, urethra, and rectum. By tightening vaginal muscles, Kegels can also increase sexual sensation.

Locate these muscles by voluntarily stopping and starting a flow of urine at midstream. Once located, tighten for three seconds, then relax for three seconds. Don't strain, and breathe naturally. You can tell if you are doing the exercises correctly if you can tighten your vagina around your finger.

Once you find the right muscles, start with 20 contractions a day. Try to build to 100 a day. These can be done in groups of ten or all at once. You may not see results from these contractions for two to three months. In the meantime, they can be done any place and at any time. No one needs to be the wiser.

Resources

RECOMMENDED READING
General:
1. Beard, Mary, M.D., F.A.C.O.G., and Lindsay Curtis, M.D., F.A.C.O.G., *Menopause and the Years Ahead* (Tucson, Ariz.: Fisher Books, 1988).
2. Burnett, Raymond G., M.D., *Menopause, All Your Questions Answered* (Chicago: Contemporary Books, Inc., 1987).
3. Cutler, Winnifred Berg, Ph.D., *Hysterectomy: Before and After* (New York: HarperCollins, 1990).
4. ———, Celso-Ramon García, M.D., and David A. Edwards, Ph.D., *Menopause: A Guide for Women and the Men Who Love Them* (New York: W. W. Norton, 1985).
5. Doress, Paula Brown, Diana Laskin Siegel, and the Older Women's Book Project in cooperation with the Boston Women's Health Book Collective, *Ourselves, Growing Older* (New York: Touchstone/Simon & Schuster, 1987).
6. Ehrenreich, Barbara, and Deirdre English, *For Her Own Good: 150 Years of the Experts' Advice to Women* (New York: Anchor/Doubleday, 1979, 1989).
7. Fairlie, Judi, Jayne Nelson, and Ruth Popplestone, *Menopause, a Time for Positive Change* (New York: Javelin Books, 1987).
8. Fisher, Sue, Ph.D., *In the Patient's Best Interest: Women and the Politics of Medical Decision Making* (New Jersey: Rutgers University Press, 1986).
9. Friedan, Betty, *The Feminine Mystique* (New York: W. W. Norton, 1963).
10. Gillespie, Clark, M.D., *Hormones, Hot Flashes and Mood Swings* (New York: Harper & Row, 1989).
11. Greenwood, Sadja, M.D., *Menopause, Naturally* (Volcano, Cal.: Volcano Press, 1984).

12. Greer, Germaine, *The Female Eunuch* (New York: McGraw-Hill, 1970).
13. Henig, Robin Marantz, *How a Woman Ages* (New York: Ballantine/ Esquire, 1985).
14. Masters, William H., and Virginia E. Johnson, *Human Sexual Response* (Boston: Little, Brown, 1966).
15. Melamed, Elissa, Ph.D., *Mirror, Mirror: The Terror of Not Being Young* (New York: Linden Press/Simon & Schuster, 1983).
16. Ransohoff, Rita, Ph.D., *Venus After Forty: Sexual Myths, Men's Fantasies and Truths About Middle-Aged Women* (Fair Hills, N.J.: New Horizons Press, 1987).
17. Sarrel, L. J., and P. M. Sarrel, *Sexual Turning Points* (New York: Macmillan, 1984).
18. Trien, Susan Flamholtz, *Change of Life Handbook* (New York: Fawcett Columbine, 1986).
19. Utian, Wulf H., M.D., Ph.D., and Ruth Jacobowitz, *Managing Your Menopause—for Women in Their Prime Who Want to Stay that Way* (New York: Prentice Hall Press, 1990). *Your Middle Years: A Doctor's Guide for Today's Women* (New York: Appleton Century Crofts, 1980).
20. ──and Ruth S. Jacobowitz, *Managing Your Menopause* (New York: Prentice Hall, 1990).
21. Weideger, Paula, *Menstruation and Menopause: The Physiology and Psychology, the Myth and the Reality* (New York: Dell, 1975).

Nutrition:

1. American Dietetic Association Nutrition Resources, 216 West Jackson Boulevard, Suite 800, Chicago, IL 60606-6995. Send a stamped self-addressed business-size envelope and request the "Good Nutrition Reading List, 1990."
2. Bailey, Covert, *The Fit-or-Fat Target Diet* (Boston: Houghton Mifflin, 1984).
3. ── and Lea Bishop, *Target Recipes, the Fit-or-Fat System* (Boston: Houghton Mifflin, 1985).
4. Brody, Jane E., *Jane Brody's Good Food Book: Living the High Carbohydrate Way* (New York: W. W. Norton, 1985).
5. Center for Science in the Public Interest, 1875 Connecticut Avenue, Suite 300, Washington, D.C. 20009-5728. Send for the *Nutrition Action Healthletter*, $19.95 per year.
6. Clark, Nancy, M.S., R.D., *Nancy Clark's Sports Nutrition Guidebook* (Champaign, Ill.: Leisure Press, 1990).
7. Robertson, Laurel, Carol Flinders, and Bronwen Godfrey, *Laurel's Kitchen* (Berkeley, Cal: Nilgiri Press, 1976).

Exercise:

1. Bailey, Covert, *Fit or Fat?* (Boston: Houghton Mifflin, 1977).
2. —— and Lea Bishop, *The Fit-or-Fat Woman* (Boston: Houghton Mifflin, 1989).
3. Shangold, M., and G. Mirkin, *Women and Exercise Physiology and Sports Medicine* (Philadelphia: F. A. Davis, 1988).
4. Advanced yoga postures: Iyengar, B.K.S., *Light on Yoga* (New York: Schocken Books, 1966).
5. Hittleman, Richard, *Richard Hittleman's Yoga, 28 Day Exercise Plan* (New York: Bantam Books, 1973).

OTHER RESOURCES

General:

The Older Women's League (OWL)—promotes state and federal educational and advocacy activities regarding the lives of middle-aged and older women. Publishes a bimonthly newsletter, *The OWL Observer.*

 730 11th Street, N.W., Suite 300
 Washington, D.C. 20001
 (202) 783-6686

Forty-Plus—A self-help, nonprofit club located in major cities that attempts to find employment for laid-off management-level executives.

 15 Park Row
 New York, NY 10038
 (212) 233-6068

National Association of Older Worker Employment Services
 600 Maryland Avenue, S.W., West Wing 100
 Washington, D.C. 20024

A Friend Indeed Publications, Inc.—a networking newsletter for women.

 Box 515 Place du Parc Station
 Montreal, Canada H2W 2P1

Patient Care Directory
 Wulf H. Utian, M.D., Ph.D.
 President, North American Menopause Society
 Director, Dept. of Obstetrics and Gynecology
 University Hospitals of Cleveland
 2074 Abington Road
 Cleveland, OH 44106

North American Menopause Society
c/o University Hospitals of Cleveland
2074 Abington Road
Cleveland, OH 44106
(216) 844-3334

To order *Menopause Management* contact:
  The Conwood Group
  telephone: (201) 361-1280
  fax: (201) 361-1882

Beauty:
American Academy of Dermatology
1567 Maple Avenue
Evanston, IL 60201
(708) 869-3954

American Society of Plastic and Reconstructive Surgeons
444 East Algonquin Road
Arlington Heights, IL 60005
(708) 228-9900
Referral service: (800) 635-0635

Center for Human Appearance
University of Pennsylvania
Penn Tower Hotel, 10th floor
3400 Spruce St.
Philadelphia, PA 19104
(800) 234-PENN

''Look Good . . . Feel Better''
The Cosmetic, Toiletry and Fragrance Association (CTFA) Foundation
1110 Vermont Avenue, N.W., Suite 800
Washington, D.C. 20005
(800) 558-5005

Face Life
c/o Laura Hart, Ph.D.
454 Lowell Avenue
Newton, MA 02160
(617) 965-5335

Facial Plastic Surgery Information Service
1101 Vermont Ave, N.W., Suite 404
Washington, D.C. 20005
(800) 332-FACE

The Catherine Hinds Institute of Esthetics
65 Riverside Place
Medford, MA 02155

National Association of Accredited Cosmetology Schools
5201 Leesburg Pike, Suite 205
Falls Church, VA 22041
(703) 845-1333

National Cosmetology Association
3510 Olive Street
St. Louis, MO 63103
(314) 534-7980

Nutrition:
Silent Epidemic: The Truth About Women and Heart Disease. Send
self-addressed, stamped (50 cents), business-size envelope to:
The American Heart Association
Box BUL-1
7320 Greenville Ave.
Dallas, TX 75231

"The Healthy Heart Handbook for Women"
(GPO stock number p17-00117-006)
U.S. Government Printing Office
Superintendent of Documents, U.S. G.P.O.
Washington, D.C. 20402
Cost: $1.25

Sources

INTRODUCTION: SO THIS IS MENOPAUSE
McKinlay, McKinlay, and Brambilla, *Journal of Health and Social Behavior*, December 1987, 28:345–363, p. 347.

CHAPTER 1—WHO WE ARE AND HOW WE FOUND OURSELVES HERE
1. Evelyn Fox Keller, *Reflections on Gender and Science* (New Haven: Yale University Press, 1985).
2. Estella Lauter, *Women as Mythmakers: Poetry and Visual Art by Twentieth-Century Women* (Bloomington: Indiana University Press, 1984).

CHAPTER 2—MYTH 1: "NO LONGER A WOMAN"
1. Simone de Beauvoir (translated into English by H. M. Parshley), *The Second Sex* (New York: Alfred A. Knopf, 1971), originally published in France in 1949.
2. Elinor W. Gadon, "The Life Cycle of the Goddess," *Woman of Power*, Summer 1989, Issue 14.
3. Marilyn Gardner, "Older Women Expressing a New Sophistication," *Christian Science Monitor News Service*, Palm Beach: January 1989.
4. Germaine Greer, *The Female Eunuch* (New York: McGraw-Hill, 1970).
5. Betty Friedan, *The Feminine Mystique* (New York: W. W. Norton, 1963).
6. Spencer Marsh, *Edith the Good: The Transformation of Edith Bunker from Total Woman to Whole Person* (New York: Harper & Row, 1977).
7. David Reuben, *Everything You Always Wanted to Know About Sex But Were Afraid to Ask* (New York: Bantam Books, 1971).
8. Gail Sheehy, *Passages: Predictable Crises of Adult Life* (New York: E. P. Dutton, 1974, 1976).

9. Wulf H. Utian, M.D., Ph.D., *Your Middle Years: A Doctor's Guide for Today's Women* (New York: Appleton Century Crofts, 1980).
10. Paula Weideger, *Menstruation and Menopause: The Physiology and Psychology, the Myth and the Reality* (New York: Dell, 1975).

CHAPTER 3—MYTH 2: SEX AND THE
NONFERTILE WOMAN

1. Winnifred Berg Cutler, Ph.D., Celso-Ramon García, M.D., and David A. Edwards, Ph.D., *Menopause: A Guide for Women and the Men Who Love Them* (New York: W. W. Norton, 1985).
2. Paula Brown Doress, Diana Laskin Siegel, and the Older Women's Book Project in cooperation with the Boston Women's Health Book Collective, *Ourselves, Growing Older* (New York: Touchstone/Simon & Schuster, 1987).
3. Barbara Ehrenreich and Deirdre English, *For Her Own Good: 150 Years of the Experts' Advice to Women* (New York: Anchor Books/Doubleday, 1979, 1989).
4. Henry Gleitman, *Psychology* (New York: W. W. Norton, 1981).
5. Shere Hite, *The Hite Report: A Nationwide Study on Female Sexuality* (New York: Macmillan, 1976).
6. Spencer Marsh, *Edith the Good: The Transformation of Edith Bunker from Total Woman to Whole Person* (New York: Harper & Row, 1977).
7. Elissa Melamed, Ph.D., *Mirror, Mirror: The Terror of Not Being Young* (New York: Linden Press/Simon & Schuster, 1983).
8. Rita Ransohoff, Ph.D., *Venus After Forty: Sexual Myths, Men's Fantasies and Truths About Middle-Aged Women* (Fair Hills, N.J.: New Horizons Press, 1987).
9. Bernard D. Starr, Ph.D., and Marcella Bakur Weiner, Ed.D., *The Starr-Weiner Report on Sex and Sexuality in the Mature Years* (New York: McGraw-Hill, 1981).

CHAPTER 4—MYTH 3: MENOPAUSE AS A MEDICAL DISEASE: "THE WOMB IS PART OF EVERY ILLNESS . . ."

1. Barbara Ehrenreich and Deirdre English, *Complaints and Disorders: The Sexual Politics of Sickness* (New York: The Feminist Press, 1973).
2. Germaine Greer, *The Female Eunuch* (New York: McGraw-Hill, 1970).
3. Kathleen I. MacPherson, R.N., M.A., M.S., "Menopause as Disease: The Social Construction of a Metaphor," *Advances in Nursing Science*, March 1981.
4. Rita Ransohoff, Ph.D., *Venus After Forty: Sexual Myths, Men's*

Fantasies and Truths About Middle-Aged Women (Fair Hills, N.J.: New Horizons Press, 1987).

5. Wulf H. Utian, M.D., Ph.D., *Your Middle Years: A Doctor's Guide for Today's Women* (New York: Appleton Century Crofts, 1980).

CHAPTER 5—MYTH 4: MENOPAUSE AS A PSYCHOLOGICAL CRISIS: "THE DEPRESSION NATURAL TO THE CHANGE OF LIFE"

1. Simone de Beauvoir (translated into English by H. M. Parshley), *The Second Sex* (New York: Alfred A. Knopf, 1971), originally published in France in 1949.

2. Barbara Ehrenreich and Deirdre English, *For Her Own Good: 150 Years of the Experts' Advice to Women* (New York: Anchor Books/ Doubleday, 1979, 1989).

3. Henry Gleitman, *Psychology* (New York: W. W. Norton, 1981).

4. Daniel Goleman, "Wide Beliefs in Depression in Women Contradicted," *The New York Times*, January 9, 1990, pp. C1, C8.

5. Kathleen I. MacPherson, R.N., M.A., M.S., "Menopause as Disease: The Social Construction of a Metaphor," *Advances in Nursing Science*, March 1981.

6. Elissa Melamed, Ph.D., *Mirror, Mirror: The Terror of Not Being Young* (New York: Linden Press/ Simon & Schuster, 1983).

7. Rita Ransohoff, Ph.D., *Venus After Forty: Sexual Myths, Men's Fantasies and Truths About Middle-Aged Women* (Fair Hills, N.J.: New Horizons Press, 1987).

8. Melva Weber, "The Myth of Menopause Blues," *Vogue*, November 1988, p. 296.

9. Paula Weideger, *Menstruation and Menopause: The Physiology and Psychology, the Myth and the Reality* (New York: Dell, 1975).

CHAPTER 6—MYTH 5: MENOPAUSE SIGNALS THE ONSET OF OLD AGE

1. Christopher Cox, "The Power People of the 90's," *The Boston Sunday Herald*, January 7, 1990, p. 61.

2. Bob Diddlebock, "Creative departments slow to act," *Advertising Age*, May 22, 1989, p. 86.

3. Geraldine Fabrikant, "And Now a Magazine for the Over-40 Woman," *The New York Times*, February 7, 1988, p. F5.

4. Jerry Gerber and Walt Klores, "Reaching Over-50s through Kids," *Advertising Age*, December 19, 1988, p. 17.

5. Shere Hite, *The Hite Report: A Nationwide Study on Female Sexuality* (New York: Macmillan, 1976).

6. Elissa Koff, Margaret L. Stubbs, Jill Rierdan, "College Women's Conceptions of Menopause," Center for Research on Women, Wellesley College, Wellesley, Mass., 1989.

7. Jon Lafayette and Lenore Skenazy, "How to reach seniors? Be positive," *Advertising Age*, October 31, 1988.

8. Meridel Le Sueur, "Rites of Ancient Ripening," *Woman of Power*, Summer 1989, Issue 14.

9. Elissa Melamed, Ph.D., *Mirror, Mirror: The Terror of Not Being Young* (New York: Linden Press/ Simon & Schuster, 1983).

10. Wulf H. Utian, M.D., Ph.D., *Your Middle Years: A Doctor's Guide for Today's Women* (New York: Appleton Century Crofts, 1980).

11. Gene Valentino, "The Missing Generation," *Advertising Age*, June 28, 1988, p. 18.

12. Adrienne War, "Marketers Slow to Catch Age Wave," *Advertising Age*, May 22, 1987, p. F1.

13. Paula Weideger, *Menstruation and Menopause: The Physiology and Psychology, the Myth and the Reality* (New York: Dell, 1975).

CHAPTER 7—WHAT HAPPENS

1. "Review of the Literature," *Acta Obstetricia et Gynecologica Scandinavia*, September 21, 1972.

2. Jane Brody, "Personal Health," *The New York Times*, May 10, 1990, p. E15.

3. Winnifred B. Cutler, Ph.D., *Hysterectomy: Before and After* (New York: HarperCollins, 1990).

4. ———, Celso-Ramon García, Ph.D., and David A. Edwards, Ph.D., *Menopause: A Guide for Women and the Men Who Love Them* (New York: W. W. Norton, 1985).

5. Lisa Davis, "The Myths of Menopause," *Hippocrates*, May/June 1989.

6. Melvin Frisch, M.D., *Stay Cool Through Menopause* (Los Angeles: The Body Press, 1989).

7. Clark Gillespie, M.D., *Hormones, Hot Flashes and Mood Swings* (New York: Harper & Row, 1989).

9. Sonja M. McKinlay, Ph.D., *The Impact of Menopause and Social Factors on Health* (Watertown, Mass: New England Research Institute, April 1988).

10. McKinlay, McKinlay, and Brambilla, "The Relative Contributions of Endocrine Change and Social Circumstances to Depression in Mid-Aged Women," *Journal of Health and Social Behavior*, December 1987, Vol. 28.

11. Elissa Melamed, Ph.D., *Mirror, Mirror: The Terror of Not Being Young* (New York: Linden Press/Simon & Schuster, 1983).

12. G. W. Molnar, "Body Temperature During Menopausal Hot Flashes," *Journal of Applied Physiology*, 1975, Vol. 38.

13. "Should You Take Estrogen?" *Prevention*, November 1989.

14. R. Punnonen and L. Rauramo, *Annales Chirugiae et Gynaecologiae* (1977).

15. Paula Brown Doress, Diana Laskin Siegel, and the Older Wom-

en's Book Project in cooperation with the Boston Women's Health Book Collective, *Ourselves, Growing Older* (New York: Touchstone/Simon & Schuster, 1987).

16. Philip M. Sarrel, M.D., "Sexuality and Menopause," *Obstetrics and Gynecology*, Vol. 75, No. 4 (supplement), April 1990.

17. ——, "Sexuality in Menopause," *Menopause Management*, Winter 1989, Vol. 2, No. 1, p. 9.

18. Isaac Schiff, M.D., "Is ERT Cardioprotective?" *Menopause Management*, Summer 1989, Vol. 2.

19. Leigh Silverman, "Self Center," *Lear's*, June 1990.

20. Wulf H. Utian, M.D., Ph.D., and Ruth S. Jacobowitz, *Managing Your Menopause* (New York: Prentice Hall, 1990).

21. Paula Weideger, *Menstruation and Menopause: The Physiology and Psychology, the Myth and the Reality* (New York: Dell, 1975).

CHAPTER 8—THE ESTROGEN CONTROVERSY

1. A. Bergman, et al., "Changes in urethal cytology following estrogen administration," Department of Obstetrics and Gynecology, UCLA , *Los Angeles Gynecological Obstetrics Invest.*, 1990.

2. "Doctors Faulted on Reply to Patient Breast Check," *The Boston Globe*, July 9, 1990.

3. Jane Brody, "Personal Health: Estrogens After Menopause," *The New York Times*, October 12, 1989, p. B11.

4. Raymond Burnett, M.D., *Menopause: All Your Questions Answered* (Chicago: Contemporary Books, 1987).

5. Allan G. Charles, M.D., "Estrogen Replacement After Menopause: When Is It Warranted?" *Postgraduate Medicine*, Vol. 85, No. 4.

6. Graham A. Coldits, M.B., B.S., et al., "Prospective Study of Estrogen Replacement Therapy and Risk of Breast Cancer in Postmenopausal Women," *Journal of American Medical Association*, November 28, 1990, Vol. 264, No. 20.

7. Lisa Davis, "The Myths of Menopause," *Hippocrates*, May/June 1989.

8. Bruce Ettinger, M.D., "Can Menopause Be Diagnosed?" *Menopause Management*, Fall 1988, Vol. 1, No. 1.

9. Kristi J. Ferguson, Ph.D., Curtis Hoegh, M.D., Susan Johnson, M.D., "Estrogen Replacement Therapy: A Survey of Women's Knowledge and Attitudes," *Arch Intern Med*, January 1989, 149:133.

10. S. E. Fruner, et al., "A Case Control Study of Large Bowel Cancer and Hormone Exposure in Women," *Cancer Research*, 1989, 49/17.

11. R. Don Gambrell, Jr., M.D., "Endometrial Cancer from ERT:

An Unfounded Fear," *Menopause Management*, Summer 1989, Vol. 2, No. 2.

12. Robin Marantz Henig, *How a Woman Ages* (New York: Ballantine Esquire, 1985).

13. Marc L'Hermite, "Risks of Estrogen and Progestogens," *Maturitas*, December 1990, pp. 215–246.

14. G. T. Kovacs and H. G. Burger, "Endometrial Sampling for Women on Peri-Menopausal Hormone Replacement Therapy," *Maturitas*, 1988, 10:259–262.

15. Rogerio A. Lobo, M.D., "Cardiovascular Implication of Estrogen Replacement Therapy," *Obstetrics and Gynecology*, Vol. 75, No. 4, April 1990.

16. ―― and M. Whitehead, "Too Much of a Good Thing? Use of Progestogens in the Menopause: An International Consensus Statement," *Fertil Steril*, 1989, 51:229–231.

17. Kathleen I. MacPherson, R.N., M.A., M.S., "Construction of a Metaphor," *Advances in Nursing Science*, March 1981.

18. B. A. Stoll, Department of Oncology, St. Thomas' Hospital, London, "Hormone Replacement Therapy in Women Treated for Breast Cancer," *European Journal of Cancer, Clinical Oncology*, 1989, 25/12.

CHAPTER 9—EAT HEARTY, STAY HEALTHY
CHAPTER 10—ONE MONTH OF MENUS

1. *AARP Bulletin*, July/August, 1990, Vol. 31, No. 7, p. 2.

2. *AIRC Information Series*, Vol. III, p. 3.

3. Exchange Lists for Meal Planning, *American Dietetic Association*, 430 North Michigan Avenue, Chicago, IL 60611.

4. "No Time to Cook," *American Institute for Cancer Research*, 1759 R Street, N.W., Washington, D.C. 20069.

5. James W. Anderson, M.D., *Plant Fiber in Foods*, University of Kentucky Medical Center, 1980 (handout).

6. Covert Bailey, *The Fit-or-Fat Target Diet* (Boston: Houghton Mifflin, 1984).

7. ―― and Lea Bishop, *Target Recipes: The Fit or Fat System* (Boston: Houghton Mifflin, 1985).

8. Helen Nichols Church, B.S., and Jean A. T. Pennington, Ph.D., R.D., *Bowes and Church's Food Values of Portions Commonly Used*, 14th ed. (Philadelphia: J. B. Lippincott Company, 1985).

9. Jane Brody, *Jane Brody's Good Food Book: Living the High Carbohydrate Way* (New York: W. W. Norton, 1985).

10. *Nutrition Action Healthletter*, Center for Science in the Public Interest, September 1990.

11. Nancy Clark, M.S., R.D., *Nancy Clark's Sport Nutrition Guidebook* (Champaign, Ill.: Leisure Press, 1990).

12. Leonard A. Cohen, "Diet and Cancer," *Scientific American*, November 1987, Vol. 257, No. 5, p. 42.

13. John R. Erdman, Jr., Ph.D., et al., "Nutrient Interactions Involving Vitamins and Minerals," *Contemporary Nutrition*, 1988, Vol. 13, No. 2 (handout).

14. William Evans, Ph.D.: presentation at annual convention of Massachusetts Dietetic Association, 1990.

15. Robert P. Heaney, M.D., F.A.C.P., "Bone Health After Menopause—Is Calcium the Complete Answer?" *Menopause Management*, June 1990, Vol. 3, No. 1, p. 4.

16. T. H. Magnuson et al., "Oral Calcium Promotes Pigment Gallstone Formation," *Journal Surg. Res.*, 1989, 46/4.

17. Catherine H. Garner, R.N.O., M.S.N., M.P.A., "Developing a Menopause Program," *Menopause Management*, August 1990, Vol. 3, No. 2, p. 10.

18. Cheryl L. Rock, M.M.S.C., R.D., and Ann Coulston, M.S., R.D., "Do Americans Eat Healthier at Home?", *Nutrition and the M.D.*, May 1989, Vol. 15, No. 5, p. 8.

19. *Recommended Dietary Allowances*, 10th ed., National Resource Council of National Academy of Science (Washington, D.C.: National Academy Press, 1989).

20. Daphne A. Roe, *Nutrition and the Skin* (New York: Alan R. Liss, 1986).

21. Herbert Schaumburg, M.D., et al., "Sensory Neuropathy from Pyridoxine Abuse," *New England Journal of Medicine*, August 25, 1983, Vol. 309, No. 8.

22. Maurice E. Shils, M.D., Sc.D., and Vernon R. Young, Ph.D., *Modern Nutrition in Health and Disease*, 7th ed. (Philadelphia: Lea and Febiger, 1988).

23. Sue Rodwell Williams, Ph.D., M.P.H., R.D., *Nutrition and Diet Therapy* (St. Louis: Times Mirror/Mosby College Publishing, 1985).

24. Wulf H. Utian, M.D., Ph.D., and Ruth S. Jacobowitz, *Managing Your Menopause* (New York: Prentice Hall, 1990).

CHAPTER 11—EXERCISE: A SCIENCE WITH MAGIC

1. Covert Bailey, *The Fit-or-Fat Target Diet* (Boston: Houghton Mifflin, 1984).

2. ——, *Fit or Fat?* (Boston: Houghton Mifflin, 1977).

3. —— and Lea Bishop, *The Fit-or-Fat Woman* (Boston: Houghton Mifflin, 1989).

4. Richard Hittleman, *Richard Hittleman's Yoga, 28 Day Exercise Plan* (New York: Bantam Books, 1973).

5. B.K.S. Iyengar, *Light on Yoga* (New York: Schocken, 1966).

6. M. Shangold, G. Mirkin, *Women and Exercise Physiology and Sports Medicine* (Philadelphia: F. A. Davis, 1988).

CHAPTER 12—ALREADY BEAUTIFUL

1. *Advertising Age,* May 22, 1989, p. S1.
2. Center for Human Appearance, University of Pennsylvania, Penn Tower Hotel, 10th floor, 3400 Spruce St., Philadelphia, PA 19104.
3. Carol Krucoff, "You: Is Beauty More Than Skin Deep?" *The Washington Post,* May 3, 1982, p. C5.
4. Pamela Lister, "The True Importance of Looks," *Mirabella,* June 1989, p. 63.
5. *Look Good . . . Feel Better,* The Cosmetic, Toiletry and Fragrance Association (CTFA) Foundation, 1110 Vermont Avenue, N.W., Suite 800, Washington, D.C. 20005 (brochure).
6. Rodale Press Staff, *Future Youth* (Emmaus, Penn.: Rodale Press, 1987).
7. Roxanne Roberts, "First Lady Donates Gown," *The Washington Post,* January 10, 1990.
8. Alix Kates Shulman, *Memoirs of an Ex-Prom Queen* (New York: Alfred A. Knopf, 1972).

CHAPTER 13—TIME FOR A CHANGE

1. James Ayres, "MGH Gets $85 Million Grant," *The Boston Globe,* August 3, 1989, p. 52.
2. J. L. Bolognia, "Skin Changes in Menopause," *Maturitas,* November 1989, pp. 295–304.
3. Elaine Brumberg, *Save Your Money, Save Your Face* (New York: Facts on File Publications, 1986).
4. Susan Carlton, "Makeup Lessons," *Mirabella,* June 1990, p. 74.
5. The Catherine Hinds Institute of Esthetics, 65 Riverside Place, Medford, MA 02155.
6. Face Life, c/o Laura Hart, Ph.D., 454 Lowell Avenue, Newton, MA 02160.
7. Heloise, *Heloise's Beauty Book* (New York: Arbor House, 1985).
8. Carlotta Karlson Jacobson and Catherine Ettinger, *How to Be Wrinkle Free—Look Younger Longer Without Plastic Surgery* (New York: G. P. Putnam's Sons, 1986).
9. Leon Jaroff, "The Dark Side of Worshipping the Sun," *Time,* July 23, 1990, p. 68.
10. *Lahey Clinic,* Spring, 1989. Vol. 8, No. 2, The Lahey Clinic, 41 Mall Road, Box 541, Burlington, MA 01805.
11. Betsey A. Lehman, "Looking For Mr. Beautiful," *The Boston Globe,* May 7, 1990, p. 30.
12. Lida Livingston and Constance Schrader, *Wrinkles: How to Prevent Them, How to Erase Them* (Englewood Cliffs, NJ: Prentice Hall, 1978).
13. Shirley Lord, "Reshaping Russia," *Vogue,* April 1989, p. 170.

14. M. Craig, *Miss Craig's Face-Saving Exercises* (New York: Random House, 1970).
15. "The Other Jackie O," *Vanity Fair,* August 1989, p. 99.
16. M. J. Saffon, *M. J. Saffon's Youthlift* (New York: Warner Books, 1981).
17. Wulf H. Utian, M.D., Ph.D., and Ruth S. Jacobowitz, *Managing Your Menopause* (New York: Prentice Hall, 1990).
18. Christine Valmy, *Christine Valmy's Skin Care and Makeup Book* (New York: Crown, 1982).

CHAPTER 14—TAKING RISKS, MAKING NOISE, BEING COURAGEOUS
1. Marian Christie, "How Pearl Bailey Learned the Lessons of Life," *The Boston Globe,* December 17, 1989, p. B34.
2. Nina McCain, "Telling True Stories About Women," *The Boston Globe,* November 28, 1988, p. 12.
3. Georgie Anne Geyer, "Notes from a Continuing Conflict." (This column was given to me as a clipping and I have not been able to find out what newspaper or magazine originally published it!)
4. Dolores Kong, "Impatience Growing Over Breast Cancer Research," *The Boston Globe,* June 15, 1990, p. 1.
5. Deborah Mesce, "U.S. Office to Focus on Health of Women," *The Boston Globe,* September 11, 1990, p. 3.
6. Andrew Purvis, "A Perilous Gap," *Time* special issue, Fall 1990, pp. 66–67.
7. David Roberts, *"Architectural Digest* Visits: Liv Ullmann," *Architectural Digest,* December, 1989, p. 208.
8. Jean Seligman et al., "Not Past Their Prime," *Newsweek,* August 6, 1990.
9. Liv Ullmann, *Choices* (New York: Bantam Books, 1985).

Index

Page numbers in *italics* refer to illustrations. Those in **boldface** refer to recipes.

About the Authors

JUDITH PAIGE is five years postmenopausal. She is an international fashion model with Ford Models in New York as well as a registered dietitian and a former yoga teacher. Her articles on nutrition have been featured in *Shape* magazine. She lives in Massachusetts and is the mother of two daughters.

PAMELA GORDON is a free-lance writer and a former faculty member at Emerson College in Boston.